Bristol in 1807

Impressions of the City at the time of Abolition

Matthews' New and Correct Plan of Bristol, 1800.

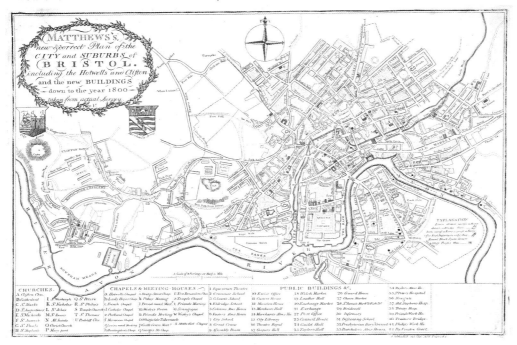

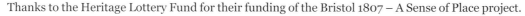

First published in 2009 by Redcliffe Press Ltd. in conjunction with Bristol Libraries

Redcliffe Press, 81g Pembroke Road, Bristol BS8 3EA

T: 0117 973 7207

E: info@redcliffepress.co.uk

www.redcliffepress.co.uk

© Anthony Beeson

ISBN 978-1-906593-26-1

British Library Cataloguing-in-Publication Data

A catalogue record for this book is available from the British Library

Design and layout Stephen Morris www.stephen-morris.co.uk

Printed by HSW Tonypandy, Rhondda

Thanks to the Heritage Lottery Fund for their funding of the Bristol 1807 – A Sense of Place project.

Bristol in 1807

Impressions of the City at the time of Abolition

Anthony Beeson

The Salop Seller, WH Pyne, 1805.

redcliffe Bristol Libraries

To David
Semper Eadem

Acknowledgements
I should like to thank my inestimable colleague Dawn Dyer for her usual enthusiastic and knowledgeable support in the preparation of this volume and in the exhibition that it commemorates. Most of the newspaper references are gleaned by her researches. Likewise I must applaud those colleagues who transcribed original and printed sources for me and Andrew Eason and Kate Pau who employed their computer skills on some of the illustrations. Thanks must also go to Jane Bradley for the part she played in the setting up of the travelling exhibitions and Jane Choules, Robert Harrison, Janet Randall for applying for funding to the Heritage Lottery Fund and in that organisation's goodness in granting the request.
My thanks also to Andrew Stevens and Michael Tozer for the loan of images and objects from their collections in the exhibition and permission to use them to illustrate this book. My ever-cooperative curator colleagues Sheena Stoddard, Timothy Ewin and David Eveleigh at the City Museum and Art Gallery are thanked for the loan of exhibits and permission to illustrate some here.

Anthony Beeson, May 2009

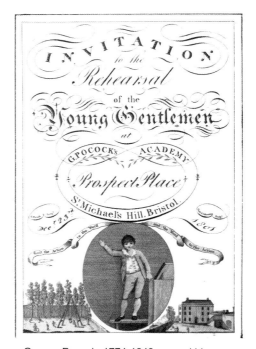

George Pocock, 1774-1843, moved his school to Prospect Place in 1800. It prospered for 43 years and trained boys to become men of business. Pocock was a remarkable man. He invented a boy spanking machine for unruly pupils (the Royal Patent Self-acting Ferule) and an inflatable 12-foot globe for travellers. His most famous invention was the Charvolant, or kite-propelled carriage, in which he took his family and horse on an excursion to Marlborough from Bristol.

Contents

Jack-Ass Place

A song by a Bristol wit about Mr Ferguson, from *The Observer*.
Being a Transient Glance at About Forty Youths of Bristol, Anon, 1794

About four years ago when the Bristolians were affected with the mania of Building, this Gentleman came in for a share of the distemper. Being asked one day in a public company 'what spot he had fixed on for his intended scheme of building?' he replied 'it was the field behind Brandon Hill, where the Jack-Asses were milked,' upon which a person in company observed, that it might with great propriety be called 'JACK-ASS PLACE.' – This anecdote, coming to the knowledge of a certain satirical Genius, produced the following song.

1.

While others sing of Richmond-Hill,
With many a pretty grace;
I'll now attempt, (tho' small in skill)
The Lad of Jack-Ass Place,
This lad so tall
With Wit so small
And stupid, vacant Face,
Has no pretence
To a grain of sense, -
Great Lad of Jack-Ass Place!

2.

Dreadful in form as Milton's Sin,
Unpolished as a Bear;
Yet wishes to be voted in,
The fav'rite of the Fair!
This Lad so tall, &c.

3.

Of contradiction ever full,
T'oppose is his delight:
In conversation he's as dull
As Twelve o'clock at Night.
This lad so tall, &c.

4.

In Jack-Ass Place, he'll rank a Peer;
An Ass among the Men;
Take him for all in all, we ne'er
'Shall see his like again!'
This Lad so tall,
With Wit so small,
And stupid, vacant Face,
Has no pretence
To a grain of sense, -
Great Lad of JACK-ASS PLACE!

(to the tune of 'Sweet Lass of Richmond Hill')

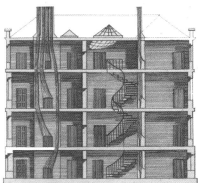

House design from William Pain's *Practical House Carpenter*, 1792.

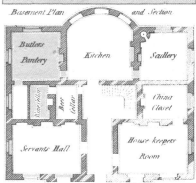

By Mud Cemented And By Smoke Obscur'd

IN NOVEMBER 2007 AN EXHIBITION ENTITLED 'BRISTOL 1807 A SENSE of Place' opened in the exhibition gallery of the Central Reference Library at College Green, Bristol, dedicated to showing what life was really like for ordinary Bristolians in 1807, the year of the abolition of the slave trade. Researched by Anthony Beeson, Dawn Dyer, and Jane Bradley, the exhibition drew on contemporary accounts from travellers, inhabitants, guidebooks and local newspapers to provide contrasting and sometimes quite startling accounts of everyday life. The exhibition was one of a series of city-wide events for library and community venues that were financed by a grant from the Heritage Lottery Fund and Abolition 200. Concise versions of the main exhibition circulated in Bristol and numerous 'Treasures in Store' days, where the public had the opportunity to handle and turn the pages of rare books and letters of the period, were held both in the Central Library and at various locations throughout the city. The artist Toby Hulse ran several creative workshops with local schools investigating the 'sense of place' of Bristol now and then. This was joined by adult education classes, craft sessions and lectures around the same theme. Events continued throughout 2008 and came to a conclusion in the early part of 2009. As a legacy Bristol Reference Library published an illustrated bibliography entitled *Slavery, Abolition and Emancipation* based on the permanent stock of the library in the relevant fields. The present volume came about through a constant wish from visitors to the exhibition that all of the research done for that should be preserved for the public in the form of a publication.

Although the major commemoration for 2007 was the abolition of slavery in Britain in 1807, from the start the Bristol project

Bristol from Brandon Hill showing the smoke pollution over the old city.

was conceived as being more encompassing. It was the intention to put abolition into the real context of the time by concentrating on what life was like for all inhabitants then, notwithstanding their race colour or creed. To a world used to observing the past safely through film and historical drama it comes as a shock to realise how dreadful everyday life was for a great number of the population. Several largely forgotten accounts of the city published around 1807 were vital to the research and have either been published here in their entirety or at least those sections pertinent to the city. The first was James P Malcolm's *First Impressions*, an entertaining yet thought-provoking Londoner's tour around Britain, and *Letters from England*, written by Bristolian and poet Robert Southey under the assumed name of a Spanish traveller Don Manuel Alvarez Espriella. In addition the poem *Bristol, a Satire*, written in 1794 by Southey's tragic brother-in-law, Robert Lovell, in response to Thorne's *Bristolia* (a hopelessly flattering

Old houses in Baldwin Street, J S Prout. Although published in 1835 the drawings by Prout are pertinent in showing the same buildings of the city that would have been seen in 1807. Only the fashions would have changed.

panegyric that equated Bristol to ancient Rome and Troy), contains both humour and venom in its description of the city and its money-grubbing merchant classes. Malcolm's horrified reaction to the Avon's mud, which before the days of the floating harbour and proper sewage treatment was even less aesthetically pleasing than today, mirrors my own on first encountering the river at low tide in the 1970s. Added to these are numerous shorter contemporary accounts and poems that have been drawn upon in part not only to elucidate the longer texts but also to alert the present-day researcher to their existence. Sometimes they appear from the most surprising places. Charles Heath's 1801 guide to Chepstow Castle includes a splendid description of the approach to Bristol from the New Passage ferry on the Severn which complements Malcolm's account of his excursion out of the city via Whiteladies Road.

As a major port, Bristol in 1807 was a cosmopolitan place visited by all nationalities. Malcolm mentions an aged Turk he encountered near Kingsweston and how a kind lady in a chaise had endeavoured to help the old man who was far from home, but newspaper reports from the 1730s onward show just how many different nationalities were commonplace in the streets.

Although there was bustle in the city Southey compared it unfavourably with the great centres like London and Liverpool and yet Londoner Malcolm took the opposite view. As a port Bristol was in some trouble. The war with France had seriously affected trade. Port duties still averaged £300,000 a year, but many ships moored in the Severn in the anchorage called Kingroad, and unloaded their cargoes rather than risk the Avon. Malcolm saw through the official propaganda about the desirability of Bristol to shipping:

what can be more absurd than to assert it is one of the 'deepest, safest, and most convenient for navigation, in England,' when ships and small craft are seen up to their wales *in mud*, and full ten feet below the surface of the indented quays?

Improvements to turn the traditional harbour into a wet dock through the cutting of the new river were underway and he mentions the continual blasting and the beauty of the red scar caused by the excavations across the verdant meadows near Bedminster. In 1807 the newspapers tell us that 800 of these workmen suddenly went on an unsuccessful strike over missing their breakfast and demanded more pay.

In these days of striving for a pollution-free environment it may be of interest that 1807 Bristol produced so much smoke from its thirteen kilns, glass houses, copperworks and houses that the city viewed from St Michael's Hill, even in high summer, was almost totally obscured during the working hours. Both Malcolm and Southey deplored the filth of the older parts of Bristol – 'The antient and unaltered parts are inconceivably unpleasant, dark, and dirty' – whilst contrasting these with the newly widened and paved streets. Malcolm in particular found the numerous tall and jettied Tudor and Jacobean houses very disturbing and whilst appreciating that some might find them picturesque, could only be thankful that the Great Fire had solved the problem in his own city. With so much reference to grime it is interesting to note that the newspapers have many cases of property owners being fined for failure to cleanse the pavements outside their premises daily as was legally required.

All was far from well in the new housing developments that had sprung up in the Kingsdown and Clifton areas of the city from the 1790s. The economic uncertainty engendered by the war with France together with an unwillingness of merchants to seek housing away from their fellows and commerce in the heart of the city resulted in the old timber houses being given smart modern facades or rebuilt by the same families on their original sites, whilst the vast new developments such as Portland Square, Royal York and Cornwallis Crescents stood as unfinished shells prey to the elements and thieves. Malcolm likened them to the ruins of a deserted city ravaged by war or pestilence and pondered upon the ruination of so many families who had invested in the developments.

There was however great and opulent wealth in Bristol, even if it did prefer to sit cheek by jowl with its grotesquely housed neighbours within the walls. The shops in the Wine Street area excited the visitor's admiration – 'very forcibly to the best articles of dress, gold, silver jewellery, and books of prints by the most eminent authors and artists.' Nor was admiration lacking for the foodstuffs available in the new markets in Corn Street which approached London prices. Bristol was surrounded by market gardens and noted for its fruit and vegetables. Even the orange sellers had their own traditional outfits that were to survive at least until the beginning of Victoria's reign. Visitors admired the Corn Exchange with its elegant, but deserted, porticoed piazza which had cost the City £50,000 whilst mocking the Bristol traders who still stuck to their traditional trading sites outside by the Nails exposed to the elements. Another Bristol peculiarity was the horse-drawn sledge or dray used for moving heavy goods about the city to the danger of pedestrians and carriages.

But what of Bristolians themselves? Southey wrote, 'The people of Bristol seem to sell everything that can be sold' and Lovell:

In all his Sons the mystic signs we trace,
Pounds, Shillings, Pence appear in every face.

As young Bristolians, both had contempt for those ruling the city and for those who only lived for profit. To the outsider however the picture looked different. Malcolm, whilst critically examining Bristolians' aesthetic appeal – 'The male inhabitants of Bristol are generally well formed; but the females are short, and few have handsome features. Neither have they that elegance of exterior which distinguishes even the nursery-maids and shop-women of London' – also advises 'that regularity, industry, and civility, distinguish the citizens of Bristol and its rural environs.'

Malcolm stressed the word rural as the immediate environs of the city he found decidedly disturbing:

The suburbs consist of numberless lanes lined by houses inhabited by a wild race, whose countenances indicate wretchedness and affright. These are the wives and offspring of the labourers at copper and iron-works, glass-houses, and many other manufactories; where they are buried from the world, amidst fire, smoke, and dust; and when released, sufficient leisure is denied them to humanize themselves and families.

Whilst deploring slavery it has to be said that in reality the profits of this despicable trade contributed only a portion to the wealth of Bristol. It was the myriad of industries both within and without the City and the sweat of the labourers and the skills of the artisans and the merchants in selling the products to the world that really gave Bristol her wealth. Those numberless wretched white labourers ('slaves' even) whom Malcolm refers to as the 'wild race', who toiled endless hours in the glassworks, potteries, copper and ironworks of the City had few champions then and are forgotten now when we look at and admire the artefacts of that era. Malcolm abhorred the lot of the workers but recognised it was for the common good that they be sacrificed:

I may lament that men should be compelled to undergo hardships almost too dreadful for contemplation; but I do not by any means wish to be understood as blaming the citizens of Bristol for employing the inhabitants in the production of those articles which support the labourer, the artisan, the retailer and the merchant, and contribute to the honour and independence of the island.

This dark side of Bristol in 1807 was joined in the exhibition by stories of crimes committed, from lead stripping to infanticide and of mendicancy and individual kindnesses that show that not all Bristolians lacked humanity.

Bristol at play featured greatly in the material assembled and included most entertainments enjoyed by the populace and visitors, from Sunday walks in the country to boxing matches. Distance sanitises the past and it is sometimes astonishing to realise how earthy even genteel life could be. Foreigners were shocked by the after-dinner drinking indulged in by gentlemen when the ladies withdrew. In particular the habit of toasting each guest as he used the chamberpots concealed in the side boards astonished them. Malcolm like others was shocked by the impropriety of St James' Fair. In his case it was not only because it was held in the churchyard, but that in putting up the booths and rides, portions of recently buried Bristolians were unearthed and trampled underfoot. College Green was a favourite promenade

A blind beggar and his dog from Smith's *Vagabondiana*. Such a beggar, but with pigeons on his head and shoulders, appears in Braikenridge's drawing of St James' Fair elsewhere in this volume.

where the regimental bands played each day, but Southey mentions that the Cathedral entrance smelled of urine as the sheltered doorway was blasphemously used as a convenience. Similarly he mentions the beauty of the crisp carving on the abbey gateway apart from where repeated watery abuse had etched the stone away.

Holidaying at Hotwells and Clifton was another topic covered by the exhibits which included examples of the famous Bristol diamonds and other fascinating rocks from the gorge that were made into souvenirs for the visitors. In 1807 the spa was in decline mostly as a result of the rapacity of the landlords and tenant, who had raised the prices for taking the waters deterring all but the wealthiest or most desperate of visitors. This affected all who relied on them for their livelihood. In 1807 the numbers were still respectable but they were soon to fall. After the end of the Napoleonic war they again rose but never achieved the early popularity. The Season for Hotwells was the summer, unlike Bath's winter one. There was much for the visitor to enjoy, from cream teas in Ashton village to donkey riding on the Downs. *Rownham Ferry*, a painting by Rolinda Sharples reproduced in the exhibition, although painted a decade later, encapsulates much that was fun about a holiday in Hotwells and its wonderful gorge. What cannot be appreciated now are the explosions emanating from the neighbouring quarries that with those from the excavations of the New Cut must have shaken the nerves of many a patient. Southey wondered how people could spend the summer here enjoying themselves whilst their fellow guests died and were buried by the same hotels that had entertained them.

Chief amongst the hotels in Hotwells was Barton's or the Gloucester, that stood south of Albemarle Row. Towering and described as 'a house upon a house', apart from its admired circular staircase and apartments overlooking the Somerset landscape, one of its attractions was a seemingly endless supply of imported live turtles that could be sent all over the Kingdom to satisfy the craze for turtle soup. With its news stories, topics and quotations, the exhibition 'Bristol 1807' contained much that was unknown and fascinating to the modern Bristolian. We hope that this book, its successor and commemorator, will continue to do the same and to reacquaint the reader with some worthy but forgotten accounts of their city.

Anthony Beeson
Art Librarian, Central Reference Library, College Green, Bristol

Blazing Furnaces: to Bristol and the Wells

Ibbetson Julius Caesar and others. A Picturesque Guide to Bath, *Bristol Hot-Wells, the River Avon and the Adjacent Country,* 1793

DESCENDING FROM KEYNSHAM, WE CLIMB ANOTHER HILL, ON THE LEFT of which, the valley and the river present themselves: we then again lose sight of them, and sink into the road, which lies between hedges, till we reach Brislington, a village two miles south-east of Bristol.

We were now warned of our approach to this city, by blazing furnaces, and glasshouses, and by meeting droves of over-burthened coal-horses &c. The coal-mines here are very numerous and productive; the veins are covered with a kind of shell or crust, of a black and stony substance, called Wark, which splits like slate, but is still more frangible. On dividing it, there is frequently to be found the print of a fern leaf, as if engraved, and on the corresponding surface, a protuberant figure, by which the impression is made.

On the right, as we leave Brislington, the valley opens, and acquires the name of Arno's vale; by what right is not easy to conjecture, as it contains nothing but smoking brick-kilns and sooty furnaces. We now again fall in with the Avon, which bears us company till we enter Bristol.

*

The city of Bristol may vie with most in England, for beauty as well as convenience of situation. It lies in a valley of an uneven surface, encompassed with eminences of various heights and forms. The air, in its natural state is remarkably pure; but the smoke issuing from the brass-works, glasshouses, &c. keeps the town in an almost impenetrable obscurity. As it stands on seven hills, and is intersected by the Avon, Bristol has been frequently compared to ancient Rome and its Tiber. On its north side, the houses rise above each other to a considerable height, and entirely overlook the lower part of the city. The most elevated point is that of Kingsdown; and of the steepness here, some idea may be formed from the flight of steps which have been hewn in the hill to facilitate the ascent. Bristol stands in the two counties of Gloucester and Somerset, and is also a county of itself, having been made so by Edward III who established a wool-manufactory here. The river Avon, which here joins the Froome, divides the counties. The shores abound with convenient quays and wharfs, far superior to any on the Thames, wet and dry docks, and a great number of dock-yards. The river, rapid in its course, and rising to the height of forty feet, brings ships, of a thousand tons burthen, up to Bristol bridge. The business of ship-building is carried on here with very great success.

The bridge, distinguished by the name of Bristol bridge, is a plain, yet elegant structure of three arches, with a stone balustrade on each side, about seven feet high, and raised foot-paths chained in. The avenues leading to this bridge have been lately much improved, and are daily mending.

Over the river Froome there are two bridges, the one, called the Draw-bridge, leads to the center of the city, and that at the extremity of the wharfs, called the Stone-bridge, communicates with the lower parts towards St James's.

In commercial importance, Bristol owns no superior in Great Britain excepting London. The merchants here freight ships to every part of the globe; and their opulence sets them on an equality with any traders in Europe. The idea of total occupation in trade, which must strike every mind, on beholding a city, in which from twenty to thirty sugar-houses, and abundance of sulphur, turpentine, vitriol, and coal-works, brass & iron foundries, distilleries, glasshouses, and manufactories of woollen stuffs, and china, are almost incessantly at work, is agreeably corrected by the great encouragement and success literature, and the polite arts, meet with in this emporium of the west, and the very liberal urbanity with which persons, of all nations are encouraged to settle here, and become free of the city. Luxury, in her passage through our island, has not forgotten to visit Bristol; but she has not been able to expel industry. The gentry, merchants, and traders, have very elegant town and country houses, and public amusements, as frequent, and as various, as those of the metropolis. A particular degree of civility and attention is remarkable in the shop-keepers, and they are in general free from the charge of extortion. The city is governed by a mayor, who, before the dispute with the colonies, had an annual allowance of fifteen hundred pounds to support his dignity; at present it is reduced to one thousand: during his mayoralty, this officer is rarely seen in the streets but in his carriage. The corporation is composed of twelve aldermen, all justices of the peace, two sheriffs, who have each four hundred pounds for the discharge of the office, twenty-eight common council-men, a town clerk and his deputy, a chamberlain and vice-chamberlain, clerks of the court of conscience, under-sheriff, sword-bearer, &c.

The approach to the Hotwell House, 1792. The Pump Room may be seen jutting out into the river in the distance beyond the ramshackle buildings then existing around Rownham. A vessel is towed down river against the tide.

The principle buildings are the Cathedral, or collegiate church, St Mary Redcliffe, the Exchange, the Custom-house, the Council-house, the Guildhall, the Post-office, the Merchants', the Coopers', and the Merchant-taylors' hall, the Theatre, and the Assembly rooms.

There are in Bristol no fewer than eighteen parish churches: the most remarkable of them, besides those we have described, are St Stephens, admired for the beauty of its tower; All Saints, noticed for its resemblance to Bow church, London; and the Temple church, the tower of which is many degrees out of the perpendicular, and which, according to Camden, when the bells are rung, moves as he expresses it, 'huc et illuc', this way and that.

Broad Street by John Bartlett.

On the side of the green opposite to the cathedral, is the church of St Mark, now called the Mayor's chapel.

The exchange is situated in Corn-street, and was opened in 1743, after fifty thousand pounds had been expended in the purchase of the ground, and erection of it. The front is one hundred and ten feet in extent, and the depth is one hundred and forty-eight. It is capable of containing fifteen hundred persons. Before the Exchange, and on the Tolsey, are some of the old brass pillars used for transacting business before this edifice was built.

The Council-house is a stone building erected in 1701. Over the chimney, in the room where the corporation meet, there is a whole length portrait, by Vandyke, said to be that of an earl Pembroke, a present to the city of Bristol.

In the Guildhall, the assizes and sessions, and the mayor's and sheriffs' courts are holden. Adjoining to it is a lofty room called St George's chapel, in which the city officers are chosen.

*

A spirit of emulation and improvement has pervaded Bristol within these few years, and contributed much to the beauty of its appearance. In that part towards Clifton its bids fair to rival Bath.

Adjoining Park-street is a stone house belonging to Mr Tyndale. It has three fronts and overlooks the principal parts of the city, the river, and the adjacent country, the vale of Ashton and Dundry hill and tower, which in the morning, and at sun set, have a very remarkable effect. This group of scenery possesses no small degree of beauty: the valley is well wooded, and breaks into forms pleasingly irregular. Close under the hill passes the Avon, and at the turn of the tide, presents the ships floating up. The greatest objection to this view is the long line of the hill of Dundry.

A purchase has recently been made of Mr Tyndale's park for

BRISTOL-HOTWELLS, 1774.

L. SHIRLEY,

Begs Leave to acquaint the Nobility, Gentry, &c.

THAT she has neatly fitted up the OLD LONG-ROOM, where the Company may be accommodated with good Beds well aired; and also good Dining-Rooms and Parlours, large and commodious, superior to any at the Wells.—A Man Cook; Dinners drest on the shortest Notice, for Company at her own House, or to be sent to them at their Lodgings.—Neat Wines of all Sorts; Coffee, Tea, and Chocolate for any Number.

BALLS, ASSEMBLIES, &c. as usual.

N. B. The PUBLIC BREAKFASTS, with Cotillons and Country-Dances, every Monday during the Season.— She returns her sincere Thanks to the Company for past Favours, and humbly hopes for a Continuance of them, which she will use every Means to merit.

☞ Good Stabling for any Number of Horses, the best Hay and Corn, and great Care taken of them.—Neat Post-Chaises and Coaches with able Horses to lett to any Part of the Kingdom.

The Assembly Room at Hotwells was run by Mrs L Shirley at the time of this advertisement in 1774. Within 20 years it would be transformed by James Barton into the Gloucester Hotel.

the purpose of building, and a number of labourers were, when we visited it, preparing the ground.

The road to the Hot-Wells leads by the bottom of Brandon-hill, on the left of which the Avon shapes its course. A short distance farther, the river is concealed from sight by a row of houses to the left, called the Hot-well road, till we reach Dowry-square, a plain, but beautiful situation, at the foot of Clifton-hill.

On the left of the Hot-well road a crescent is now building, which will, when completed, make a handsome appearance.

Beyond Dowry-square, the road leads by the Old and New Rooms, and down to the ferry, at the Rownham passage, where

Bristol Cathedral from the cloisters, Samuel Lysons, 1804. In one of the houses nestling next to the south transept, and destroyed by the Victorian nave, Mary 'Perdita' Robinson was born.

ROYAL-FORT CRESCENT,
PARK-PLACE, BRISTOL.

ON MONDAY the 20th day of this instant August, at Twelve o'clock, WILL BE LET BY PUBLIC AUCTION, on the PREMISES, in THIRTY-EIGHT LOTS, for BUILDING, the whole of this CRESCENT, for a Term of 999 Years, under the best ground-rent that can be then and there produced, and under such terms and conditions for Building as shall be then and there produced.—The plan of the CRESCENT, and the elevation of the Houses to form the same, as drawn by JAMES WYATT, Esq; Architect, London, may be seen and particulars further known, by application to the Surveyor, Mr. CHARLES MELSOM, upon the Premises, and who will constantly attend there.
BRISTOL, August 4, 1792.

The building mania that swept Bristol in the 1790s resulted in a projected development in the grounds of the Royal Fort, here advertised on 4 August 1792. When this failed, Humphry Repton was engaged to repair the damage to the landscape.

again the Avon accompanies the path, and remains with us till we reach the Hot-well house.

The Parade, leading to the Hot-well house, is sheltered on each side by trees, and has, of late, received several additions. It wants breadth, but is kept in excellent order. The road from the Rooms to the Wells has been also much improved; and, instead of a few paltry huts that skirted this avenue, there are now building some handsome stone houses.

*

The village of Clifton is accounted the largest, and one of the most polite of any in the kingdom. The houses are of late become very numerous, and, in general, are large and elegant. It has been proposed to establish a market here, independent of that at Bristol, which, if the buildings planned are erected, will probably be carried into execution. Female education is a subject much attended to at Clifton; it abounds with good schools, amongst which Miss Burnet's, of Rodney-house, is much distinguished.

From the point of view above-mentioned, Clifton, and its elegant buildings, are seen to great advantage, immediately over-looking the river and Hot-wells. The houses now erecting by Mr Watts, will, when finished, form a very grand and singular feature in this prospect, as, for the purpose of making an artificial terrace, they are raised to a remarkable height. The expense attending this undertaking is very great; but it will give Clifton, still in a greater degree, the superiority over all villages. This eminence commands the river, and every thing passing on it, the whole of the vale of Ashton, the hills of Dundry, and great part of Leigh downs, and the adjacent country to the west. The parade, and close by the Well-house, opposite to which are the cotton mills.

Outdone by None: trade and industry

BRISTOL HAD LONG ENGENDERED ENVY, ADMIRATION AND CONTEMPT from other British cities, but especially London, in its successful and wholehearted pursuit of wealth. Apart from the industries and professions intimately connected with shipping itself, the city was the great emporium of the west, supplying purchasers over a wide area. A small collection of bills from around 1807 survive in the Reference Library's collection. They were originally sent to Sir Charles Morgan of Tredegar House, near Newport and chronicle some of the purchases made by his household in this era. All of the purchases were made from Bristol tradesmen and they cover all manner of things from mops and baskets to loaves of sugar. Alternatively producers and manufacturers from outside saw it as a good place in which to sell their wares. The city's imports and exports overseas are chronicled in the *Bristol Presentments* that are also in the Reference Library. These volumes contain the weekly printed lists that show the ships leaving the harbour and their destinations. Apart from British destinations (and the trade with Ireland was very great) the great majority were bound for the West Indies who relied on Britain for most of their goods. They had little or no manufacturing of their own and were not encouraged to trade with foreign powers, especially during this time of war.

The cargoes are quite astonishing and show the great variety of produce that Bristol was making and sending out. On 19 October the *Concord* left for Barbados carrying four cases of marble monuments from Henry Wood (architect and builder of College Place and Hotwells) and also four more from Forster and Co. In addition there were coffin ornaments, beer, glassware, toys,

Redcliffe Street, W H Bartlett. In this lithograph of the ancient street Bartlett has restored the spire of St Mary Redcliffe which was then still missing.

Windsor chairs, hats and hatbands, soap, pipes, paint and refined sugar, to list but a fraction of the cargo. The export of sugar back to the Indies is interesting as it was refined in Bristol first. On 24 February the *Rossetti* had left for Demerara including on board the materials for building a complete sugar mill from Dobbins, Stephen & Co, clothes, pans, millinery and 20,000 bricks! A glance at the classified and professional lists in any Bristol city directory of the period shows the myriad of small concerns that were at work within the city. The guidebooks of the era provide a full and yet still not comprehensive survey of the city's manufactures that brought her wealth. Accounts from two here follow.

Coal heavers, WH Pyne. These men sorted coal into different sizes to send to customers. Bristol was surrounded by coal fields and the miners were often unruly and feared.

The New Bristol Guide
Containing its Antiquities 1804 Section VII

The inhabitants of Bristol were very early addicted to trade and manufacturers. Several ancient authors represent Bristol as 'the most famous place of commerce in England, next to London, frequented by Merchants of many nations.' It took early to the Newfoundland Cod-fishing, and had trade to Andalusia in Spain, and many other foreign parts. By the charter of Edward III it appears that it was so considerable as to obtain the reputation of being the second City in England, for trade and populousness; and was of so much importance as to be constituted a County within itself. The King established the Manufactory of Cloth at Bristol, where it flourished for a long series of years to the middle of the last century, but is now much declined, and removed to other places where labour is cheaper. Bristol has been anciently and frequently celebrated by the writers of our own and other countries. Busching wrote that 'this City, for its prudent regulations, is perhaps outdone by none; and for its vast commerce, Wealth, and Shipping, by very few trading Cities in Europe.' And Dr Campbell: 'as to foreign Commerce, if we view it in gross, Bristol is next to London; but if the value of that Commerce is compared with the size of the respective Cities, Bristol has the start; and, except in a few branches, to the participation of which, of late, she begins to put her claim, in point of inter-course with all parts of the World, her correspondence is as extensive.' Such are the accounts of it by a foreigner and by a Britain.

The Bristol and Hotwell Guide containing an Account of that Opulent City
E Shiercliff 1805

OPPOSITE THE HOT-WELL-HOUSE, ON THE BANK OF THE AVON, IS A large building that lately contained a mill for spinning worsted, which was worked by a stream of pure water that springs immediately from the rock behind, runs through the house, and falls into the river.

The woollen manufactory is most entirely taken away from Bristol; some woollen stuffs, serges and other cloths, are made here. The manufacturers of silk, lace and fringe, and of sail-cloth, must not be omitted, nor those of Queen's and different sorts of earthen-ware; of toys, pins, and tobacco-pipes, which last are exported in great quantities.

The Cotton Manufactory, instituted in Temple-street, which in 1793 employed upwards of 250 persons, still continues, thrives, and increases. And the new manufactory of Pontipool, or japanned ware, on Temple-backs, meets with great encouragement.

A considerable number of builders, masons, and carpenters were lately engaged in the several new buildings in and about the City. But a temporary stop has been put to these desirable ornaments.

No place in England can boast of greater advantages by nature than Bristol now enjoys, owing to which its merchants trade with a greater independence upon London, than any other town in Britain; whatever exportations they make to any part of the world, they are able to bring back the returns to their own port and can dispose of them there, which no other port in Britain can do; for in general the merchants of other ports are obliged either to ship part of the effects they have abroad, on ships bound to London, or else consign their own vessels there, to sell their cargoes and get a freight: but the Bristol merchants, as they have a very great trade abroad, so that they always have buyers at home for their returns, and such buyers that no cargo is too large for them. The shopkeepers also are in general wholesale dealers, and have so great an inland trade, that they maintain riders and carriers, in the same manner as the Londoners, to all the Western counties, and principal counties and towns from Southampton in the south, even to the banks of the Trent in the north. Add to this, as well by sea as by the navigation of the two great rivers the Severn and the Wye, they have almost the whole trade of South Wales, as it were, to themselves, and the greatest part of North Wales; and their trade also to Ireland is very considerable.

There are about 300 sail of ships and vessels employed in foreign trade belonging to Bristol only, (exclusive of those who arrive here from different parts of the world, either to dispose of their cargoes or get freight,) besides coasting vessels, trows, market boats and other craft, which amounts to a very great number.

The customs and Excise of this port are immense, exceeding half a million annually.

The revenue of the Post-office is about 20,000l of the Land-tax about 10,000l and of the Poor-rate 14,000l.

Although the chief dependance of Bristol is upon its foreign trade, yet there are almost all kinds of business carried on in this city; and in the shops are seen as great a display and choice of every sort of goods, as are to be met with anywhere in the kingdom, and they are sold at as cheap rates. There are also very many capital works here and in the neighbourhood, which by reason of the great plenty and cheapness of coal and other fuel,

The piazza of the Exchange, Edward Bird. Visitors mocked the merchants of the city for not using this £50,000 building. Even after 50 years, for fear of losing trade they still preferred to stand outside in Corn Street by the Nails in the traditional place of business. The piazza was roofed in 1872.

On the banks of the Avon, near Hanham, about two miles East from Bristol, are situated the Spelter and Brass Works established by Mr Emerson, where the contents of several large furnaces are in continual fusion. These works are said to produce some of the purest and most valuable brass that has ever been manufactured. Its peculiar fineness of texture, tenacity of fibre, and malleability, render it in great demand among the more curious artificers at Birmingham, and other places; and considerable quantities of the spelter are exported, being much purer than any now manufactured on the continent.

*

In the parish of St Philip and Jacob, are three iron founderies for casting all kinds of iron work and artillery; and here is a steam engine for boring cannon when run solid. And in the same parish are considerable Lead Works, where lead is smelted from the ore, and rolled, or cast into sheets, pipes, and various articles for plumbers' use; and adjoining, the same proprietors have erected a house of great extent for making white and red lead.

It may not be amiss to remark that Bristol is famous for its manufactures of small lead shot, which on account of the roundness and colour, are preferred abroad to any other; and also that the Patent shot, so much esteemed, was the invention of Mr William Watts, of this city, who first made it here, and obtained a Patent for his discovery.

A Patent has likewise been granted to Mr John Garnett, of Bristol, Esq. for his invention to lessen friction in all kinds of

with the easiness of land and water carriage, the proprietors are enabled to sell on as low terms as can be done elsewhere. The brass-works at Baptist-Mills, at the distance of about one mile to the north-east of the city, was the first place where brass was made in England, and the original workmen were brought over from Holland for the purpose; the quantity made here is prodigious, it is drawn into wire, or formed into what they call battery, for the Guinea trade and other purposes, from whence it is sent to London, Liverpool, and every part of the kingdom. Another work of the same kind was also carried on at Warmley, about five miles from Bristol but it has been discontinued for some time.

wheels, blocks for ships, grindstones, rollers, and the like machinery; this invention is of great importance to persons concerned in mill-work, where great powers are required, for by the use of it, a far less force answers every purpose, and the movements being rendered more easy, the works of course last longer, and seldom want repairs. The works are carried on near College-street, and are called Garnett & Co's Patent Wheel and Block Manufacture.

The Bristol soap, for goodness, is not equalled by any that is made in England, large quantities of it are sent to London, and most parts of the kingdom.

As there is more sugar imported into Bristol from the West India islands, in proportion, than there is even into London, so there is also a greater number of sugar-houses, by which means loaf sugar is made here, and sold on better terms than can be done elsewhere, and in general, the single refined sugars of Bristol, are held in a higher estimation, and will fetch a better price abroad, than that which they receive from other places.

There is more glass manufactured in Bristol, than perhaps in any other place in England; the wine cyder, beer, and other liquors, together with the Hotwell water exported from hence to most parts of the world, cause so great a demand for bottles, as to employ several houses for making them. And of window glass also there are vast quantities sent to America, and other parts; and the home consumption must be very great, for glazing windows and other purposes, not only in this city, but in Bath, and in the many towns and villages round about; as also the western counties, Wales and every place north and south, wherever the Bristol trade extends. Here are likewise two houses, wherein they make white or flint glass, and phial-bottles; and to those who have never seen the manner of working this material,

A potter specialising in sugar loaf moulds, by John Smith. The child below turns the potter's wheel.

it may be a pleasing entertainment to attend the process particularly of window-glass; nor is the blowing of white, or flint-glass unworthy of their attention, as it is formed into such a variety of articles; strangers are never denied the liberty of seeing the people at work, on a small gratuity being given to the men employed. To such of our readers who are desirous of seeing these manufactures, we think it necessary that they be informed of the days on

'New scissors!', RM Bryant. Pedlars were a common sight both in the streets of Bristol and the countryside around.

which they work at each house, and the sort of glass made on those days, that they may not be disappointed by going at a wrong time.

*

The distilleries carried on here are in a very extensive line, the demand for spirits for the African trade and internal consumption being very great.

A manufactory has been instituted and established with great success by Mr John Thomas from London, for preparing red, blue and yellow Morocco Leather; green and black Spanish: also red, blue, yellow, green, and black Roans: which, we are credibly informed, are superior to foreign skins in colour, gloss, and lustre; and are vended on the most reasonable terms. There is only another manufactory of this sort in England, and that is in London. It was carried on at first on the Broad Ware, but is since removed to convenient buildings erected for it at Baptist Mills, near to the river, on the western side of the Fox.

We shall lastly remark, that the many ships and vessels which are built at Bristol, with the various trades require to compleat them for sea, must necessarily give employment to a very great number of people, besides the seamen who navigate them in their respective voyages.

There are two fairs usually held in Bristol, which formerly began on the 25th of January, and the 25th July; the first continued nine; and the last eight clear days, besides a day for what is termed the packing-penny. These fairs were formerly of very great importance, as traders almost in every line, and from all parts of Great Britain and Ireland, resorted to them, for the purpose of buying or selling. The time of year, for each, being judged inconvenient, is now changed, the one being held on the 1st of March, in the Great-gardens, in Temple Parish; the other on the 1st of September in St James's Church Yard. At this last, there is generally a large number of horses of all kinds, for sale, which seldom continues more than two or three days; at present, the principal traders, who frequent these fairs, are the clothiers, either to sell or receive orders for their goods; also dealers in tanned leather, there being more of this article sold during those periods, at the Back-Hall, than at any other fair in England, and of ticking for bed cases there is likewise a very considerable quantity vended at the Tick-Hall. But besides these, there are only a few hardware-men, from Birmingham, Wolverhampton, Sheffield, and other places, and some cotton stocking makers from Tewksbury, the rest consisting merely of shops and stands wherein millinery wares, toys, or some trifling articles, are exposed for sale by the towns people.

There are two principal markets in this city for butchers meat, poultry, butter cheese, bacon, eggs and all kinds of vegetables, held on Wednesday and Saturday in every week. We shall first take notice of the most capital one, which by way of eminence, and as being the oldest, is generally styled the Market, this is situate on the south-side of the Exchange, on a large, commodious square piece of ground, which was cleared for the purpose, soon after that edifice was compleated; it consists of eight double rows of sheds, or stands, covered with Cornish slate; on the end of each row is painted a large capital letter, alphabetically, from A. to H. and every stand in each row is numbered from 1 to 157, this is done for the mutual convenience of buyer and seller, as by this method any person wanted is immediately found, without the trouble of enquiry. Those sheds are always occupied for the sale of butchers meat. There are also three market houses of considerable length and breadth, under cover, wherein the farmers and country people sell butter, cheese, poultry, eggs, bacon, and other articles. One is in the piazza of the south front of the Exchange, and is called the Glocestershire market, being occupied mostly by people from that county; the stands or seats here are likewise numbered, beginning with No. 1 and ending with 62.

On the west-side are piazzas also that support a range of buildings, called the Somersetshire market, most of the farmers, and country people therein being of that county: the stands and seats here are also numbered from 1 to 68. And on the east side, which leads to the market-house gate next High-street are other piazzas with buildings over, the stands and seats are here also numbered as the former, from 1 to 52. Opposite to this last, are eight separate stands or shops for all kinds of garden produce, which is raised early, and in great perfection. At the entrance into the market from Corn-street, by the Post-office, are thirteen other shops, also

The Baker, W H Pyne, 1805.

a range of ten stands, extending in front of the Glostershire market on the south side of the Exchange, where the like articles are sold. And there is another row of ten stands on the west-side of the butchers, facing the Somersetshire market, wherein are sold flowers and roots in pots, or plants and shrubs for the green-

Castle Bank (The Dutch House) on the corner of High Street and Wine Street, J S Prout.

house or garden. When we consider the whole of this as being but one market, and the abundant quantity of articles with which it is supplied, we may venture to affirm, that for plenty, goodness, and cheapness, it is scarcely equalled by any market in Great Britain.

The Corporation have advertised for building a new Market in addition to the above, behind Nicholas-Street, and contracts have been drawn for the same.

But notwithstanding the largeness of the above market, and its extensive supply, together with the situation nearly in the centre of the city; yet on account of the many additional buildings, and increase of inhabitants of late years, it was found inadequate to the demands of the people, therefore the Corporation have erected another market, on a very convenient spot adjoining Union-street, near Broad-mead, called St James's-market, where every sort of provisions are sold as in the other market, and the shops and stands here are numbered in like manner. Here also the market for Fish is kept on Wednesday and Friday, on which days it is plentifully supplied with every kind in proper season. The two market houses formerly made use of for the sale of Corn, between Wine-street, and Maryport-street, were opened by order of the Magistrates on the 3d of January, 1787, for

Trade card for W Collins, wine merchant.

A slaughterman, WH Pyne, 1805. In England the time-honoured way of despatching cattle and sheep had not changed over the centuries. Cattle were struck on the head with a pole-axe to kill them and sheep and pigs had their throats cut.

bottom right:
A receipt for 7/- for six baskets from Henry Warner's Warehouse at 21 Maryport Street, bought for Sir Charles Morgan's household at Tredegar near Newport.

the sale of Cheese only; the market days are every Wednesday and Saturday. There are likewise shambles for butchers meat without the place where Lawford's-gate stood, but not being in the liberties of the city, they are scarcely frequented by any except the inhabitants of adjacent streets.

The markets for the sale of Raw Hides, Calves Skins, and all sorts of unwrought Tanned Leather, is held at the Back-Hall every Wednesday and Saturday throughout the year. And at the same place is held a market for Tanned Leather every Thursday.

In that part of the city called the Back, there is a market-house erected for the mutual convenience of the inhabitants, and the people from Wales, who bring hither for sale, every Wednesday, roasting pigs, poultry, and different kinds of fruit, walnuts, filberts, and common hazel nuts, during their seasons; and farther on are houses for the lodging of corn, faggots, stable brooms, and other articles. There is also a very considerable market every

Thursday in St Thomas-street, for horses, pigs, and live cattle. And in Broad-mead, is a market for Hay and Straw every Tuesday and Friday.

Bristol, as well as all the country round, is in general supplied with coals from Kingswood; (there are also pits in Bedminster, Ashton, Nailsea and Brislington, besides extensive ones at Coalpit-Heath). The colliers' houses, when seen from St Michael's-Hill, Kingsdown, or any other eminence, seem to stand so close to each other for miles together, as to have the appearance of being a part of the suburbs of the city: some of these pits are not more than two miles distant from the town, and to those who choose to fetch their own coals, they are sold there at 4d. per bushel for large, and 3d. per bushel for the small; it is brought in waggons and carts, often on horses and asses, and sold to the inhabitants at 15d. the sack, containing about two bushels. There is also coal brought hither by water from the Forest of Dean in Glocestershire, and other places, which is sold at the head of the Quay by the ton weight; which being all large coal, and making a cheerful fire, though not very durable, is chiefly used for burning in the parlour and chamber.

The pumps, both public and private, are numerous, and all of them emit from the sand, rocks, and strata beneath, the clearest and most excellent water.

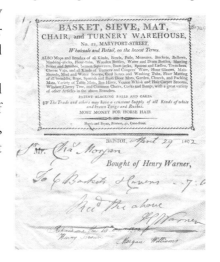

A drink of ass's milk

Hotwells and Clifton as holiday resorts

BY 1807 HOTWELLS' GLORY DAYS AS A SPA WERE SERIOUSLY ON THE wane but it was still reasonably popular. The next few years would prove to be very difficult for the resort. Up until 1789 it had been crowded with fashionable visitors but the greed of the spa's tenant and the short-sightedness of the landlord, the Merchants' Company, saw the pleasure-seeking fashionable trade go elsewhere as the fee for taking the water was raised to £1-6s per month. Raised charges for the bottled water saw its popularity plummet amongst distant customers. Only the most desperate invalids or the most wealthy pleasure seeker could now countenance the new charges. The decline in visitors through the increased charges resulted in bankruptcies and ruin to many of the lodging houses and places of entertainment and, even in Bristol itself, the Prince Street Assembly Rooms became a warehouse for iron for a while after 1810. Added to this was the fact that with the cessation of hostilities with France the wealthy flocked to experience Europe again and rejected the old resorts. By 1816 the Pump Room was described by the Clifton physician

But the goddess of love, and the graces and all.
Must yield to the beauties I've seen at the ball.

Thinks I 'tis all over, my sentence is past.
And now he is counting how long I may last.

How the Ladies did giggle and set up their clacks:
All the while an old women was rubbing their backs.

Dr Carrick as having 'the silence of the grave, to which it seems the inlet. Not a carriage to be seen once an hour, and scarcely more frequently does a solitary invalid approach the neglected spring. One of the ballrooms and taverns has been long ago shut up, and the other with great difficulty kept open'.

Hotwells faced competition from the gradually expanding village of Clifton high on the cliffs above with its rival pump room, although there and in Kingsdown and Portland Square the frantic and ruinous property speculations of the 1790s had resulted in the blight of long rows of roofless and unfinished terraces such as Royal York Crescent and Cornwallis Crescent. In the years following 1807 both Hotwells and Clifton were to feel the effects of a serious decline in visitors caused by the greed and mismanagement of the spa owners. Even Bath was feeling the effect at this time from the new craze of sea bathing which saw the winter Season now spent at such resorts as Brighton and Southend.

Unlike Bath's winter visitors, however, Hotwells had always been a summer resort, as the water was believed to be at its most efficacious in warm weather. In 1807, whilst the sun still shone on Hotwells, a typical day for the patient or pleasure seeker started at six am with a drink of ass's milk. It seems that the asses were kept and milked in fields beyond Brandon Hill. At half past seven the first glass of water was taken at the spring and after a short walk the second was swallowed. Horse or carriage exercise followed until about nine o'clock, when breakfast was taken either at the public rooms or privately. A second course of waters followed about noon followed by riding exercise until the dinner hour at four. Tea was taken at about half-past six. Regular balls, visits to libraries, sitting for portraits and shopping for souvenirs occupied other minutes of the day. Thomas Rowlandson's rare

top: *View of the Avon Gorge from Clifton Downs*. TE Chapman, lithograph.

above: *The Old Hotwell House*, Samuel Jackson, lithograph. The actual spring was below the high tide mark and so the house had to built out into the river in order to capture it. As a result it became a shipping hazard and was finally removed and the water piped to the new Pump Room below the cliff. The steep stairway up to Clifton and terraced gardens can be seen to the right.

27

A card party from the 1807 edition of Anstey's *New Bath Guide*.

And at cards all the night take the trouble to play,
To get back the money they spent in the day.　　page 59.

series of satirical prints *The Comforts of Bath* (published in 1798, and held by Bristol Reference Library) can equally be used to illustrate most of the holiday activities in Hotwells and Clifton, as can the various plates in editions of Christopher Anstey's amusing *New Bath Guide*.

The 1807 visitor would not have experienced a quiet stay at the spa as the area must have been rocked by regular explosions as the stone was blasted from the cliffs by the quarrymen and lime-burners. At the same time the new river (the 'New Cut') was being blasted through the countryside opposite and beyond. The meadows of Rownham Mead were themselves in the process of being transformed into the Cumberland Basin.

Rownham Ferry, Cream Teas and Fossilists

Fair Nymphs more blooming than the flow'rs

'Many ladies and gentlemen cross the River at Rownham-ferry, and walk to the sweet and wholesome village of Ashton, to eat strawberries, or raspberries, with cream, a delicious and salutary repast.'
The New Bristol Guide

ALTHOUGH PAINTED SOME YEARS LATER THAN 1807, ROLINDA Sharples' charming painting of the Rownham Ferry is a marvellous record of the characters and activities witnessed in the resort of Hotwells. The ferry was a direct route for traffic between Somerset and Hotwells and up to the Edwardian era provided passage for travellers and their mounts and those wishing to sell their produce in Bristol and the resort. It also afforded holiday-makers the opportunity to explore the wonderful scenery of the west bank of the Avon and for sportsmen to hunt game. It was believed to have been a Roman crossing point of the Avon, a belief further advanced by the antiquarian interest of the two encampments on the heights either side of the gorge.

Pleasure trips down the Avon were popular and when accompanied by music in the boats the sound was echoed and re-echoed by the rocks either side of the gorge. Here a lady waves from a small boat to an army officer on board the departing Dublin packet that sailed every Thursday. Her companions include a naval officer. In 1807 Bristol and the spa must have been bright with uniforms. Passengers for the packet stayed at the towering Gloucester Hotel in Gloucester Terrace.

The packet's sail covers the site of the old Pump Room which was under demolition at the time Sharples painted the scene. The old Pump Room had jutted out into the river and was a navigational hazard. Its removal allowed the cutting of the new road up to Clifton to spare the nervous the terrifying carriage ride down Granby Hill. At the same time a new pump room in the Tuscan style was built under the cliff and for the first time had baths attached. Although the dreadful situation of 1816 had by now improved the spa never really prospered financially. The water also lost its original temperature through being piped from its original source.

Those gathered on the riverside in Sharples' painting and awaiting the next ferry provide a microcosm of some of the pleasures and hazards available to the visitors of Hotwells and Clifton.

Apart from thrilling scenic walks and rides on both sides of the gorge and on the Downs, donkey riding might also be enjoyed and in Sharples' painting (see colour section) a small attendant with a whip steadies a mount whilst a little girl is placed on the saddle. James Malcolm noted with amazement in June 1805 that he had seen a sight ridiculous to a Londoner of 'an elegant young lady clad in black silk, with a white beaver bonnet, and laced veil, bearing a parasol of green silk' riding with her brother on donkeys on the Downs. It seems that riding donkeys on the Bristol Downs for enjoyment whilst on holiday predates the pastime at seaside holiday resorts. By January 1806 the craze had spread to Brighton and was mocked by Gillray in his engraving *Morning promenade*. By 1825 it had certainly become commonplace as the *Matthews' Bristol Guide* declares 'There are at the Hotwells and also at Clifton, neat Pony Cars and Donkies for riding, which may be hired at any time of the day.' Probably it was seen not only as a convenient and less energetic way in which to see the country whilst avoiding the hazards of mud and dust but may also have been rustic novelty for the town dweller to

The Morning Promenade, James Gillray, 1806. Gillray's caricature of the brand-new fashion for riding donkeys whilst on holiday. The ladies with the parasols and veils echo Malcolm's lady encountered on the Downs at Clifton the previous year.

engage in. The Bristolian, Mrs Elton, sums up the practice in Jane Austen's 1815 novel *Emma*. 'I wish we had a donkey. The thing would be for us all to come on donkeys, Jane, Miss Bates and me, and my Caro Sposo walking by. I really must talk to him about purchasing a donkey. In a country life I conceive it to be a sort of necessary;—-very long walks you know…in summer there is dust, and in winter there is dirt.' A painting by Charles Branwhite in the Bristol City Art Gallery dated 1846 shows two donkeys and their child attendant on the Downs.

In the Sharples' painting, a gentleman marksman quizzes two Italianate street entertainers who hold a tambourine and small guitar whilst another hunter rides by frightening a fruit seller in the process. Wild fowl were hunted along the river for sport and especially in the woods and on the coast at Portishead. For the

Details from *Rownham Ferry*, Rolinda Sharples (see colour section for complete painting):

left:
Donkey rides at Hotwells. The little girl has a specially adapted saddle and a smartly-dressed child attendant.

opposite:
Passengers on the Rownham ferry leaving for the Somerset bank.

asleep, possibly from enjoying the inns that were on both sides of the river. His makeshift bed includes a box addressed to the artist inscribed with the instruction 'To be kept very dry' that has already been engulfed by the rising tide. A black sweep boy uses his brush to sprinkle soot on the man's face, whilst his white companion touches it with a stinging nettle. They are regarded by the wild-fowler's silver-collared dog.

The occupants of the wide ferry boat are painted with Sharples' usual humorous observation. An artisan flirts with a girl loaded with fruit and flowers and so captivates her that she does not realise that her other flower basket has fallen off the boat and is floating away, nor that her admirer has stolen a bunch of grapes. A partially sighted man holds his penny fare up to his eye whilst a lady offers her purse to a country woman in a red cloak. Ibbetson on his visit in the early 1790s found the ferry very picturesque:

A view of the opposite side where the boat lands, affords a subject for the artist; and though not in the grand gusto, may, by the addition of the ferry-boat, and groups of rustic figures and horses, frequently to be seen there, be formed into a good landscape. The eye now looking towards the Hot-well house, will catch another subject; but here the formal hand of art has destroyed the bolder features of nature, by the interposition of some huts, still in their outline, and mean in their general character. About four o'clock in a summer's afternoon and when the tide is high, one of the broadest and best effects of light and shade may be seen, by looking from the tree where the ferry-boat lands. On the western side the rocks rise to a considerable height, and are covered with wood almost to the summit;

more energetic genteel sporting visitor the chance of riding to hounds at Ashton Court was always on offer when the Smyths arranged a meet. Bristol was noted for its fresh-fruit sellers and two of these may be seen carrying baskets on their heads. A young artist carrying a portfolio is approached by an elderly beggar with a bowl whilst a gentleman makes use of his telescope to appreciate the view or his companions more intimately. In the distance a couple walk along the tree-lined promenade in front of St Vincent's Parade whilst their boys enjoy the age-old childhood sport of wall-top walking.

Less innocent amusements occupy the two boys in the foreground. A porter or tapster (to judge by his apron) has fallen beneath them the Avon forms a broad sheer, and loses itself imperceptibly behind the rocks of St Vincent. On the east, the bed of the river is bounded by rocks familiar to those on the opposite shore, but not wooded. At the above-mentioned point of time, the sun declining just overlooks the western rocks, and reflects the shadow from the woods beneath it, to about mid-way on the river, where a broad light unites the remaining part of the scene into an harmonious composition.

The habit of crossing the river to walk the short distance to Long Ashton for cream teas started in the previous century following the visit of a predecessor, the Rev Mr Wickham, to Holland for the purpose of finding new culinary plants. He returned with several different species of strawberries which the cottagers cultivated, along with raspberries, and thus started a thriving series of tea gardens. William Morgan of Bower Ashton was inspired to write a substantial poem in two parts entitled 'Long Ashton' in praise of the local scenery:

And fragrant Raspberry scents the gale,
From every cot throughout the vale
Fair Nymphs more blooming than the flow'rs
In crowds, pass on to Ashton's Bowers,
Adorn'd with youth in beauty's pride,
The Swains attendant by their side.—
Now in the woodbine Arbours sweet
Mirthful partake the luscious treat.
Some to the swing for pastime fly
And swiftly circling mount on high,
A mingled Crowd in groups display'd

Stroll in the Orchard's cooling shade;
The Dulcimer and Viol's note
Amid the verdant scen'ry float,
And many a Fair beside her Swain
Sits list'ning to the joyous strain.

Ibbetson was in complete agreement with Morgan on the subject of the village's charms:

Ashton is one of the pleasantest villages in the vicinity of Bristol, and famous for fine fruit: an attraction which draws abundance of company thither in the summer evenings. At the back of the houses in the village, alcoves are fitted up for their reception, where they may be accommodated with tea, &c.

His wanderings on the Leigh side of the river brought him to the cotton mills that were still operating in the 1790s opposite the Hotwells Pump Room. These would soon turn to worsted production and by 1806 to grinding logwood. They are referred to as the Red or Scarle(t) Mills in some accounts:

> The mills are happily situated under an immense mass of lime-stone rocks, on the surface of which is a profusion of wood. These rocks lie in broad strata, shelving over one another, and declining gradually down to the bed of the river. A spring of water issues behind the mills, and is conducted to turn them. It empties itself into the river, at the Hot-well house.

Exploring further he found Nightingale Valley:

> … a path leads through a shady retreat, and up a coomb of some length, to Leigh-down, which separated the Roman camps. Frequent parties are made to this spot, for the purpose of drinking tea: an old oak's projecting withered branch serves to sling the kettle from, while a piece of rock and a felled tree, supply the deficiency of a table and a chair: a small band of music is often an adjunct to this rural scene; and the reverberation of the sounds among the rocks produces a sort of gentle confusion, that is, at least in perfect harmony with the wildness of the scene, if not to the advantage of the performers.

> From the rising ground, a very good view of the Hot-well house may be taken; but the stiff forms of the buildings now erecting above it, on the rocks of Clifton, however they may, when finished, embellish the scene, have totally ruined a once magnificent landscape.

One class of visitor that Sharples did not include, unless one appears without an attribute in the composition, is the 'Fossilist' or palaeontologist. The gorge and surrounding rocks were a magnet for gentlemen interested in this relatively new hobby, and Bristol had already one of the first (if not the first) publicly displayed collection of fossils in the country at the Library in King Street. In Georgian Bristol the Rev Alexander Catcott was a well-known collector of fossils. He used his collection to preach that fossils were evidence of the Biblical Deluge that had melted the surface of the planet and deposited the remains of sea creatures far away from their original habitat sometimes high on newly formed mountains left by the receding waters. In his will, dated 24 March 1778, he left two cabinets of his fossils and minerals to Bristol Library together with all his books on the subject. This 'fossilary' became the earliest museum collection in Bristol. When Bristol Museum was established the collection was transferred from the library and became part of the fabulous, internationally important, collection of fossils.

In 1924 the Catcott Cabinet, as it was then called, was cleaned and put on display in the Geological Room of the Natural History Museum (now Brown's restaurant). Unfortunately it appears to have been destroyed in the Blitz along with the greater part of the fossil reptile collection so it is believed that only Catcott's books now survive in the Reference Library.

The watercolour artist and writer on art, George Cumberland, moved to Bristol in 1807 and lived at 1 Culver Street until his death in 1848. He amassed a large and important collection of fossils and published several works on the subject including

Reliquiae Conservatae in 1826. He was the first to recognise the general resemblance of ichthyosaurs to the modern porpoise and to suggest a dorsal fin, although this was not included in restorations for many years.

Other collectors of fossils in Bristol in 1807 and still around in 1814 when G B Greenhough drew up a list, were George Weare Braikenridge of Brislington (who also collected historical prints and watercolours of the city now in the possession of the Reference Library and City Art Gallery) and James Johnson of Colston Parade. Both possessed ichthyosaur specimens from the Lias beds of Somerset. Braikenridge's 'crocodile' was found in a quarry at Keynsham where finds of ammonites were commonplace. His fossil collection was to be a great influence on his neighbour, the Rev William Conybeare, one of the joint founders of the Bristol Institution. James Johnson of Hotwells (c1764-1841) and his son, John (c1789-1841), collected fossils at Lyme and discovered two enormous ichthyosaur skulls in 1813. The same poetical William Morgan (c1773-1848) of Bower Ashton mentioned above uncovered an exceptionally well preserved ichthyosaur at Watchet that was drawn in great detail by Cumberland. Morgan could not resist including references to fossil collecting in his poem:

Now vent'rous up the rugged steep,
Or climbing in the Cavern deep,
Yon Fossilist will oft explore
With curious eye each Stratum o'er.
His hammer's stroke, the stone divides-
From him, no treasure Nature hides.

The gentleman fossilist *par excellence*. Gideon Mantell complete with hammer watches quarry workers uncover a fossil at Tilgate quarry in Sussex. A lithograph by P Gauci from a drawing by F Pollard.

The Bristol Diamonds

In the fissures and cavities of the rocks, are found those fine chrystals called Bristol Stones or Diamonds, some of which are so hard as to cut glass, are extremely clear, colourless and brilliant; and when set in rings in their natural state, have appeared of as high a polish and lustre as if they had been wrought by the most skilful lapidary.

It will be proper to observe to the purchasers of clusters of stones, apparently chrystal, that are sold in the shops, that many of them are nothing better than spar, and much softer than the true Bristol Stones, which will cut glass, and bear the fire and Aqua Fortis without alteration; but glass breaks the spar, aqua fortis corrodes it, and fire calcines it into lime. Also the shoots of spar are triangular or pentangular, but those of chrystal are hexagonal, and terminate in a point.

New Bristol Guide

Male and female quarry workers in the Avon Gorge. J Laporte, aquatint, 1793.

THE AVON GORGE IS REMARKABLE FOR THE GREAT VARIETY OF geological strata that occur in it. Although much of the stone quarried in the eighteenth and nineteenth centuries was used for building stone or burned to make lime, there were certain ones that were destined for more ornamental uses. Black Goethite seems to have been polished to resemble marble as did a Carboniferous Coralline limestone that may have been the stone used for producing mantelpieces. The outcrop known as 'Black Rock' not surprisingly produced a dense black stone that would also bear a polish. The Triassic limestone, known locally as Cotham Marble or Landscape Marble, also produced an effect of a painted landscape with trees when polished.

Certainly at a later date and probably also in 1807, visitors could purchase mineral specimens or rulers, paperweights and other ornamental items made from one or a variety of these stones. When the new Tuscan-style Pump Room was opened following the demolition of the historic one, we know that the new shop in the building sold not only such useful devices as flesh rubbers and brushes, respirators; portable seats and stools, cigars, umbrellas and Hotwell toothpowder, but also boomerangs, fancy objects in lava and fossils from the neighbourhood, both in their natural state and also made into inkstands, brooches and so on.

These rocks, for the most part, when broken up, are of a dusky red, brown or chocolate coloured marble, very hard and close grained, and being hit with a hammer emit a strong sulphurous scent. This stone will bear a polish equal to any foreign marble; and when sawed into slabs and polished, it appears beautifully variegated with veins of white bluish grey, or yellow. It is frequently used for chimney-pieces (of which there is an agreeable specimen in that of the Pump-room); but principally for making lime, for which there is not any stone in England so good as this; nor is there any lime so strong, fine and white, which excellent properties occasion a very great demand for it abroad.
New Bristol Guide

The most sought-after geological delight that most visitors desired either in searching the gorge or more likely the shops of the spa, were the famous Bristol diamonds. These were actually quartz, but quite remarkable in their clarity and hardness. They were made into jewellery or used as mantelpiece or grotto ornaments. Goldney Grotto in Clifton had a very fine display of them. Ibbetson goes in to some detail over the different diamonds that occurred in the quarries around Bristol:

The miners of the neighbouring country bring great quantities of fossil to this place, and in the city is of such common use, that it is rare to see a chimney not decorated with pieces of spar. Specimens have been dug of the weight of half a hundred.

The stones, known by the name of Bristol stones, are dug out of St Vincent's rock, and are of a crystal kind, as perfectly polished as possible. In general they are clear and destitute of colour, but some are of a whitish hue. They are found in the neighbourhood of the iron ore, and when dug, are often fit for the purpose of setting in rings, &c. Many grottos in the vicinity of Bristol are ornamented with them, particularly one at Clifton. They rise in a variety of forms; in some places resembling rose diamonds, and in others table diamonds. Those about Clifton often look like clusters of small brilliants; those of King's Weston are remarkable for the whimsical singularity of forms into which they shoot. In some there seem to be little hairs in others, white specks; in many bubbles of air or drops of water. Those that are pure are clear, and such as are tinged with color, are hard enough to bear a strong fire without alteration; such as the imperfect turn white in this trial. They generally adhere to one side; some are pointed at both ends, some are pyramidal and sexangular. The small ones are more frequently coloured than the larger ones.
Ibbetson

The Gloucester Hotel

such a Lodgement can scarcely be paralleled

> Gloucester House, formerly the only hotel of any note, and whence the steam packets to Ireland regularly sail, is still much frequented, from its proximity to the Hot Wells.
> *A Topographical History of England*, 1848

FOR OVER A CENTURY AND A HALF THE ESTABLISHMENT THAT BECAME known as the Gloucester Hotel reigned paramount in Hotwells and Clifton and was renowned not only for its hospitality but for its astonishing architecture. It has now been generally forgotten.

The original Bath-stone building which was also the Assembly Rooms was constructed at the beginning of the eighteenth century and opened in 1722. From the outside it appeared to be two storeyed, but descriptions suggest that the rooms reached to the full height of the building. It had a central doorway set between six pairs of large round-topped windows. It was from the first the most impressive structure in the landscape.

In 1774 the proprietor was a lady called L B Shirley who advertised accommodation and stabling, a 'Man Cook', and balls, assemblies and public breakfasts. It is not known exactly what the hotel part of the building was like at this time, but it may have formed the ground and first floors of what was to come later. The Assembly Room itself occupied the entire front of the building. The southern façade was fronted by a raised terrace or parade for the company. The front wall of this held brackets for flower urns. Fronting this was a rectangular walled Paradise or garden. The latter gave the name of Paradise Row to the street, until it later changed to Gloucester Terrace in the early part of the next century. The central path through the Paradise led to a flight of

'Turtle sent to all parts of the Kingdom.' The Gloucester Hotel in the 1820s from an advertisement engraved by J Price. That Price's engraving is incredibly accurate can be seen by comparing it with the newly-discovered photograph shown on page 40. Even the slope of the roof above the rooms is exact.

steps and was approached through gate piers topped with richly carved stone pine cones and closed by elaborate wrought iron gates. The building was also backed by a large walled garden with ornamental beds holding trees and shrubs. A landscape of Hotwells and Clifton around 1730 in the Red Lodge, Bristol (K4646) shows the new building and its gardens.

Later in the century under its proprietor James Barton, the hotel was turned into the luxurious towering building that was to dominate Hotwells for many years. Described as 'a house upon a house' it appears to have been about five or six storeys high with three sets of bay windows attached to the southern façade. The effect was very seaside... very Brighton! This extension was built in the back garden of the Assembly Rooms, behind and to the right of the old building, and overlooked Albemarle Row and Green Street to the north. The steeply ascending hillside behind the Assembly Rooms no doubt contributed to the towering effect but architecturally the result was very striking. A grand panorama by Col William Booth in 1822 from Granby Hill, Clifton, now in the City Art Gallery (K101), shows the spectacular view across the river that guests at the hotel would have enjoyed. Of greater importance though for the study of the building, it also shows that the rear or northern façade also had three long rows of bay windows. The lower houses of Granby Place, with their four-storeyed bays may have been influenced by the Gloucester Hotel or have possibly been, in fact, the work of the same architect. Booth's watercolour also tells us that the famous circular staircase below a skylight was placed in the centre of the tower block in the manner of a light well. Around the same time the south façade of the Assembly Rooms was engrandised with an attached and pedimented entrance façade, although it copied or reused the existing early eighteenth-century windows. The new entrance copied that of the New or Lower Rooms. For additional accom-modation Barton also built Paradise Row, the series of three smart, bow fronted houses adjoining the property that still survive in Hotwell Road.

George Heath's guide of 1797 contains an excellent description, proving that the alterations had been achieved by the 1790s at the latest:

Here are two sets of large, elegant, public Rooms; and three Hotels. But of all the Hotels, here, or indeed in these Parts, that named GLOCESTER HOUSE or BARTON's HOTEL is the principal, compleatest and grandest. The unremit-ting exertions of Mr James Barton, to render it so; and the great expense he has been at, to make it more than a convenient, a truly excellent Hotel, merit the Public notice and encouragement. On the northern side, he has enlarged it by building a lofty House, rising story over story to a remarkable height. In this, are, a beautiful circular Stair Case, which perforates the whole from the bottom to the top, which ends in a Sky-light; also many spacious, airy, Bed Rooms, sitting and dining Rooms, which command such delightful Prospects of the River, the Hills and Country, that such a Lodgement can scarcely be paralleled. He had added to it, on the western side, a series of handsome Buildings, in Paradise-row, in which he has opened for the better accommodation of the Nobility and Gentry, a Table de Hote, on such terms as meet with general approbation. The Assembly Room, was originally built, very early in this century, and was then one of the principal Rooms in the Kingdom: a few years ago, it was totally rebuilt, and is now the best at the Wells. It is 90 feet long, 35 wide and 35 high; has Glass Chandeliers, a Music Gallery, and presents lovely views of the adjacent Paradise, from which the row in which it stands was denominated.

The next Assembly Room and Hotel, stands on the opposite side of the Street, and is called the Lower, or New Long Room, this is built on arches and fronts to the River. At these, are public Breakfasts, during the Season, every

Monday and Thursday alternately; with Cotillions and Country Dances; for which each person pays 1s. 6d. The Balls are on Tuesdays; subscriptions to which is one Guinea at each Room; and for walking in the Rooms and Gardens and reading the Papers. 5s. Subscribers to the Balls are allowed two Tickets, which admit two Ladies: Non-subscribers pay 5s each Ball. There is also, the New Inn or Hotel, a good House in Dowry-square.

The New or Lower Rooms were opened in 1774/5 and were to survive until 1963, having become a school after 1870, until the roadworks of the Cumberland Basin unfortunately swept them away. In general shape they mimicked the older rooms but had square-topped windows and a high-pitched roof. They can be seen clearly on two watercolours in the City Art Gallery collection, one by an anonymous artist and dating from around 1780 (M4178) and another by the Irish artist George Holmes (K2356), who had set up a purveyor of local souvenir landscapes to the visitors at the Wells in 1802.

By the early-nineteenth century the Paradise, although still functioning as a garden, had been provided with a double carriage drive for the convenience of guests. Either at this time or during Barton's redevelopment the parade and front steps were provided with simple railings of a rectangular pattern that may also have functioned as trellis for the plants in the beds fronting them. An iron arch rose from the top of the steps and originally held a central flambeau. The front garden wall was also by now replaced by lengths of plain spiked railings topped with the occasional urn finial. An engraved trade card by Price gives a wonderful and accurate portrayal of how it appeared, even down to the design of the gates and the glass flambeaux either side of

the main doors. Its general accuracy is confirmed by the recent discovery of a photograph taken of the building from the same viewpoint shortly before demolition in the 1880s. Not only can one trace the ruins of the design of the ornamental ironwork of the gates but pasted notices appear on the gate posts in exactly the same places where they appear on the engraving sixty years before.

With the falling off of visitors to the Spa, by 1815 the Lower Rooms across the street were described as 'void' in the guide book, there no longer being enough business to support the two. As was expected, the hotel also had a thriving funerary business for those guests who did not survive. *Matthew's Guide* for 1819 confides 'Mr Barton also carries on the business of Undertaking to any part of the kingdom, and keeps a rich assortment of real ostrich funereal plumes, both white and black'. Amongst the other delights the establishment offered to its guests was a seemingly endless supply of freshly shipped turtles to cope with the craving for turtle soup. Remarkable as it seems, live turtles could be sent anywhere in the kingdom on demand. By the 1820s the Hotel had changed hands and was now called Warne's Hotel and Ballrooms, after its new proprietor. Matthew's 1825 *Guide to Bristol* described them thus:

WARNE'S HOTEL AND BALL-ROOMS, (late Barton's) a short distance from Rownham. These Rooms are rendered eligible and elegant by Mr Warne, who has made several improvements in his Hotel, and his Coffee-Room we pronounce to be the handsomest in the West of England. On the northern side over the Ball Rooms is a lofty house, in which are many spacious and airy dining, sitting, and bed-rooms, which command delightful prospects of the river, the hills, and country. The Assembly room is 90 feet long and 35 wide, and 35 high: has glass chandeliers, and a music gallery. Near the Hotel are excellent stabling for horses and good coach houses. This Hotel is admirably situated for its nearness to Cumberland Basin, or entrance to the harbour, where the Steam packets and other vessels arrive, being well calculated to accommodate those families who arrive and leave by steam conveyance.

The following year Chilcott's *Guide* could add:

THE GLOUCESTER HOTEL is a very remarkable building – one large house being, as it were, planted on top of another... The Coffee Room is also of large dimensions, and the whole of the sitting and sleeping apartments spacious and airy. The present proprietor, Mr G. Warne, has done much for the improvement of this hotel, and under his direction it rivals the first establishment of the kind in the kingdom. It's peculiar convenience for steam packet passengers is apparent from its proximity to the Basin, and the ease with which goods and luggage are immediately conveyed to await ulterior destination: in a word, no one can witness the bustle and regularity of this house during the steam packet season, without being convinced that its success and prosperity are consummate with the good management and courteous conduct of the host and hostess.

In the Assembly Room of the hotel the various meetings of the Bristol and Clifton Horticultural Society, established in 1829, were held. It was said that the room, large as it was, was still insuf-

The Cumberland Basin in the 1850s (detail from *Clifton and the Harbour at Hotwells*) E T Dolby lithograph. The Gloucester Hotel can be seen directly above the fore-mast of the first steamer. By this time it had lost its bay windows.

ficient for the purpose, so numerous were the members and occasional visitors who crowded in to see the beautiful spectacle of flowers, fruits and vegetables on display. Five meetings of the society were held in the room each year, in April, May, June, July and September. By 1833 the hotel had again changed hands and around this time a lithographic view of Clifton by John Willis shows that its name 'Royal Glocester Hotel' was painted across the towering façade. Chilcott afforded more information:

> The present proprietor, Mr Ivatts, (late of the Guildhall Coffee-house, London) has done much for the improvement of this hotel, and under his direction it equals any establishment of the kind in the kingdom.

> The regularity and good order with which this commodious Hotel is conducted, at all times, and more especially during the steam packet season, when the influx of visitors is very considerable, reflect the greatest credit on the proprietor: and it may with truth be added, that the mild temperature of its situation, the attention, comfort, and cleanliness in every department, render it a desirable winter residence for families, who wish to divest themselves of the trouble and inconvenience attendant on house-keeping.

By 1849 the 'Royal Gloster Hotel', as the directories called it, was still surviving albeit in competition with younger establishments, and according to Chilcott's *Clifton Guide*, 'from its ensconsed position, strongly recommended by Dr Granville and others to the invalid for his temporary residence'.

It had, however, seen its glory days even if tradition still treated it with respect. By the 1850s two of the bow-fronted properties in the row next to the hotel (by now called Gloucester Terrace) had become boarding houses, possibly separate from the main establishment, although one was named Ivatt's after the Gloucester's previous owner, and the other Redman's Hotel. Around this time the front of the towering structure was visually severely marred by the removal of the three rows of bay windows. No doubt after fifty years they had become unsafe. Their removal and replace-

The Gloucester Hotel in 1889. The three rows of small-paned bay windows that had been such a prominent and attractive feature of the original building had been long removed. The old building was soon to be demolished.

ment by single plate glass sash windows robbed the tower block of much of its interest visually. The distinctive profile of the building can be seen on ET Dolby's lithograph of Clifton and the harbour at Hotwells.

In 1851 The Royal Gloucester's proprietor was listed as R. Chappel and various members of that family continued to run it until the final entry in the directories in 1889. From 1859, however, it seems as though its days as a fashionable hotel had come to an end as it was then listed as a public house under the name of the Gloster House Tap. At this time part of the vast building was used for military purposes as a recruiting office. The building appears on Lavar's aerial view of Bristol of 1887 but within two years would be replaced by Lady Haberfield's Almshouses, which now occupy the site. The recently discovered photograph now in the Tozer Collection, and published here for the first time, presumably shows Lady Haberfield and others connected with the purchase of the property standing on the parade of the sadly derelict hotel.

Agriculture, Horticulture and Gardening

BRISTOL WAS FAMOUS FOR THE QUALITY OF THE NATURAL PRODUCE available to its inhabitants and visitors. Although some foodstuffs such as oranges and turtle were obvious imports, the farms in the area were well stocked and the country fertile. Most travellers' accounts mention the rich, well stocked pastures along the Severn that were visible on the way to the New Passage, and the size of many of the still remaining farm houses in the area hint at the comfortable lifestyle that could be maintained by a well managed farm. Mr Marshall's two-volume *The Rural Economy of Gloucestershire; including its Dairy* is a marvellous review of all manner of aspects of contemporary agriculture in the county from the farm labourer who were 'noticeable as being simple, inoffensive, unintelligent, and apparently slow. How different from the farm labourers of Norfolk!'…. to how to feed a harvestman.

Fruit was something that Bristol was particularly noted for. Apart from the many orchards for commercial and private use and the production of soft fruits in the Long Ashton area, the local geography of the Avon gorge meant that in certain places the hillside had been terraced to take full advantage of the sun and to provide early ripening gardens. An advertisement in the local newspaper for 21 January 1775 announced that the Spring Gardens along the Hotwells Road were available for letting. 'All those Hanging Gardens, so remarkable for their early Produce, situated in the Road leading from Bristol to the Hotwells; where great Advantages are made in the Season by the Sale of the Fruit' they were 'full planted, with the best Fruit Trees, now in their Prime.' The Season of course was the summer months when Hotwells was full of visitors who would provide a ready market for fresh fruit.

The present Whiteladies Road was, in 1807, the main route to Wales and to the Passages. It got its name at some time in that century from an inn called White Ladies (or singular White Lady's) that had long stood approximately where the T.A.'s rifle range now stands. On maps it is generally just referred to as the route to the Passages. For most of the road's length it was bordered by high stone walls which are commented on by both Malcolm and Heath in their accounts of leaving and arriving in the city by this route. Apart from those bordering the Tyndalls' estate, the others shielded farmland and nurseries from the light-

Slut, the pointer pig, J Landseer, 1805.
A pig unparalleled. William Barker Daniel's *Rural Sports* tells us that she was called Slut 'in consequence of soiling herself in a Bog.' She lived wild but her 'owner' taught her to act like a pointer dog and she accompanied him on his hunting expeditions and would point and retrieve as well as a dog. Slut was slaughtered when she was ten years old, which Daniel said was 'animal murder'.

Miller and Sweet's Nursery Villas which still survive in Chantry Road, were originally a seventeenth-century farmhouse. The perimeter wall near the main gates has been lowered by the artist to show the buildings, but was originally high on both sides for most of the length of Whiteladies Road. Engraving by R W Silvester.

fingered. Miller and Sweet were the most important nurserymen, seedsmen and florists in the area. Their gardens stretched on the west side of the Whiteladies from what is now Alma Road up to the present Apsley Road. King's Parade, the terrace of houses that Malcolm mentions as on the eastern extremity of the Downs, jutted into their property near Apsley Road. Their main buildings, Nursery Villas, were situated where Chantry Road is now. The buildings that were adapted from a farm house of about 1670 are still in existence. On the eastern side of Whiteladies the nursery covered the land from Woodbury Lane down to Cotham Hill and stretched across to the eastern side of Redland Lane (now Hampton Road) at one point. These nurseries were laid out with a grid system of roads and paths. The main entrance was near the Nursery Villas buildings and the roadway eventually became Chantry Road itself, but there were other entrances strategically placed including a southern one so as to avoid the toll-gates where Cotham Hill met Whiteladies Road. The illustration used

on the firms' trade cards shows a low wall near the main gates, but this is artistic licence to display Nursery Villas the better.

A catalogue of the firm, dating from 1808, survives in the Bristol Reference Library and illustrates what an astonishing choice of plants was available to the buyer. In these days of huge garden centres throughout the country one assumes that they offer their clientele a wide range of plants. However, compared to 1807 the selection is quite pathetic. For example, Miller and Sweet could offer 113 different varieties of apple trees, 99 varieties of gooseberries, 34 different peaches and 58 different grapevines. Added to this were page after page of shrubs, trees, bulbs and flowers, nearly all species with multiple choices of colour and variety. Pages of flowers for the green house and plants for the hot-house completed the ensemble. Hot-houses had long been the rage amongst the wealthy both as a status symbol and for the variety of exotic plants and fruit that they afforded the owner. Plans for their construction appeared in such useful architectural volumes as William Pain's 1792 *Practical House Carpenter; or Youth's Instructor*.

Miller and Sweet's name regularly appears on the list of importers to the port, bringing in seeds, bulbs and tubers by sea to add to their stocks. In addition to the plant catalogue that survives, they also produced a catalogue of the seeds that they stocked and advertised that 'Best double or single mats, garden-tools and almost every article for the Use of Gardens' was available from them.

The tradition of nurseries continued in Whiteladies Road until 2008 when Garaways' garden centre, on the approximate site of Miller and Sweet's Nursery Villas, unfortunately closed. Garaways seem to have taken over at least part of Miller's business by 1839 and it was called Durdham Down Nursery. Members of

left:
Butchers, W H Pyne 1805. England was famous for the care with which meat was bred and slaughtered and for the cleanliness of the meat markets.

right:
A trade card of John Waldron, the gardener of Love Street, Hotwells, engraved by Doddrell c.1807.

the family were soon living at Nursery Villas. Before the 2008 closure the other surviving remnant of the Whiteladies' nurseries tradition, Forest and Orchard Nurseries (but latterly Severnvale Garden Centre), on the corner of Queen's Road and Richmond Hill had closed in the late 1970s.

There was much interest in gardening in the late Georgian period and John Narraway (q.v.) writes to Thomas Coutts of a new garden he has made at his farm in Horfield with the fashionable railed flower beds. Such railed beds of the period can be seen in the series of watercolours of another garden in St James' Square owned by the Pole family that are now in the City Art Gallery collection. An example of an older-style Bristol garden appears in an early-nineteenth-century painting now in the Red Maid's school and in a second version in a private collection and reproduced here in this volume for the first time. The garden of the school in Denmark Street, behind College Green and St Mark's Chapel consisted of a gravelled space bordered by long straight beds planted with fruit trees and shrubs. In the centre of the garden two opposed triangular beds and four sub-rectangular beds gave the effect to the eye of a Maltese cross. All of the beds were bordered by small clipped box hedges, a remnant no doubt of earlier knot gardens within the city.

On a considerably grander scale Humphry Repton had been engaged by Thomas Tyndall of the Fort in 1799 to repair the damage caused to his park following a failed building speculation in the 1790s and to shield it from the expanding city. In 1801 Repton produced one of his famous Red Books of his projected improvements. The original is now in the Yale Library, New Haven, Connecticut but a facsimile is in the Art Reference Collection at the Bristol Reference Library. Repton also accepted commissions at Blaise Castle (1796) and at Brentry Hill (1802) and Cote Bank (before 1803).

Prose run mad

The Observer
Being a Transient Glance at About Forty Youths of Bristol. Anon, 1794

Romaine Joseph Thorne

Fade ye writings of Shakespeare, of Milton of Dryden, and of every other genius of eminent abilities, when placed in competition with the effulgent productions of this transcendant Poet! He is the Author of several pieces, every one of which scarcely dragged out of the miserable existence of a day; they were equally as short lived as the Ephemera; the contempt with which they were treated, is a convincing proof of the public judgement; for of all attempts at writing Poetry, Mr Thorne's are the most insignificant; his blank verse is really ludicrous, it is in its best stage nothing more than 'Prose run mad.' In the 'Mad Gallop, or a Trip to Devizes,' a production of his recent date; he has placed Barbers distinct from Tradesmen; and then with an insolence to him peculiar apologizes to 'the honourable fraternity of shavers' for it observing that he did it 'merely to accommodate the construction of the verse,' which abusive epithet is again an aggravation. I am inclined to think that when Mr Thorne wrote the alluded to expressions, he must have forgotten when he convened his Tradesmen, in order to offer them Ten Shillings in the Pound, (from the embarrassed situation of his affairs) that his Hair-dresser was among the number! We here see to what lengths prejudice and pride will carry a man; what if he were a chimney-sweeper and a virtuous man, ought his situation in life to preclude him from our esteem? Would the Merchant toil unless something pecuniary were attached to his labours? Certainly not. The Hair-dresser toils from the fame consideration; of course the one is not a step higher than the other. 'Ere I finish I must recommend the Youth in question to let his future Works breath somewhat more of originality than those which have appeared, as in many passages plagiarism is a prominent feature: I would likewise recommend him to preface them in such a manner as not to deceive with respect to the after matter.

BRISTOLIA,

A POEM:

BY

ROMAINE JOSEPH THORN,

AUTHOR OF

CLITO AND DELIA, --- THE MAD GALLOP,
OR TRIP TO DEVIZES, -- RETIREMENT,
&c. &c.

𝔅𝔯𝔦𝔰𝔱𝔬𝔩 :

Printed for OWEN REES, No. 10, WINE - STREET, and
J. N. LONGMAN, LONDON.

above:
Watercolour by William Milton of the goddess Bristolia.
A design for a Bristol merchant's ex-libris plate, c.1745.

left:
Clare Street and the drawbridge by Edward Bird.
Fruit sellers await customers by the harbour rails whilst
beyond St Stephen's Church the city is enveloped in smoke.

Watercolour looking towards Bristol Cathedral from Lime-kiln Dock at the bottom of Wells Wood Lane (Jacob's Wells Road).

TO THE NUMEROUS
AND RESPECTABLE INHABITANTS
OF THIS GREAT COMMERCIAL CITY,
THE FOLLOWING SMALL POEM
IS MOST SUBMISSIVELY DEDICATED,
BY THEIR FELLOW CITIZEN,
AND VERY HUMBLE SERVANT

Romaine Joseph Thorn
Bristol, 25 March 1794

BRISTOLIA,

A POEM.

ARISE, my Mufe, attune thy trembling ftring,
In lofty notes, of fam'd BRISTOLIA, fing;
And, as old HOMER did to lafting fame
Commit his *Troy's*, fo, thou fhalt BRISTOL's name.
Forthwith, then, Mufe, thy tuneful airs refound;　5
And publifh, far, her deathlefs praife around.

　Majeftic Briftol! to thy happy port
Prolific COMMERCE makes its lov'd refort;
Thy gallant fhips, with fpacious fails, unfurl'd,
Waft, to thy fhore, the treafures of the world!　10
With each production of the Eaft, and Weft,
Thy favor'd citizens are amply bleft;
Thy active fons, unceafingly, are fway'd
By HONOR, JUSTICE, and a thirft for TRADE;

Around thy Quay, in countless heaps, appear   15
Bales, pil'd on bales, and loads of foreign ware:
There, the strong porter, constantly, is seen,
With brawny arm, to work the pond'rous crane:
There, groves, on groves of tow'ring masts, arise,
In stately ranks, and penetrate the skies;   20
There, too, resounds the jolly seamen's cry,
As they their handspikes, to the windlass, ply:
With shouts, sonorous, shakes the neighb'ring shore,
Whilst they, with cheerful souls, their lofty ships unmoor.

   Majestic Bristol! in thy ev'ry street,   25
Thy fam'd inhabitants, by hundreds, meet!
So vast their number, and so great their throng,*
That strangers wonder, as they pass along:
Absorb'd in *Trade*, within thy limits, dwell
Dutch, *Irish*, *Spanish*, *Jew*, and *Infidel*!   30
Thy spacious shops with works of art are stor'd;
Thy plenteous markets ev'ry good afford;
Thou wear'st the form of old, majestic ROME,†
And (save great LONDON) second art to none;

   * According to a recent computation, Bristol, and its environs, contain upwards of an Hundred Thousand inhabitants.

   † Bristol is thought very much to resemble old ROME. It stands, as did that celebrated city, on seven hills.

Large, splendid buildings, in thy streets abound;   35
Thy suburbs, too, delightful walks surround;
Without thy walls, array'd in smiling green,
Are tow'ring hills and charming landscapes seen.

   Majestic Bristol! CHARITY is thine;*
To speak thy goodness high and low combine: 40
Thy lib'ral hand provides the needy old
A blest asylum from the winter's cold;
Where, whilst they sit, around the cheerful blaze,
Their grateful tongues are lavish of thy praise.
Immortal COLSTON first devis'd a plan   45
That breath'd of Heav'n, and dignify'd the man;
An *hundred boys*, by him, are daily fed,
Cloath'd by his bounty, and to *learning* bred;†
These, in his school, with gratitude, declare
His *worth*, how sacred! and his *name*, how dear!   50

   * It would engross whole pages to enumerate the various charities with which Bristol is endowed. To such of my readers as may wish for a particular account of them, I would humbly recommend the perusal of *Mr. Matthews's* Bristol-Guide, recently published.

   † Independent of this most excellent charity, which is too well known to require any further comment, Colston established several others; amongst which is a school in Temple-Street, for the cloathing, and educating, forty poor boys.

Lo! mid the fpacious walks of COLLEGE-GREEN,
What num'rous crowds of blooming nymphs are feen!
Beneath the branches of th' extended trees,
They take their circuit, and imbibe the breeze.
Not HELEN's face, which prov'd the fall of TROY, 55
Outfhone the charms BRISTOLIA's FAIR enjoy;
With thefe, DIANA, and her virgin train,
May vie for beauty, but, may vie in vain;
Nor VENUS' felf, were VENUS to appear,
Could look, in figure, or in face, more fair: 60
The graceful form, with rapture, I furvey;
And piercing eyes, where fportive Cupids play:
The fwelling breaft, more white than Alpine fnow,
Where HONOR triumphs, and the VIRTUES grow;
In charms, like thefe, *Bristolia's daughters* fhine,   65
And boaft a femblance equal to divine.*

* I have frequently heard the obfervation made, that the generality
of the *Bristol Ladies* were *formerly* noted for *homelinefs of person*, and
an *ungraceful appearance;* but, I believe, I may venture to affert,
that, at prefent, *the contrary is absolutely the case;* and I make no
doubt of there being thoufands, of my own fex, in this city, who very
readily coincide in opinion with me: therefore, I hope the panegyric
I have beftowed on the ladies of Briftol will not be confidered as adu-
lation; for I can affure my readers, that it is no other than I think
they really merit.

But, hark! the COLLEGE ORGAN's blifsful found
Salutes my ear, and ftrikes an awe around;
Oh, let me hafte within the facred dome,
From whence thefe pleafing, folemn accents come; 70
There, whilft I hear the heav'nly notes arife,
My raptur'd foul fhall mount into the fkies;
In grateful praife, adore th' incarnate God,
Of all our fins who bore the mighty load;
Who hung, extended, on the curfed tree,   75
And fhed his blood, his precious blood, for me!

From COLLEGE GREEN to REDLAND I repair,*
Its vifta traverfe, and enjoy its air;
Delightful fpot! 'mid *Summer's* piercing heat;
How oft I've wander'd to thy bleft retreat!   80
Beneath thy trees, fecur'd from *Phœbus'* rage,
How oft I've rov'd, and read th' inftructive page!
Soon as thy lovely folitude I fpy,
What rural beauty burfts upon mine eye!
Enraptur'd FANCY, with ingenious hand,   85
Depicts a fcene refembling fairy land.

* Redland, the beautiful feat of Jeremy Baker, Efq. forming one
of the moft romantic and pleafing profpects imaginable, fituated about
half a mile from the city, on the road to Weftbury.

Two rows of trees, at proper diftance, fhew
The planter's tafte, and rural genius too:
Thefe, when array'd in Spring's enliv'ning bloom,
The profpect heighten, with romantic gloom;   90
A verdant walk, and cooling zephyrs blefs
Th' enchanting region of thy fweet recefs:
The owner's manfion, on a gentle rife,
Appears a palace to th' admiring eyes;
Its noble fabric is, encircled, feen,   95
With groves of lofty elms, and fhrubs of lafting green.

Dear fpot, adieu! from thy lov'd haunt, I bend
My devious courfe, and CLIFTON HILL afcend.
Fam'd CLIFTON HILL! thy various charms invite
The great, the gay, the wealthy, and polite!   100
On thee, both *Health* and *Pleasure* keep their court;
To thee, old age and blooming youth refort;
Thy balmy breezes have the magic pow'r
The *weak* to ftrengthen, and the *sick* reftore;
Who, when they find their wonted vigour fail,   105
Fly to thy fummit, and imbibe thy gale,
Whofe ev'ry zephyr, pregnant with her charms,
HYGEIA owns, and with her fpirit warms.

And now, HOTWELL, on thee, my mufe would fain
Beftow a portion of her humble ftrain: 110
Salubrious fountain! How can language tell
What wond'rous virtues in thy waters dwell?
When dire CONSUMPTION, with corroding fway,
Afflicts the fair, and makes their bloom decay,
Thy healing ftream invigorates their fouls,   115
The monfter baffles, and its rage controls;
Reftores them, once more, to their lover's arms,
Replete with health, and fraught with blooming charms.
Dear, valu'd fount! to diftant countries, Fame
Hath loudly borne thy much-diftinguifh'd name: 120
To diftant countries is thy wave confign'd,
In copious floods, to benefit mankind.*

But yonder, tow'ring o'er the fwelling tide,
St. VINCENT's far-fam'd, awful ROCKS, abide!
Heav'ns! what tremendous precipices, there,   125
Exalt their heads, and fhoot into the air!
Say, craggy rocks, what rude convulfion tore
Thefe clifts from thofe on yon adjacent fhore?

* Vaft quantities of the Hotwell Water are exported, particularly to the Weft Indies and America.

You look as though, in ages paſt, you'd been
In contact cloſe, without a gulf between;   130
Perhaps, *you*, alſo, when the LORD was ſlain,
With *Nature*, groan'd, and, ſtraightway, rent in twain !*

To BRANDON HILL my journey I purſue,
From whence BRISTOLIA forms a pleaſing view.
Now, on its ſummit, as I, muſing, ſtray,   135
I trace the ſpot where hoſtile Britons lay ;†
But *diſcord*, now, and *civil wars*, are o'er,
And joy, and *commerce*, bleſs BRISTOLIA's ſhore:
Now, from each quarter, clouds of ſmoke appear,
Mount their black columns, and diſſolve in air ; 140
Buildings ſuperb, and lofty ſpires, ſurpriſe
The gazer's ſenſes, and enchant his eyes;
Whilſt, to his ears, in quick vibration, come
The noiſe of trucks, and city's ceaſeleſs hum :
The ſhouts of ſailors, as their caſtles ride,   145
With waving ſtreamers, on the chryſtal tide;

* Many are of opinion, that St. *Vincent's rocks* were formerly united,
and were ſeparated by ſome very great convulſion of nature.   Some
will affirm, that it is *more than probable* St. Vincent's rock was one of
thoſe, which, at the crucifixion, are ſaid to have been rent in twain.

† The top of this hill, during the civil wars, was alternately occupied
by the monarchial and parliamentary forces ; the trenches are yet to be
ſeen.

All which declare, to Briſtol's buſy throng
That *commerce*, *wealth*, and *industry* belong.

Hail, Briſtol, hail ! whilſt Gallia's cities groan,
'Neath *blood* and *slaughter*, PEACE is all thy own !   150
Thy loyal thouſands bleſs their monarch's ſway,
Revere their COUNTRY, and its laws obey ;
They, for its welfare, in the time of need,
Would ruſh to battle, and, in battle, bleed ;
Thy fearleſs youth already feel the flame   155
Of martial ardour kindle in their frame :*
They long, they pant, 'gainſt Gallia's ſons, to bear
Their ſacred ſtandard, and to mix in war :
To ſhew them Britain yet can boaſt a few
Who love their country, and their ſov'reign too ; 160
Who'd joy to puniſh, with their vengeful ſword,
A race of caitiffs vile, and murd'rers of their LORD.

* I am informed, that many young gentlemen, in this city, have,
much to their honor, agreed to incorporate themſelves into a body ; to
provide themſelves with arms, and to prove ready, at all times, to ſtand
forth in defence of their *Gracious King and Glorious Constitution*.

Talent perverted to indifferent purpose

The Observer
Being a Transient Glance at About Forty Youths of Bristol. Anon, 1794

Robert Lovell

This young man could if he were inclined to stick more closely to the cultivation of his mind, make a distinguished figure in the school of science; his abilities are surpassed by few, though his education is not so great as the preceding two Gentlemen.* It often happens that good talents are perverted to indifferent purposes; this Youth is a living instance of it: his attachment to that meanest of all sciences, Pugilism, much lessens him in the estimation of the world; his frequent appearance in the Racquet-court still tends to depreciate his character. 'Bristol, a Satire,' is a production of his; it is not illy written, but I think it favours much of the ill-nature and disappointment: it is penned with virulence, and it is venting a spleen to little purpose; there are many glaring truths in it, and I am inclined to think there are many more untruths.

*Southey and Coleridge

BRISTOL:

A

SATIRE.

By Robert Lovell

" *Urbs hæc sublimis, spatiosa. fidelis amœna,*
" *Dulcis et insignis, prisca, benigna, nitens,"*

" *Bristolia, lofty, spacious, faithful, fair,*
" *Sweet, famous, old, kind, neat beyond compare."*

MATTHEWS BRISTOL GUIDE.

PRICE ONE SHILLING.

LONDON:
PRINTED FOR THE AUTHOR,
AND SOLD BY THE BOOKSELLERS OF LONDON, BATH, HOTWELLS, AND BRISTOL.

1794.

PREFACE.

A TURNPIKE GATE does not more certainly precede a Town than a Preface precedes a modern Book, and though both Traveller and Reader would often be willing to dispense with them, they generally obtrude a Tax both on his Patience and his Pocket, why then should I write a Preface? Why truly gentle Reader I do it not for fashion's sake, but because (unlike the generality of Authors) I have something to tell thee.

1st. I have as much as possible avoided personal reflection in the following Satire.

2d. I have annexed notes in explanation of some circumstances, which being generally known here, the Bristol reader may deem superfluous; they are intended for the information of those who reside at a distance, (if any such may read them) to whom the subject is not so familiar.

BRISTOL:

A

SATIRE.

LOW in a drear and gloomy Vale immur'd,
By mud cemented, and by smoke obscur'd,
A City stands, and BRISTOL is its name,
By trade and dullness consecrate to fame,
5 *That* o'er her Sons in form of Plutus reigns,
And binds their groveling hearts in golden chains;
This to their brain a leaden mask imparts,
And makes their heads as callous as their hearts.

In mingled heaps here mud and misery lie,
10 Here vice and folly rear their standard high;
Here sweating dustman, sweating dustman meets,
But all their efforts ne'er can cleanse their streets.

B   Like

Like Sifyphus they toil with endlefs pain,
And find like Sifyphus, their labor vain;
15 While heedlefs Magiftrates recline in peace,
Content to mumble o'er the good Police *
But ne'er effay its bleffings to fecure,
Nor ftretch the hand to help the fuppliant poor;
Suffice to them the *name*, the important air,
20 The *Fur-Clad Gown* and *Magiflerial Chair*.
Hail! BRISTOL hail! and hail thy " bufy throng
Whom thine own bard † has famed in matchlefs fong,
Thy Thorn for thee has tun'd the trembling ftring,
And bade his Mufe in lofty notes to fing"
25 " Forthwith the Mufe's tuneful airs refound,
And publifh far thy deathlefs praife around;
No common theme demands his founding ftrain,
No common praife his Mufe afpires to gain,
But as old Homer did, to lafting fame,
30 " Commit his Troys, fo he will BRISTOL's name."

Thrice happy bard, of fuch a theme poffeft,
Thrice happy town with fuch a Poet bleft;

* The Briftol Police Bill contains many good Regulations, which if attended to would refcue the City from much of its filth and infamy.

† Romain Jofeph Thorn, Author of Briftolia a Poem, from which thefe Quotations are taken.

How

How fweet the lay which gives thy charms to fame,
How fweetly claffic thy poetic name:
35 BRISTOL no more a vulgar found we hear,
But foft BRISTOLIA foothes the lift'ning ear;
Or if per chance, the gothic word we trace,
'Tis dubb'd " Majeftic" and affumes a grace,

But who can read, and reading not admire,
40 The lay replete with warm poetic fire,
Which fweetly fays " BRISTOLIA's Sons are fway'd
By honor, juftice, and a thirft of trade."
And tells how " Porters conftantly are feen
With brawny arm to work the pondrous crane"
45 While " handfpikes, bales, and windlafs" *terms divine*,
With harfh confufion jumble in the line.

And now the Poet mounts up Brandon Hill,
But turns his thoughts to lov'd BRISTOLIA ftill,
And marks on every fide with eager eyes
50 Black clouds of fmoke in mounting columns rife,
Whilft " to his ears in quick vibration come
" The noife of trucks and City's ceafelefs hum;"
Delightful founds which BRISTOLS' Sons revere,
Which more than mufic charm the tradesman's ear.

B 2

55 Proceed

55 Proceed great Poet in thy path sublime,
And deign to give us more BRISTOLIAN Rhyme,
Still praise our far-fam'd City, for we see
The song, the subject, and the bard agree.

Anxious we wait thy future verse to gain,
60 T'imbibe instruction from the learned strain;
Thou who hast said within our City " dwell
" Dutch, Irish, Spanish, Jew and Infidel."
Oh! curious wight in future song declare
If only these inhale BRISTOLIAN air:
65 Does never Scotchman to our precincts roam,
Does never Welshman find with us a home;
Or dwell none with us of the race abhorr'd,
" The race of Caitiffs vile, and murderers of their Lord?"*

Thy pious thoughts dwell on " the cursed Tree,
70 " Where GOD extended, shed his BLOOD for thee;"
And *aptly* deem " those rocks which now abide,
" Awful and tow'ring o'er the swelling Tide"
Yclep'd St. Vincents " when the LORD was slain,
" With Nature groan'd and straightway rent in twain."

* We conceive the *ingenious* Author means the *French*, though he characterizes the *Jews*.

75 Oh!

75 Oh! say sublime in science as in song
When first the river roll'd the rocks among,
Tell us how long the current shall remain,
And when the parted rocks shall meet again?

Ev'n on this theme, 'twere easier far to dwell
80 Than praise the City which thou lov'st so well;
Easier than proving (which thy strains presume)
That BRISTOL wears the form of ancient Rome.
That all her streets are *grand* beyond compare,
Her Sons all *gen'rous* and her Daughters *fair*.

85 Turn Muse of Satire devious now too long,
And for the mighty subject leave the song.

BRISTOL in thee has dullness fixed her throne,
(Congenial seat) and marks thy Sons her own;
On thee the Goddess cast her cloudy eyes,
90 And saw sublime thy welcome fogs arise;
From Owl-like sleep, with secret joy awoke,
Pleased with the incense of thy curling smoke.
To guard her laws, and aid her mighty reign
All-powerful Plutus fills the busy brain;
95 Full oft the God inspires the golden dream
Of cent per cent, and many a goodly scheme:

In

In all his Sons the myſtic ſigns we trace,
Pounds, Shillings, Pence appear in every face.
Here worth is prized, if worth will *aught* obtain,
100 And truth is judg'd by rules of *loſs* and *gain*.
The love of virtue's loſt in love of pence
And mean, low cunning holds the place of ſenſe.

In clouded ſtate Oh! dullneſs dwell in peace,
Thus firm'd thy throne, thy reign ſhall never ceaſe,
105 Secure in BRISTOL of eternal ſway,
And all the honors which her ſons can pay;
No blaze of wit thy palace ſhall illume,
No ray of ſcience pierce the ſacred gloom;
But gathering fogs and vapoury miſts ſhall ſpread
110 Their murky honors round thy royal head;
And oft to thee thy Sons ſhall ſacrifice
With lifted hands, wide mouth, and rayleſs eyes.

Majeſtic Goddeſs who doſt rule ſupreme
Thy favorite City and its *muddy* ſtream;
115 The ſtream which chill'd by thy lethean force
Sleeps on the dull banks in its ſluggiſh courſe:
A ditch, a ſtagnant pool, a lazy flood,
A rill flow creeping through a world of mud.

Thou

Thou who doſt guide full many a rhyming wight,
120 And make them fondly fancy they can write;
Thou who did'ſt bid thy *Thorn* his verſe produce,
And ſpoil the paper meant for better uſe.
On * Vapid's head thy drowſy dews diſpenſe,
And bad him verſes write, who ne'er wrote ſenſe.
125 Long haſt thou held illimitable power,
And cruſh'd young merit in its riſing hour.
If ever ſcience in thy region gleam,
If ever wit its hated radiance beam,
If o'er ſome mind bright genius ſhed her ray
130 No friendly foſterer brings it forth to day;
But mark'd by dullneſs and contempt, a foe,
Roams the ſad child of penury and woe.

Here let me pauſe o'er genius' hapleſs Son,
Here drop the penſive tear for CHATTERTON.

135 Ill-fated youth whoſe proud yet gen'rous Soul,
Glowing with ardor ſpurn'd the baſe controul;
He ſaw the Sons of wealth in pamper'd pride,
He ſaw the poor the ſcanty boon denied;

* A contemptible poetaſter who publiſhes under that name. Author of Cannalling, &c.

Saw

Saw vice ennobled on its titled feat,

140 While worth unfriended fought a lone retreat;

He faw proud folly catch the admiring eye,

And modeft genius unreguarded die:

He felt that juftice from the world was driv'n

And rufh'd to meet her in her native heav'n.

145   Oh! ill-ftarr'd youth, how lucklefs was thy birth,

Where never friend was found to fofter worth;*

Sad was thy life, a fhort and cloudy day,

To cold neglect and penury a prey;

Death, only death thy juft reward could claim,

150 The meed of genius, an immortal name:

Like mighty HOMER's was thy haplefs fate,

Scorn'd by the world, and known alas! too late;

To thee the pofthumous applaufe they pour'd;

When living ftarv'd thee, and when dead ador'd.

155   Return oh! Mufe to BRISTOL's matchlefs Sons,

In avarice *Dutchmen,* and in fcience *Huns.*

Say, in their brains what varied paffions rule,

What mingled character of knave and fool!

* CHATTERTON was born in BRISTOL; his ftory is too generally known to require a repetition here.

See

See yon high tower* now leaning to its bafe,

160 What myftic rites once fill'd the facred place,

Credulity defcended in a Cloud,

And with ftrange wonders drew the gaping crowd;

Her fav'rite † Children aid her caufe, and fix

Yon Church the high fcene of her monkifh tricks.

165   Lo! LUKINS comes, and with him comes a train

Of parfons famous for a lack of brain;

With Owl-like faces and with raven coats,

Their folemn ftep, their folemn tafk denotes;

By exorcifings, prayers, and rebukings,

170 To drive feven fturdy *Devils* out of LUKINS.

   High founds the alarm, the wond'rous tale is told,

The gathering crowd affembles, young and old;

Nor might credulity an audience fear,

Her flighteft tale will call forth thoufands here;

175 Still lives that fpirit which in former days

Drew all the city to the fancied gaze;

When father, mother, join'd with fon and daughter,

To fee the conjurer walk upon the water.‡

* Temple Church, where George Lukins was exorcifed.
† Seven Clergymen of this city.
‡ It is a well known fact that many thoufands of the inhabitants of this city affembled in full expectation of beholding this miracle.

C

Now

Now in loud tumult prefs the expectant throng,
180 The fable train moves heavily along;
They gain the church, wide opes the facred door,
And the rude mob their mighty numbers pour;
And now the devil-hunters fet to work,
Fierce as Crufaders to attack a Turk;
185 Some read, fome pray, to end the ferious evil,
And fome more learn'd, talk Latin to the Devil.
The baited fpirits held the conteft long,
But found at laft the parfons were too ftrong;
Then in ftrange tongues they fpake with wild affright,
190 And begg'd to make fome decent terms of flight.
The holy feven denied the mild requeft,
But on the foe with double ardor preft,
And drove the demons from the poor poffeft;
The Devils grumbling left their lov'd abode,
195 And the freed LUKINS thank'd the men of God.

But who can tell where fixed their final doom,
If in the *red fea*, or the *river Froome*;
Whether they fojourn with the men *divine*,
Or entered (as of old) the *herd of fwine*.*

200 Trade, mighty trade, here holds refiftlefs fway,
And drives the nobler cares of *mind* away.

* Briftolmen proverbially called *hogs*.

To

11

To this fole object every effort tends,
And virtue dies and *pliant* honor bends;
No foft humanities are cherifh'd here,
205 No fympathetic feeling prompts the tear;
No mild urbanity attracts the fight,
No arts of fkill or elegant delight;
But fordid wealth infpires the general cry,
And fpeeds the ftep and fharps the eager eye;
210 Foul as their ftreets, triumphant meannefs fways,
And grov'ling as their mud-compelling drays;
Difcordant founds compofe the babel hum,
'Tis " how goes fugar? what's the price of rum?"
" What fhips arrived? and how are ftocks to-day?
215 " Who's dead? who's broken? and who's run away?"

Thefe conftant cares with conftant gain requite;
Hence BRISTOL boafts full many a wealthy wight;
Yet not benevolence is here difplay'd,
No generous impulfe warms the fons of trade:
220 Avarice *firft* taught the golden ftore to *heap*,
Her *next* great leffon is that ftore to *keep*.

See yonder pile* unfinifhed ftill remains,
See ftill deferted, charity complains;

* The Infirmary.

C 2

Penfive

Penſive ſhe mourns her ſolitary ſeat,
225 Where her ſad children might have found retreat;
'Twas heaven's own ſpirit form'd the great deſign,
The approving virtues hail'd the work divine;
Hope o'er the ſcene her brighteſt radiance ſhed,
And pain and ſorrow rear'd the drooping head;
230 But BRISTOL's evil genius hov'ring here,
Forbad one virtue to illume her ſphere:
Hope then retired,--for avarice appear'd,
Refus'd his mite, and lo! the pile unrear'd.*

Amid the mantling gloom which long has ſpread
235 Its thick'ning darkneſs over BRISTOL's head,
The muſe beheld a ſpark of genius riſe,
Like the bright meteor in the midnight ſkies,
But foe to dullneſs and her ſable train,
The trembling luſtre beam'd, but beam'd in vain;
240 Her votive minions quench'd the riſing ray,
And the dark Goddeſs holds unrivall'd ſway.

Thus through the ſeries of full many an age,
(Annals of infamy) her bluſhing page

---

* We ſhould be unjuſt did we not remark as an exception, the generous and liberal contri-
bution of William Turner, Eſq. who gave 100l. to this excellent charity: an example worthy
the imitation of thoſe who are bleſſed with ability.

Records

Records alone *one* ſolitary name,
245 To generous virtue dear, and dear to fame;
Benevolence gladden'd at her COLSTON's ſight,
And ſickening avarice ſought the realms of night;
He fear'd the bright example might inſpire,
His choſen children with the gen'rous fire;
250 But fear not, BRISTOL ſhall uphold thy ſtate,
Tho' all ſhall *praiſe* him, none ſhall *imitate!*

COLSTON deceas'd, now from the dark retreat,
See avarice welcom'd to his ancient ſeat;
No ſecret foe ſhall riſe in his domain,
255 No voice oppoſe his univerſal reign,
Sooner his wily ſons ſhall ceaſe to range,
The open ſtreet, and fill the vaſt exchange*
Sooner ſhall ſeek the concert's coſtly ſong†
Or dam the river now propos'd ſo long;
260 But loyal ſtrains the motley crowd ſhall ſing,
Dullneſs their queen, and avarice their king.

Tho' not thy ſtream in amber waves is roll'd,
Nor like pactolus flows o'er ſands of gold,

---

* That Briſtolmen ſtill continue to occupy the Tolzey in utter contempt of their elegant
Exchange, has been long a matter of ſurprize.

† This populous and wealthy city has not been *able* to ſupport a winter concert, tho' pro-
poſed at ſix for a Guinea.

Yet

14

Yet rides the rich store o'er the sullen flood,
165 And wealth comes wafted by its kindred mud ;
From diſtant realms, the mighty veſſels fraught,
From either zone the native product's brought ;
But chief the weſtern iſles attention gain,
Where grows the ſaccharine and juicy cane :
270 Wide ſpreads the ſail from BRISTOL's buſy quay,
To Afric's coaſt directs the eager way,
Their motive avarice, and trade their plan,
Their means oppreſſion, and their commerce man.*

The hapleſs victim ſold to till the ſoil,
275 Reaps only miſery for his lengthened toil ;
To us the grateful plant is freely given,
A feaſt unguilty by the hand of heav'n ;
But the ſad ſlave the unbleſt produce rears,
" Fans with his ſighs, and waters with his tears"
280 Thus man perverts what heav'n intended good,
And dies the growing plant with human blood ;
Slaves torn and mangled, cultivate the ſweet,
That trade may thrive, and luxury may eat.

Nor leſs is fam'd the bridge, whoſe arches ſtride
285 O'er the dull ſurface of thy turbid tide.

* Next to London and Liverpool, Briſtol employs moſt ſhips in the ſlave trade.

Since

Since Calcot firſt, (who ſighs to gain a name,
And madly climbs up half-built ſpires to fame)
Croſs'd o'er the pile with proud triumphant air,
And riſk'd his life to make the ſtupid ſtare.*

290 But memory turns from folly's tranſient ſway,
To mark the horrors of a ſadder day,
When ſacred Juſtice bad the toll to ceaſe ;
But oppoſition chas'd the form of peace ;
The hand of power the rightful claim withſtood,
295 And ſtain'd the ſtreets with many a victim's blood.†
Still the dread thought the indignant heart appalls ;
Still from their graves the voice of vengeance calls ;
The widows mourn, the fatherleſs complain,
But (ſhame to BRISTOL) ſtill they call in vain :
300 Tho' unreveng'd it dies, nor fate nor time,
Shall blot remembrance of ſo foul a crime ;

* Mr. GEORGE CALCOTT, ambitious of the honor of firſt paying the toll on the erection of the new Bridge, procured himſelf the privilege of croſſing on horſeback, when the boards placed as a temporary ſcaffold, were ſcarcely able to ſupport the weight.

† The killed and wounded on this fatal day, amounted to upwards of *ſeventy*, their names will remain an eternal monument to the infamy of thoſe *who ordered the Militia* to fire ; and to the diſgrace of the inhabitants of this City, who have neglected to ſupport an inveſtigation of the cauſe of ſo horrid a maſſacre. Yet the efforts of E. L. Fox, Eſq. and his diſintereſted aſſociates, will ever demand our applauſe, and excite regret, that their good intentions were fruſtrated by the influence of thoſe who were too conſcious of their guilt, not to fear an impartial enquiry.

But

Humanity ſhall drop the pitying tear,

In penſive ſorrow o'er each timeleſs bier;

While injur'd boſoms heave with deep'ning ſighs,

305 And call from Heav'n the vengeance man denies.

Oppreſſion, frequent as the varying hour,

Still marks this mighty *ſelf elected* power;

To them the excluſive charter'd powers belong,

" The right" and privilege "of doing wrong"

310 But ſuffering thouſands fear their awful frown,

And fancy terrors in an old red gown.

For freedom dwells not in theſe dark domains,

For crouching avarice ever hugs its chains,

And heedleſs, views the violated truſt,

315 Unguarded rights, and murder moſt unjuſt;

Meanly ſubmits all evils to endure,

And knows no ſorrow while its wealth's ſecure.

Hence BRISTOL rous'd with money, ſaving zeal,

When its great rulers plann'd a new Baſtile; *

320 Briſtol, tho' dormant long, the ſcheme withſtood,

Yet mean the *motive,* tho' the *act was good;*

In 1792 the Corporation wiſh'd to build a new Goal, and obtained an Act of Parliament, empowering them to raiſe for that purpoſe a *perpetual* and *unlimited* tax.

Yet

17

Avarice, not *virtue* form'd the ſole pretence;

Not to guard *freedom,* but to ſave *expence.*

Hail! *ſons of power,* hail! *turtle loving* throng,

325 To whom great BRISTOL and its ſons belong,

Still you may keep the path you've long purſued,

You wiſh to rule them, and they chuſe you ſhould;

One only care the Citizens implore,

Oh! *"ſave their pockets"* and they aſk no more;

330 Grant but this boon, they fear no other ill,

Oppreſs them, ſtarve them, murder if you will,

Still ſhall they kneel ſubmiſs to kiſs the rod,

And thank the hand that thus protects their God.

F I N I S.

E R R A T A.

Page 5,——Line 88,——for mark, read marks.

Page 15,——for Calcot, read Catcott.

Believe me love

Robert Lovell's last letter to his wife discovered during the mounting of the 1807 exhibition in an uncatalogued autograph collection. Lovell died in Bristol on 3 May 1796, from a fever contracted in Salisbury. He was 24.

Dearest Love

You would have heard from before this time, but being somewhat unwell a few days since, I determined to wait some change either happily for the better, or if I became worse, I proposed to return home.

It is now more than four days since I first felt indisposed, and without any present appearance of getting better. I was seized with that fainting and giddiness which often oppresses me in very hot weather, accompanied by a most violent head-ach and pain in many parts of my body. I have however contrived to get on in my journey tho slowly, being soon fatigued by the exercise – I do not know that I get worse, nor should I perhaps think much of this complaint if at home but to be ill on a journey is very comfortless. I have sent to my Father, shall get an answer from him tomorrow at South[amp]ton, and then if not better shall most probably return.

Believe me love, it is a task to write on such an occasion to one who will be magnifying the danger by her fears – but it would be unpardonable not to give you some account, and it is hard for a sick person to describe a fictitious complaint when wholly engaged in his real one. Neither is it easy to paint them lighter than reality, as most invalids feel a pleasing relief in enlarging on every piece of pain they suffer. You will therefore be assured that my head-ach is to all intents and purposes a common head-ach such as people feel every day and my weakness and giddiness nothing more than ordinary – and not expect to see me come home dreadfully ill and unable to stand.

A man requires good health and spirits to support the exercise and business of a journey and when he has not, he had better return home. My spirits are still tolerably good – when writing yesterday I felt a trembling and dimness, but now I grasp the pen firmly, and see clearly – and perhaps if I set off for Bristol shall be well before I get there – but shall hardly trust to that in expectation – I have only rode eleven miles today, lay by yesterday entirely, but Saturday [came] two stages in [a day] about 25 miles – twas rather too much [but I] got on for the conveniency of reach[ing my quarters, the little pot houses in th[e villages?] are very annoying to me. I cannot [think?] non connectidly you will excuse [me if I do not?] tell you where to write me. If I don't return my route will be alter'd, in that case you will wait till you hear again from
Yours most faithfully
Lovell (please to turn over)

A thousand kisses to the dear little boy – while he is well I cannot be unhappy for my own indisposition – I do not cease a moment to think of him.

You will give my Love to Mrs Southey, <u>particularly</u> and many others generally whom I don't now remember. Saw the Davis' at Bath but forgot all about it.

Winchester Monday eveng. April 18. '96

An excerpt from ONE HOUR after MARRIAGE. A Tale.

HARRY CROKER was a buck of the first water in the city of Bristol; he was known at every brothel in town, and of great consequence at the American. The American, gentle reader, is the only polite coffee-house in that city of commerce and avarice. Here the rage of trade subsides for a few moments; and the young bloods endeavour to appear tolerable. Elegance is utterly unknown; the city is the very fag end of fashion; no favourite dresses appear there till they are familiar among the valets in the metropolis. Harry, however, by often taking a voyage to Bath, in the one day barge, prudently maintained the reputation of being the tip of the mode; and by the dint of a gold button and loop, and a large oak-stick, headed with iron, has won many a tender unexperienced virgin's heart. Add to his other qualifications, Harry was a patriot, and could speechify much better than the town-clerk, who did not understand grammar. He was a tory, and wore upon extraordinary occasions a piece of blue incle (ribbon would have been a stretch of expence unknown in that prudent place.) He was a true-blue and swore by his Maker that no whig minister should cheat him of his rights and liberties. Upon these principles he presented the Bristol petition, intreating his majesty to kick all wicked whigs out of place; when it is notoriously known that there are none but tories in administration. But Harry is still so much a Bristolian, as to prefer interest to popularity. Having waited on a tool of the ministry, to solicit a place for an agent of his, in one of the colonies, his application met with the desired success, and in consequence of some private instructions from lord D--------, Harry has done all in his power to suppress a remonstrance from that city of meanness.
Town and Country Magazine

The Very Fag End of Fashion

Bad company at the tavern from Trusler's *Proverbs Exemplified*, 1790.

Days Out and Kingsweston

No Views can strike with greater Force the Eye,
Than those fair scenes that round Blaise Castle lie

When people come into a beautiful country of this sort,
you know, Miss Woodhouse, one naturally wishes them to
see as much as possible; and Mr Suckling is extremely fond
of exploring. We explored to King's–Weston twice last
summer, in that way, most delightfully, just after their first
having the barouche-landau.
Jane Austen, *Emma*, 1815

FOR THOSE VISITORS IN 1807 WHO TIRED OF THE IMMEDIATE DELIGHTS
of Hotwells and Clifton, there were plenty of delightful villages
such as Shirehampton only too willing to profit by their presence,
and places of interest and beauty to hand within a short distance
of the resorts. Walking, riding and carriage driving could soon
present objects of interest or picturesque beauty for the genteel
eye to praise. Boat trips on the river, with or without music, or to
the tidal islands of the Severn to take a slightly alarming alfresco
tea at low tide vied with embarkations from Pill or Hotwells to
sample Portishead with its woods and Point, where picnics and
views might also be had. The following passages from Ibbetson
illustrate the typical excursion.

Passing around this peninsula, we are brought to an
opening of meadows on each side of the river: the footpath
leads to Sea-mill dock, and over a plank bridge that
communicates with the meadows on the bank of the Avon.

The scenery on each side of the Avon now gives up all claim
to beauty of any kind; the fir-woods in Lord de Clifford's

The Excursion, Thomas Bewick.

park, terminate the prospect one way; the Folly wood is
another conspicuous feature; but beyond it all is a confusion of objects.

At the bottom of Lord de Clifford's park, the river again
alters its course, and continues westward by the powder
mills, as far as Hunger-road; at which place ships are
moored, and wait, as at Gravesend, for orders or clearance.

We now reach the village of Pill, which is situated on the
Somersetshire side of the river, a place famous for pilots
and boat-men, who conduct the vessels to and from
Bristol. It is principally inhabited by this description of
persons, and by fishermen, and it is an irregular, ill-built,
dirty place. There is a never-ceasing enmity between this

village and Bristol; the people of Pill vent their rage on those of Bristol, by every species of imposition and rapacity; while contempt and opprobrium are liberally returned to them.

Opposite to Pill, and consequently on the Gloucestershire side, is a well known house, known by the name of Lamplighter's Hall: it is a place of resort for parties of pleasure, and particularly frequented by the captains of vessels, lying in King-road.

At this place we embarked for Portishead woods, taking with us a cold collation; a necessary precaution on such an excursion, as there is no house within a mile of the landing place.

The river from Pill is open on each side, with the Monmouthshire mountains in the distance, and the small island of Denny near the middle of the Severn. The seat of Lord de Clifford, which we shall hereafter describe, lies on the right hand.

Two miles from Pill, we entered the Bristol channel; and the tide being high, passed over the flats on the west side. Unless it is a very high tide, this passage is inconvenient, on account of a shoal, where vessels are often detained till the tide rises sufficiently to take them off.

An hour's pleasant sailing brought us to the woods at Portishead point, the western extremity of King-road, and which, stretching for a considerable distance into the Severn, forms an extensive bay, where ships may ride the worst weather.

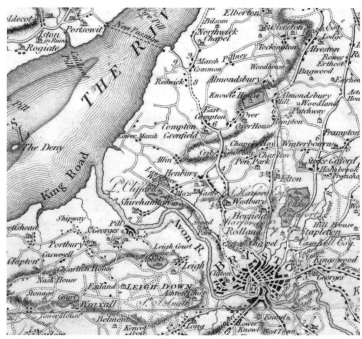

A Map of the Country Twelve Miles around Bristol. In the *New Guide or Picture of Bristol,* John Evans.

The shore is bold, and the combination of objects about it very pleasing. Parties are often made to this place and its neighbourhood, for the purpose of shooting water-fowl. A wish to visit Leigh-house, made us determined on returning by land to Bristol, from which place it is distant about eleven miles.

From Portishead woods, the road led us by some fisher-men's huts; we then entered the village, and kept the lower road through St George's and Portbury, by Pill to Leigh-house, which stands near a mile from the village of the same name, and between the high road and the river Avon.

The eighteenth-century Coombe Mill at Coombe Dingle, Samuel Loxton.

The ride was beautiful, and abounded with views, worthy [of] an artist's attention. Mounting a hill, we had a very extensive prospect, on both sides, of the Avon, the Severn, and the Welch coast, towards Henbury. The inns at King's-Weston, the windmill beyond it, and Blaize castle, are all conspicuous objects.

Day visits to Monmouthshire by road and ferry were also possible, given the right tides and an early start from one's lodgings, taking in several towns and beauty spots like Chepstow Castle or the picturesque wonders of Piercefield Park. The visitor of 1807 was surprisingly mobile. To the south of the city the stone circle of Stanton Drew and historic Wells beckoned, whilst into Gloucestershire, Henbury or Thornbury and its castle were other delights. Possibly for convenience it seems that most excursions were to the north of Bristol.

Among the rides around Bristol, are French Hay, where the Duchess of Beaufort has a seat; and Penpole park and hole. Of this singular cavern, Mr Doddrell, of Bristol, published a description, with a map and accurate dimensions. Some years since a melancholy accident happened here. The curiosity of a gentleman led him too near it, and he fell to the bottom.

Our last excursion from the Hot-wells was an aquatic expedition round the Holmes: the scenery on each side of the Bristol channel is the same as that described from Lord de Clifford's, till we are within sight of Cardiff and the islands. The castle-rock on the Holmes is worthy of notice; as are also the town, and the entrance of the Taafe. Having dined on the island, we embarked and sailed round both the steep and the flat Holmes, and returned with the tide and a brisk gale, the same night to Bristol Hot-wells.

Of all destinations, none seem to have rivalled Kingsweston, Blaise and attendant Coombe Dingle for popularity or longevity of interest. As late as the 1930s, the beauties of Coombe Dingle and its surroundings would attract Bristolians and visitors alike, traditionally seeking countrified walks, lovely views and obligatory cream teas. As a result several tea gardens still then flourished in the hamlet's old cottages around Grove Road, to which local tradition imputed a Roman origin. The area's importance in the history of early tourism in Bristol can scarcely be matched as the contemporary accounts from travellers and guidebooks reprinted here testify. The ancient and famous inn survives as houses still at Kingsweston Down although the slicing out of the cutting now spanned by the Iron Bridge in late Victorian times to by pass the old steep road up to the hostlery has isolated it and no doubt eventually brought about its demise. 'Blaise Castle', the Rev Edward Davies' delightful poem of 1783, describes the charms of the Dingle at a time when the Hazel Brook had been dammed and aided in its picturesque course by Doctor Skeet, the then proprietor, prior to Repton's landscape amendments after 1796.

No Views can strike with greater Force the Eye,
Than those fair scenes that round Blaise Castle lie;
Look here, look there, look every where around,
Look were you will – 'tis all enchanted Ground.
Pan, from his Throne, determin'd to retreat,
Found out this Spot, and here he fix'd his Seat,
Not all the Tears th' Arcadian Shepherds shed,
Can make him abdicate his *Ebon Bed;
For round his Couch here Fauns and Dryads sing,
Praise in soft Notes the Shepherd, not the King;
Lull him to Rest, prepare his mental Ears,
To listen to the Musick of the Spheres.
Deep in the Fissure of the Rocks below,
Where stately Trees the Dingle overgrow,
There SKEET directs the Waters how to flow;
Till now unnotic'd, the rude Valley stood,
Horrid and dark, as Orcus, since the Flood,
When Heav'n in Torrents pour'd on Earth the Rain,
And strong Convulsions cleft the Rocks in twain:
Each side the Dell the Counterparts appear,
Call'd now the Lover's Leap and (Goram's) Chair
Here sat in State the Giant of the Dale,
For so Tradition hands to us the Tale;
Old prattling Gossips may believe it true,

Blaise Castle and Coombe Hill from Coombe Dingle, JS Prout.

But that's no Proof to me, my Friend, nor you,
Such Legends now in England will not pass,
Where artful Popish Tales are turn'd to Grass.
With frequent Dams here SKEET the Stream restrains,
Which falling thence in murm'ring Notes complains,
Join'd to the plaintive cooing of the Dove,
It fans in youthful Breasts the Flames of Love;
And the same Notes, that raise impure Desires
In Youth, excite in Age seraphick Fires.
Here Contemplation sure would wish to dwell,
And here the World-sick Hermit fix his Cell:

Here Poets and Philosophers will find,
Each in his Way, Provision for the Mind.
O'er broken Rocks here rattles the Cascade,

'No unpleasant feature to the eye, whatever it may appear to the pocket.'
The turnpike gate on the Downs at Clifton, JC Ibbetson, aquatint.

The lost Grecian-style Coombe House with its Doric portico and apsidal rear façade was typical of the new villas built around Bristol at this period by wealthy Bristolians. A detail from a drawing of Blaise Castle and Coombe House, around 1807.

Here hanging Woods afford a cooling Shade,
Here ev'ry Night the merry Fairies sing,
Led by Queen Mab and Oberon their King;
Here Hand in Hand in Circles dance around,
And trip it to the falling Water's sound:

*

There is set up in the Castle a Bedstead of Ebony, taken in a Spanish Ship by a Privateer belonging to MrFARR, who built the Castle, and is kept there as a Curiosity, as well as an honourable Memorial of Victory.

It may be difficult to appreciate today the effect that this area had on visitors of the past with the wonderful views now marred by the immediate presence of the housing estates of Lawrence Weston and sullied by the industry of Avonmouth, but those very views do survive on the wider scale if one could only see them still. Unfortunately since the 1950s scrub land at Penpole Point has been allowed to turn into thick woodland so that this famous viewpoint is now smothered and no longer affords views up and down the Severn and across to 'the Silurian Alps'. The famous sundial with its circular bench now looks out forlornly on a wall of greenery, a monument to inactivity and lack of historical awareness in the local government department that oversees the woodland. The overall grandeur of the view is still there and awaits unveiling. The same situation occurs at the other view point on Kingsweston Down near the site of the old windmill, and near the old inn. Alas the present-day visitor, whether genteel or not, searches in vain for a view! In the days when the down was grazed, views could be had not only of the Severn but also looking back towards Bristol, although these are rarely referred to. Thomas Hobhouse's poem 'Kings Weston Hill' of 1785, whilst praising the charms of the location and mentioning this southern

Blaise Castle from Coombe Hill in 1825.

view, recounts an ancient romance between Eugenio, a Roman, and Sylvia, a maiden living in a villa in the Trym valley.

Fair seats diversify the smiling scene,
And farms, and villages, appear between:
Ashton, for summers choicest gifts renown'd,
Henb'ry's proud woods, with gorgeous turrets crown'd;
Westb'ry, where Trim in brawling shallows glides,
Shirehampton, bounded by the marshy tides;
And Durdham's Lodge, that views the shaggy caves,
Whence tow'ring Vincent threats his subjects waves;
And winding Stoke, and brooky Cote appear;
And Barrow's hills their nodding forests rear;
And Redland's smoky villas spot the ground;
And Dund'ry's tow'rs the swelling prospect bound.
Here too old Leigh his sunny plains extends,
And to the main in lengthening verdure bends;
Leigh, that to Charles unconscious refuge gave,
The British king degraded to the slave;

Of the exploration of Kingsweston, the following by Ibbetson is perhaps the most comprehensive and gives the fullest idea of the delights waiting to be explored within three miles of Hotwells.

Visitors to the Hot-wells derive great advantage and equal pleasure from the number and variety of rides and walks the neighbouring country affords. Durdham-downs, King's-Weston Hill, and the banks of the Severn, are the situations most resorted to. This noble river adds more than its own peculiar charms to the beauty of the country, by presenting an inexhaustible variety of shipping. The usual morning-ride is round Wallis's wall on Durdham-downs, where horses and carriages are to be seen, as in Hyde-park. The air of this down is esteemed the purest of any in England; and in its temperature, is neither too cold for tender constitutions, nor too warm for the purposes of healthy exercise. It has always a gentle breeze passing over it; and the morning and evening tides of the Severn bring a great quantity of the saline vapour hither.

Wallis's wall is an erection by a Bristol gentleman, whose name it carries, for the benevolent purpose of rendering a ride on these downs perfectly safe. From it there is an extensive view of a long vale, in which are seen the villages of Pill, Portbury, St George, and Portishead, with the Avon gliding close under the eye.

*

'Parties are often made up to Portishead for the purpose of shooting.'
Hunting near the shore, Thomas Bewick, wood engraving.

On the right of Durdham-down, an extensive, but very unattractive prospect, offers itself. Crossing from Wallis's wall, towards an inn called the Ostrich, we turn into the road that leads to Shirehampton, King's Weston, and Lamplighter's hall. The walk across the fields from Durdham-down, by Pitch and Pay farm, to Lord de Clifford's, is preferable to the high road.

Below the down on the right, we pass the elegant mansion of Lady Lippincott, situated at the summit of a hill, and commanding extensive prospects, nearly the same as those of Durdham-down. The house has a singular appearance, and is surrounded by a small park, paddock and gardens. A little below the house, through an opening in the tree, is seen Blaize-castle. Opposite to lady Lippincott's and by the foot-path, is the farm called Pitch and Pay.

Descending rather abruptly, we enter the village of Stoke, on the left of which, a lane branches off, leading to Sea-mill dock, a rural and pleasant ride. Stoke lies in a compressed valley, at the foot of inconsiderable hills, whence the road continues to the right. Intermitting spaces admit of views on both sides; on the left, are the houses of Mr Harford, Miss Jackson, and Mr Skidmore.

At the termination of the road, leading to the inn at King's Weston, another road passes through Lord de Clifford's park, to the pleasant village of Shirehampton. A number of remarkably large elms extend on each side of the road, their boughs spreading to a great distance. The park, which is planted with oaks and pines, is by no means so considerable a space of ground as is usually allotted to parks. The road declines gradually till we are brought to the lodge, at the other extremity of these grounds, from whence we immediately enter Shirehampton.

There is but one view from the park that deserves notice, and this includes the river Avon and Sea-mills; they appear at a short distance, and are backed by the Folly-wood. During a spring tide when the banks of the river are flooded, and the shipping are floating up to Bristol, the scene is pleasant; but its claims to praise, even at the best, are very slender.

The village of Shirehampton is prettily situated under a gentle eminence, called Penpole hill, and it surrounded by lofty and numerous groups of ash, oak, and elm trees. The vicinity of this village to Bristol, and the easy conveyance thither by water, are circumstances that render it an inviting summer-residence to the gentlemen of that city. At the entrance of Shirehampton, and in the centre of the green, opposite the George inn, is an elm tree of a very great height; but still more remarkable, on account of the manner in which the root has twisted itself into a parcel of rock, that lies beneath it; in many parts, it has perforated the solid stone, and comes out at an opposite part. It makes an appearance that cannot fail of exciting every passenger's curiosity.

There are several genteel houses in this village, among which Mr Seager's claims a superiority; his garden and grounds which surround the house, are laid out with taste, and the avenues to the summer-house and grotto, present a sudden and extensive view of the Severn, King-road, and Portishead-point and bay, with a considerable distance to the westward, and the Monmouthshire hills to the north. It is to this gentleman's politeness and patronage, that we are indebted for much of the pleasure we derived from this part of our tour.

From Shirehampton, a back-road leads to Pen-Pole, an abrupt knoll at one of the terminations of Lord de Clifford's park. On the extreme northern point of this knoll is a dial pedestal, which attracted us to the best view we had yet found here, though it presented only the vale of the Severn, which Somerville has so exquisitely introduced in his Hobbinol. It extends to the Old or Aust passage house, where a gentle, but formal swell of hills closes the view. The New passage house in Gloucestershire,

and the opposite one in Monmouthshire, are very discernible, as opaque white spots, which are relieved by woods and fields. The valley is decked with a richness rarely to be met with; coppices and hedge rows are grouped in graceful confusion, till the whole resolves itself into a continued wood. Immediately above the vale, and on a gentle acclivity, stands the mansion of Lord de Clifford, surrounded by woods, and sheltered by King's-Weston down.

Passing through the lodge, we entered the private grounds, from whence, by a broad gravel walk, and a flight of steps, we approached the house. The time allowed by his lordship for the admission of strangers to see the pictures, when he is resident there, is from ten in the forenoon, till two in the afternoon; when he is absent, they are shewn at all times.

[Here continues an extensive and detailed tour of the house and its collections]

The gardens belonging to the seat are laid out with suitable taste, and may be seen at any time, a gardener attending expressly for the purpose of conducting strangers. On a knoll of inconsiderable height above the eastern extremity of the park, is a house called King's-Weston Inn, much resorted to by those who visit Lord de Clifford's, as being a convenient place to leave their carriages and servants at. The down above this house is frequented by morning parties from the Wells; its elevation and pure air are great inducements with invalids. The walk across the fields to King's-Weston is about three miles and an half from Park-

'The setting sun takes its leave and retires behind the Silurian Alps.'
Sunset from Penpole Point, Samuel Jackson, lithograph.

Street, Bristol, through a shady path.

From the down, and near the wind-mill, an extensive prospect may be seen: a surface of about thirty miles appears declining on all sides below the brow of this hill: all the passage-houses on the river Severn, and the boats crossing it, may be distinctly seen: the river may be traced eastwards far beyond Newnham, and to the west as low as Cardiff; the entrance of the Wye, and the lofty mountains about Piercefield; the mountains in Monmouthshire, which pass in flowing lines on the opposite shore, and lose themselves in pleasing confusion; and the infinite variety of verdure observable in different spots of this sublime landscape, render it one of the first in the kingdom.

To the south are Lansdown hills and Dundry. The eye is instantly, on turning this way, attracted by the artificial

building called Blaize Castle, situated at the very summit of a spiral rock, and surrounded with wood. From hence it appears considerably higher than any ground within the same distance of Bristol. The road from Kings-Weston continues under the brow of this hill, and has the vale of Severn, with the river, and its accompaniment of rude scenery on the opposite side. A short mile from hence is the village of Henbury, where a number of the inhabitants of Bristol have country houses.

At the foot of Blaize-castle wood, and adjoining the church, is the seat of Mr Harford. Since the castle and grounds have been in his occupation, he has made very considerable improvements; the battlements form a terrace, on which he has mounted eight cannon. In the walks up to it are many objects of curiosity. The only day when strangers are admitted, is Thursday. From the top of the castle, we look down a coomb of considerable length. On each side of which are high perpendicular rocks, with a great quantity of wood beneath them. A particular part of the rock resembling a seat, is called the Giant's chair. Blaize-castle has been celebrated in a poem, named after it, by Davies.

Leaving the pretty village of Henbury, we proceed up Gloucester-lane. On the left hand, and half way towards Cribb's causeway, is the seat of Mr Battersby, a merchant of Bristol. It stands about half a mile out of the road, and on the brow of a hill that commands the Severn, and has the same view from it, as that seen from King's-Weston hill. At the end of this lane, we enter the high-road to the New and Old Passage houses. The road is now hemmed in on each side by the hedge-rows, with little variation, for a considerable distance. The seat of Mr Daubigny, and another more elevated near Almondsbury, are very conspicuous, and are not inferior, in beauty of situation, to any on the banks of the Severn.

Manby's account of a visit to Kingsweston gives us another narrative of how the place affected the susceptible viewer of the picturesque.

At the back of St Vincent's Hill, an excellent road, with agreeable winding, leads to Kingsweston; on it the turnpike gate is no unpleasant feature to the eye, whatever it may appear to the pocket; beyond it the view stretches over an extensive variety of pleasing objects and country; as part of the Downs, Black-rock, Cook's Folly and woods: and the low country, being so thickly grouped with trees, appears like a mass of wood, reaching to the Severn, and bounded by the Cambrian Hills. The Avon steals on the eye in the vale below, with inexpressible pleasure; and its contrasting shores are truly picturesque, being a proud elevation, richly clothed in foliated attire, in every fanciful variety of its hue, except where the quarrymen have laid open its bosom, and are tearing out its bowels with irresistible force.

I think I see you startle at another innovation of leaving Clifton; but as no place affords such picturesque variety as is to be seen within the pale of Lord de Clifford's park, I trust you will consider it quite allowable, as the eye is bewildered in confusion, which object should be first or most admired, as all that imagination can suggest is here realized; however, I think you will agree with me, from the

Kings Weston, the seat of Lord de Clifford, CV Fielding after F Mackenzie, 1816.

conveniences and indulgence granted to strangers by its possessors, they are certainly entitled to that claim.

This spot is covered by woods, groves, stately trees, and verdant lawns, enjoying a display of the most picturesque scenery; its shrubberies and gardens are extensive, and its hot and green-houses furnish a great variety of curious flowers and rare plants; the whole is laid out with such peculiar taste and fancy, that it would be impossible to improve the spot, or render it more beautiful: here many a seat is placed for the hospitable purpose of resting the wearied traveller, whose curiosity had led him to that distance to gratify himself by its attractive charms. A neat thatched cottage serves as a lodge, where the woodbine and other negligent shrubs are climbing up the pillars of its

Lady Lippincote's house, Stoke House. Blaise Castle is on the hill to the left of the house. Lithograph, 1820.

rustic alcove; pursuing the road, it leads to a point of land called Pen-pole, perhaps rivalling the kingdom for its pleasing and extensive view of land and water; here the elegant mansion of its possessor (partly concealed by a few trees), presents itself at the extent of a vernal lawn, whose sides are thickly grouped with stately elms, with long pendant branches sweeping the surface of that soil which yields them support; this fabric is built of stone, and its range of chimneys has a singular effect; the situation of Blaize Castle, above it, is very happy, adding consonant beauty to the whole, appearing as an elegant crest to a richly emblazoned escutcheon. Visiting the house, it corresponds with the exterior for variety and elegance; its collection of paintings is numerous, highly finished, and extremely valuable, being by celebrated masters; they are in fine preservation, and the animated power of the pencil is called forth to give the highest gratification to all lovers of the polite arts, and fan a flame of approbation on the feeling, from the spark kindled by the happy imitation of nature.

The elegant village of Shirehampton is below the hill of Kingsweston, sheltered from the north-east and east winds, which renders it a desirable winter situation; and the beauty of its country, and the scenery that surrounds it, makes it much frequented by fashion in the summer. It is composed of elegant villas and neat cottages, most of them having good gardens and orchards, which, in spring, when arrayed in all their blossoms, is not only enchanting to the eye, but most grateful by the perfume.

The little port of Pill is seated in the vale, where vessels wait to take in pilots to conduct them to Bristol, or for a fair wind to waft them towards their destination; and often with pleasure have I witnessed characteristic traits of their conductors…'The Avon bathes its shore', forming a labyrinth of windings, fearful lest regularity might fatigue the eye. At its mouth nature has placed a little island called the Swash, to check the unruly force of tempestuous waves; and beyond it is Kingroad, where large ships lie in perfect safety, from good shelter, and firm ground.

Here the Avon forms a junction with the Severn, dividing the English from the Welch coast, and uniting with that magnificent sheet of water forming the Bristol Channel; often studded with vessels bringing increase to individual and national wealth, when, should nature be at rest, without a breeze to disturb its glassy face, it presents a dazzling mirror almost too powerful for the eye, by the playing of the sun's golden beams.

The confines of the Severn to the north, is by the dark shores of Monmouth and Glamorganshires, where, should the elements be disturbed, its spray forms dazzling rainbows, finely contrasted by the white shining waves breaking on them. The vale towards the Severn is decked with a richness not often to be met with. In many places its inclosures are so closely grouped in graceful confusion, as nearly to resemble a wood, while in others it possesses all the beauties of nature, decorated by the charms of art. On it the mansion, the villa, the farm-house and most enviable cottage, appear as daisies spangled on a beautiful lawn, emblems of opulence, comfort, prosperity, and content.

I often visited Penpole to see the setting sun take its leave and retire behind the Silurian Alps, whose bright rays caused such a rich glow on the earth, pencil cannot imitate, nor pen describe.

Shiercliffe in 1805 mentions the legend of Goram and Vincent:

KINGSWESTON about four miles N. W. from Bristol, the seat of Lord de Clifford, a noble mansion of stone built by Sir John Vanbrugh. Here are a capital collection of paintings, extensive gardens and plantations, and an incomparable hothouse. From this House, Kingsweston Inn, and Penpole Hill, are some of the most beautiful prospects imaginable, of the mouth of the Avon, Kingroad, the Denny Island, Ships at anchor and under sail, Glamorgan, Monmouth

Pill, 'an irregular, ill-built dirty place.' Early-nineteenth-century watercolour.

and Glostershires, mouth of the River Wye and the Old and New Passages. This hill on which the Inn stands reaches eastward from thence about a mile. There is scarcely a spot in the kingdom that affords a more pleasing and extensive view of land and water than is seen from this hill; at the East end of it are the lines of an old Roman camp, terminated by a deep glen; on the summit of the hill, which stands to the East, on the other side of this glen, is Blaize-Castle, and to the South is Comb-hill. On the side of this last projects a rock to which the country people have given the name of Goram's Chair: this Goram was a hermit, anciently of great reputed sanctity, who resided in a cave somewhere near this place, and of whom many fabulous stories have been related by the vulgar; they will have it he was a wonderful great giant, and that he lived in the time of St Vincent, who was also another wonderful giant; each of these giants, they say, endeavoured to open a passage for

A hand bill advertising the Old Passage house.

a river to Bristol by cutting through the rocks; Goram would have effected it first, had he not spent so much of his time every day in sitting in his chair, to take a nap, and wash his feet in the brook that ran below, by which means Vincent got the start of him, and completed the work.

Kingsweston and its surroundings also provided excellent subject matter for the artist both amateur and professional for nearly 200 years. Much has been made of the Avon Gorge as a subject but the Kingsweston area was equally popular and is generally overlooked in the study of local art history.

A ludicrous sight to see
The New and Old Passage

THE TWO FERRIES ACROSS THE SEVERN WERE VITAL FOR COMMUNICATION and commerce, as well as providing new scope for entertainment to the visitor who wished to travel further afield. The Old Passage was at Aust and the New three miles to the west at Chessell Pill. The distance by ferry from the Old Passage to Beachley was two miles and it was used to reach Newent, Newnham, north Monmouthshire and the Forest of Dean. The New Passage was a voyage of three miles and took an hour longer. This opened up a direct route to all parts of South Wales and south Monmouthshire. Crossings depended on a rather complicated table of tides and wind direction and passengers needed to arrive at least an hour before departure. Ibbetson advises the traveller:

The price of passage by the horse-boat is, for a four-wheeled carriage, ten shillings; for a two-wheeled carriage, five shillings; for a man and a horse, one shilling; for a horse alone, eight-pence; for a foot passenger, six-pence; for cattle, six-pence per head; for sheep and pigs, two shillings and six-pence per score. For a small boat to cross over with a private party, five shillings, exclusive of six-pence for each person.

The New Passage-house has long been resorted to by companies for dinner and tea. The accommodations and entertainment have been much and justly complained of; but new inhabitants have retrieved its character.

A coach sets out every morning, at seven o'clock from

BEACHLEY HOUSE, OLD PASSAGE.

The Old Passage house on the other side of the Severn at Beachley.

Bristol for the New Passage-house; and another at eight o'clock for the Aust. The mail-coach from Milford, with the Waterford mail, leaves Bristol about eleven in the forenoon in Summer, and is a sure conveyance across the Severn in the packet-boat, which is kept in the pay of government for this express purpose.

At low water, when the horse-boat is ready to receive its passengers, the boatmen sound a horn as a signal for embarkation; and it is a ludicrous sight to see the whimsical groupes that have attended Bristol market hastening to secure their passage. Great inconvenience often attends the embarkation at low water, from the roughness of the shore and the rapidity of the current; but when the tide is up, the boat takes in its freight at Pill, close to the house it goes from, and there is no difficulty.

Accidents in this short, yet critical passage are very rare.

*

In Summer the small express-boat is always to be preferred to the horse-boat, as it makes a quicker passage, and the company is more select. With a little wind in its favour, it crosses usually in half an hour.

*

To those who love rural or aquatic excursions, nothing can be more delightful than to leave Bristol with the latter part of a summer afternoon's tide, sail down the Avon to King-road, and wait at the New Passage-house the return of the tide. The accommodations here are good, and the assiduity of the inhabitants has ranked this amongst the best inns in this country.

To those visitors of the Hot-wells who cannot spare even as much leisure as we devoted to this trip, it may be gratifying to know, that they may see Chepstow, Tintern-abbey, and Piercefield, and return to Bristol the same evening, if the tide happens to serve early in the morning.

An advertisement for the Old Passage for visitors to the Piercefield walks and beyond. Piercefield House in Monmouthshire was famous for its picturesque and romantic gardens and was a favourite with the polite tourist.

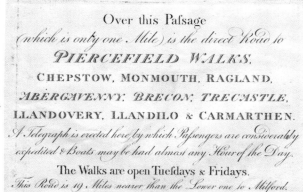

Over this Passage
(which is only one Mile) is the direct Road to
PIERCEFIELD WALKS,
CHEPSTOW, MONMOUTH, RAGLAND,
ABERGAVENNY, BRECON, TRECASTLE,
LLANDOVERY, LLANDILO & CARMARTHEN.
A Telegraph is erected here by which Passengers are considerably
expedited & Boats may be had almost any Hour of the Day.
The Walks are open Tuesdays & Fridays.
This Road is 19 Miles nearer than the Lower one to Milford.

The Road to Bristol

ten such miles are rarely to be equalled in England

Historical and Descriptive Accounts of the Ancient and Present State of Chepstow Castle. Charles Heath, 1801

THE PASSAGE HOUSE

On the Glocestershire shore, is a very spacious commodious INN, equally pleasantly situated as its opposite neighbour; and commands a grand range of country; comprehending a beautiful part of Monmouthshire, terminated by the Welch Hills.

FROM THE PASSAGE HOUSE TO BRISTOL

We travel on one of the finest public roads in the kingdom, abounding with rich and varied views the whole of the way, – in short, ten such miles are rarely to be equalled in any part of England. In coming FROM Bristol TO the Passages we particularly enjoy the fullness of its beauty; because the Severn Sea, from many of the hills, is a splendid object in the different views which here meet the eye. The first scene presented to us, was a spacious lawn, about a mile in diameter, the area of which was flat; and the boundary a grand woody bank; adorned with towers and villas, standing either boldly near the top, or seated in woody recesses near the bottom. The road is carried, for a considerable way, through these fine lawns, which are open, under certain restrictions, to the different parishes, for the support of their stock. Large and valuable herds of cattle are spread over them from one extremity to the other, which add a peculiar interest and animation to the scene. The dwelling houses of the farmers exhibit a great degree of comfort, increased by the surrounding fertility.

When we left the plain, the road carried us into shady lanes, winding round woody eminences, one of which was crowned with an artificial castle. The castle indeed, which consisted of one tower, might have been better imagined; the effect however was good, tho' the object was paltry. (It is 'Blaise Castle', built by Mr Farr, a merchant, in Bristol. It is situated on the top of a hill, in a sugar-loaf form, whose sides are cloathed with wood. A very pleasing object.)

About three miles on this side of Bristol, we had a grand view of rising country. It consisted of a pleasing mixture of wood, and lawn: the parts were large: and the houses and villages scattered in good proportion. The whole when we saw it, was overspread with a purplish tint, which, as the objects were so near, we could not account for; but it united all the parts together in a very pleasing harmony.

The village of Westbury, through which the road passes, is extremely pleasantly situated, and many families of fortune reside here, as well as Henbury, the adjoining parish. The plain called Durdham Down, is much frequented by pleasurable parties from the City, Clifton, and the Hot Wells, for the salubrity of its air, as well as for the many agreeable rides with which it is intersected, and pleasant views it presents of the Avon and surrounding country.

The Approach to Bristol is grand; and the environs every where show the neighbourhood of an opulent city; tho' the city itself lay concealed, till we entered it. For a considerable way, the road led between stone walls, which bounded the fields on each side.

This boundary, tho' of all others the most unpleasing, is yet proper as you approach a great town: it is a kind, connecting thread.

From hence – a fine driving road, corresponding with those that generally adjoin populous and opulent places, conducts to Bristol, the entrance into which is through Park Street, a spacious and well built street (little inferior to the entrance into London at Oxford Street), situate on the declivity of a hill; which, with its neighbourhood, forms one of the most genteel parts of the City. Passing through the College Green and over the Draw Bridge, we enter Corn Street, one of the four fine streets that branch off from the centre.

The Clifton Turnpike and Gorge, GW Manby, 1806, aquatint.

The narrowness of the port of Bristol, which is formed by the banks of the river, is very striking; it might be called a dry harbour, notwithstanding the river: for the vessels when the tide ebbs, lie on any ouzy bed, in a deep channel. The returning tide lifts them to the height of the wharfs. It exhibits of course none of those beautiful winding shores which often adorn an estuary. The PORT of BRISTOL was probably first formed, when vessels, afraid of being cut from their harbours by corsairs, ran up high into the country for security.

The country around BRISTOL is beautiful. The scenery about Hot-wells is in a great degree picturesque, familiar to that at New Wear, on the Wye, before described. Between these hills stands the pump-room, close to the river; and every ship, that sails into Bristol, sails under its windows.

The Miseries of Human Life

10. (T.)

While you are out with a walking-party, after heavy rains – having one shoe suddenly sucked off by the boggy clay; and then, in making a long and desperate stretch, (which fails,) with the hope of recovering it, leaving the other shoe in the same predicament:– the second stage of ruin is that of standing, or rather tottering in blank despair, with both feet planted, ancle-deep, the quagmire.—The last (I had almost said the dying) scene of the tragedy, that of deliberately cramming first one, and then the other clogged polluted foot into its choaked-up shoe, after having scavengered your hands and gloves in slaving to drag up each, separately, out of its deep bed, and in this state proceeding on your walk – is too dreadful for representation. The crown of the catastrophe is, that each of the party floundering in his, or her, own gulph, is utterly disabled from assisting, or being assisted by the rest.

12. (T.)

Setting out, on a fine morning, for a review – and, on your arrival at the ground, violent rain coming on, which continues without one moment's intermission during the whole of the spectacle; just at the close of which, the sun peeps out from his hiding-place, and laughs in your face.

left: The Misery of a broken parasol and *right*, The Misery of a high wind, one lost glove and trying to look fashionable at the same time. From *The Miseries of Human Life*.

80

Hazards of Crossing the Road

An excerpt from ONE HOUR after MARRIAGE. A Tale.

It will be necessary to inform the reader before we proceed farther, that in Bristol it is morally impossible to walk strait through a street; the drays which are used there oblige the passenger to travel in this direction.

This inconvenience may indeed be remedied, when you are acquainted with the place; and, by the principles of mathematics, know how to accompany the horses.

As Harry was pensively swinging himself along, he spied the goddess of his heart on the opposite side of the street: he flew with the wings of rapture; but Pallas, an enemy to love, had in the shape of a dray driven her to the other side: again he altered his course; and behold! she was again removed: he skipped once more over the mountains of dirt; but, unhappy lover! his planet was still in opposition; he continued this zig-zag motion for about ten minutes of insupportable anxiety, when his goddess dived into a blind alley, and was hid from his straining eyes.

The hazards of crossing the river: a ferry scene from *The New Bath Guide* of 1807.

right: a dockside view with a typical Bristol dray or sledge and a crane. From an engraving on pewter.

Sea Mills: in Search of Ancient Rome

the grand naval magazine of the Romans

It is recommended to visit the Roman Camp on the top of Clifton hill, and the summit of St Vincent's Rocks, where the remains of a windmill now stand; and to observe the marks of the ancient intrenchments and fortifications, where the coins of the later Roman Emperors have been frequently found. A peep from the edge of the rock into the gulph beneath never fails to excite surprise, admiration, and horror.
New Bristol Guide

FOR THOSE VISITORS TO THE SPA WITH AN ANTIQUARIAN INTEREST, NOT only did the earthworks on the Downs by the observatory and those on the corresponding heights at Leigh Woods bring immediate relief, but at a further distance there were other sites such as on Blaise Castle-Hill and Kingsweston Down that also held evocative earthworks. It was, however, the picturesque Roman harbour at Sea Mills that probably brought the majority of visitors, not withstanding the decayed state of the old warehouses and parts of the hamlet. Of course to the artistic eye this decay may well have contributed to the whole experience:

Sea-mill dock, like all other places that have been rivalled successfully, is left a prey to time. The store houses, that were here in great numbers, are now fallen to decay: scarce a roof remains perfect; and those buildings that are occupied, the inhabitants are as wretched as the hovels. This dilapidation is in some measure the consequence of a

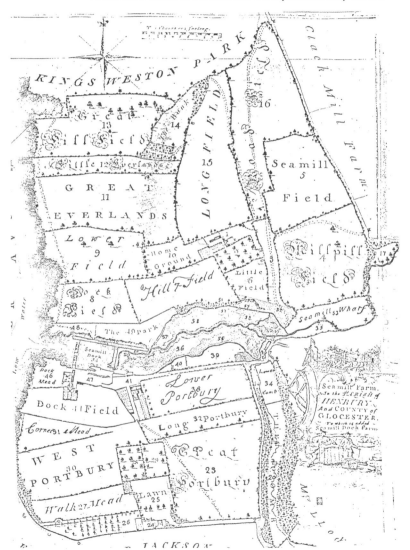

Detail of a map of Sea Mills Farm and Sea Mills Dock Farm about 1750. The harbour works at the mouth of the Trym are clearly visible.

tremendous litigation, in which the proprietors have been involved; but it is now designed to repair the dock, and make it once more fit for the reception of vessels. Before this place was converted in to a dock, a great number of roman coins were dug up; and when the dock was making, in the year 1712, an arched gate-way was discovered, and abundant coins of Constantius, Constantine and Nero.

On the Somersetshire side, and directly opposite to this place, is a beech-tree, beneath the branches of which a troop of horse might shelter.

Ibbetson

Decay notwithstanding, two substantial gentlemen's houses had been built in the previous century overlooking the inner basin, perhaps encouraged by the promised economic development of the harbour improvements but otherwise it was remote and isolated from the fashionable world.

This isolation might soon have changed. Although it has now been generally forgotten, in 1839, a serious plan to expand the Sea Mills dock in order to accommodate Brunel's steam ship *Great Western* and other large ocean steamers of the age was proposed. However, vested interest in the city of Bristol coupled with the Council's incompetence saw this plan fall through. Writing in 1885, Leonard Bruton, the Secretary to the Bristol Chamber of Commerce from 1853 until 1887, regretted the failure and pointed out that had the plan succeeded 'it would have retained the *Great Western* steamer here, and have led, in all probability to Bristol instead of Liverpool, being the Ocean mail Steamship port to New York'.

No evidence of the ancient name of Sea Mills has ever been

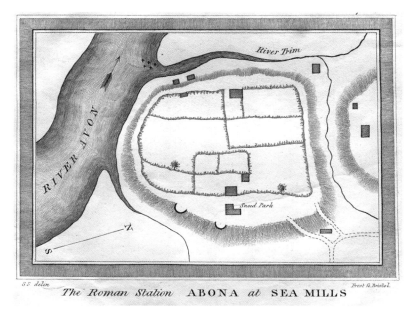

The Roman site at Sea Mills From Samuel Seyer's *Memoirs Historical and Topographical of Bristol*.

found at the site but a second- or third-century document called the Antonine Itinerary survives which lists all of the posting stations on the main roads of the Roman Empire. On this the last place on the road from Bath before the town of Caerwent (Venta Silurum) in Monmouthshire is reached on the other side of the Bristol Channel is Abonae. This was presumably a port and ferry crossing.

William Barrett in his *History and Antiquities of the City of Bristol*, 1789, quotes a document from the time of Henry VIII which refers to a field below Kingsweston Hill 'in campo Abone town' which suggests the identification is correct. The name Abonae may well derive from the river Avon. Samuel Seyer in 1823 was one of the first to suggest that Sea Mills was Abonae. In his book *Memoirs Historical and Topographical of Bristol* he

83

proposed that the town took advantage of the natural defences of the hill and covered the entire area of the plateau on which it sits. Manby's account, reprinted below, predates Seyer by 17 years.

It is highly likely, however, that the town also spread on to the northern shore of the harbour and even more likely on the western, or Somerset bank of the Avon in the area still covered by fields. Settlement on the west bank of the Avon would cater for exports and imports for the villas and inhabitants of that part of Somerset, in particular the great walled complex at Gatcombe. A Roman road has been traced running towards Sea Mills from Gatcombe which further suggests a western settlement. A ferry across the Avon at this point would also have given travellers from the west access to the road to Bath and beyond.

A very interesting map of Sea Mill Farm and Sea Mill Dock Farm made in the mid-eighteenth century contains much indirect evidence of Abonae, the Roman town. It shows that before the construction of the weir in the twentieth century the Trym valley flooded at high tide as far as the bridge at Trym Cross Road. The field called Sea Mill Wharf suggests that the port may originally have stretched as far east as there. This would have made a considerable haven for small shipping especially in Roman times before so much silting occurred.

Fields on the map covering the site of Portus Abonae are named Portbury suggesting a memory of its Roman function. Interestingly the field boundaries appear to run in the same direction as the Roman streets that have been found, suggesting perhaps that they formed natural borders once the buildings had been robbed of masonry. The footpath crossing the fields of Great Portbury and Long Portbury seems to follow the likely course of the Roman Road from Bath as it entered the town at the present Roman Way.

Manby was greatly interested in Sea Mills:

The Julia Strata, or Via Julia, already mentioned, is one of those Roman roads, formed in order to connect their great stations one with the other, and to facilitate the marching of the troops in case of insurrection, or other military purposes.

It meets the Down near a tree at Redland, where there are pointed directions to King's Weston, and the Passages, it is there observable and may be traced, running S.E. and N.W. to Durdham Lodge, running in front of Sir Harry Lippincot's Mansion, continuing under the wall at Snead Park, and over the adjoining hill, where it enters the great station of Sea Mills, a place which has involved such variety of opinions, relative to its being the Abone, the grand naval magazine of the Romans.

'Which had thy title graced it had aspired
To the first naval honors and look'd down
On Carthage.'

Nor has it been determined whether the walls which compose a large floating dock, are of their construction, as my opinion is but a streamlet contending against the ocean of the better-informed, I shall therefore humbly 'kiss the rod,' and content myself by transmitting what little history has furnished, with a few circumstances that came under my own observation.

Here the River Trim mingles its waters with the Avon,

which though now to look at appears an insignificant little brook, yet if there is any reliance from the records of ancient authorities, it has not only been of great importance for its size, but that Roman gallies and boats were secured on it, for in Wantner's manuscript, in the Bodleian library, it is stated that 'at Polbury where Trim goeth into the Avon, much coin has been found, conjectured to be the ancient station of the Romans between Bath and Avington, mentioned by Antoninus the Emperor in his journal-book.'

A more appropriate situation for command and security, could no where be found for affording the best shelter for the gallies, convenient as an arsenal, a plentiful supply of water, and capable of corresponding by signals from the adjoining eminence on King's Weston-hill, whose lofty scite commanded a view extending to Bath.

The adoption of a place of this description must naturally be an object, to a vigilant and enterprizing people like the Romans, having an immediate connection with their princely station at Caerwent; nor was the lowness of the situation of less consequence for a winter retreat, probably containing the Castra Hyberna.

In the year 1712, when the dock underwent a reparation and cleaning out, numerous coins were found, they also met with a fine arch gate-way under ground, rudera of buildings and numberless foundations of walls and inscribed bricks. Coins are found to this day, fragments of urns, scorious relics of iron-ore (called Roman cinders) and bricks eight inches and a half in length, four inches and a half in breadth, and one in thickness, all being scribed down on one side.

Bridges at Sea Mills dock, GW Manby, 1806.

These are in my possession, which I principally found on the lower part of a field, called the three Acres, south of the buildings, where the workmen informed me many had been turned up in ploughing.

Viewing the structure of the dock, the exterior walls are of large regular hewn stone, whose vacuum appears to have been filled up with loose stones and liquid lime.

As it is not allowable to consider this to be Roman masonry, it cannot fail to demand our admiration for the close resemblance of that sciented nation, and creates much surprise, that the very docks in the city of Bristol, have not copied this specimen of their own elegance applying stone and workmanship, so much inferior to what is here presented; nor is it less attractive for the arches through the west-end and two large ones at the bottom of the dock, on the north and south sides.

From the vale below Stoke-house, and passing close by the Sea-mill Tavern, the water has been denied the readiest approach to the Trim; and has become obedient to the hand of man by running parallel with it, forming a reservoir on the south side of the dock, (near the slip or landing-place) at which extremity, to discharge the superfluous water, is an arch of more modern construction and materials.

Returning to the Sea-mill Tavern, near it the Trim has been interrupted in its course, at the bridge A, by a barrier of regular stones to turn and share its waters, up to the bridge B; beyond it, it is confined by a regular and beautiful wall, as if formed for an aqueduct or bath. Between this barrier and the bridge, another wall has confined it to the north, having had abutments, and appears that an arch had been springing from it; this demands the particular attention of the antiquary and learned, to decide on its original purpose, who I am sure will feel amply requited, by such determination, as well as by viewing the arches of those two bridges; their construction being so happily imitated from the Roman mode of architecture.

The Cathedral Robin

THE REDBREAST.

THIS CHARMING STORY IS RECOUNTED BY SEVERAL COMMENTATORS and would have been well known in 1807. The author of the poem was Samuel Love, a minor canon of the Cathedral and fellow of Balliol College. The Rev Love died on 18 October 1773 aged 29 at his father's house in Bristol and was buried in the south aisle of the Cathedral chancel. His funeral was said to have attracted the greatest number of mourners known for a private clergyman. A marble mural monument in the form of a sarcophagus was erected to his memory and remains on the south wall, inscribed with a three-verse epitaph by Hannah More, then well known in the poetical world but now more for her charitable works for the poor. Unfortunately the robin has no artistic memorial in the Cathedral but perhaps deserves one.

Manby says of it:

A singular story is told of a robin-redbreast, who for fifteen years inhabited the cathedral, and received its sustenance from the hands of the verger; during the time of divine service it usually perched on one of the mitres of the organ, and accompanied the solemnity with offering up its harmonious praise. The following elegant lines were written by a member of that church, on this little chorister:

Sweet social bird ! whose soft harmonious lays
Swell the glad song of the Creator's praise,
Say, art thou conscious of approaching ills,
Fell winter's storms – the pointed blast that kills?
Shun'st thou the savage North's unpitying breath;
Or cruel Man's more latent snares of death?
Here dwell secure: here with incessant note
Pour the soft music of thy trembling throat
Here, gentle bird, a sure asylum find;
Nor dread the chilling frost, nor boisterous wind.
No hostile tyrant of the feathered race
Shall dare invade thee in hallowed space;
Nor while he sails the liquid air along,
Check the shrill numbers of thy cheerful song,
No cautious gunner whose unerring sight
Stops the swift eagle in his rapid flight,
Shall here disturb my lovely songster's rest,
Nor would the plumage of his crimson breast.
The truant school-boy who in wanton play,
With vicid lime involves the treacherous spray,
In vain shall spread the wily snare for thee,
Alike secure thy life and liberty.
Peace then, sweet warbler, to thy fluttering heart,
Defy the rage of hawks. And toils of art;
Now shake thy downy plumes, now gladlier pay
Thy graceful tribute to each rising day;
While crowds below the willing voices rise,
To sing with holy zeal Jehovah's praise;
Thou, perch'd on high, shalt hear th' adoring throng,
Catch the warm strains, and aid the sacred song;
Increase the solemn chorus, and inspire

Each tongue with music, and each heart with fire.

Shiercliffe adds the following note in his account. From his dating the poem must have been written about the first year of the bird's tenancy in 1772 and the year before Love's death:

[It] was so tame as to follow the verger to be fed. It continued its habitations till its death, which happened some time in the winter, 1787.

＊

Some of our readers may perhaps think fifteen years a great age for a Robin-red breast, and therefore doubt if it was the same bird. The Author begs leave to remark, that one of those little domestic songsters has frequented a hot-house, belonging to him several years past in the winter months, during which he makes it his chief abode a small aperture is purposefully made for him to go in or out; he is exceedingly tame, and usually comes in September, and goes away in February.

Memorial to Samuel Love in the south aisle of the chancel at Bristol Cathedral.

Taking the Waters

The lower part of the town, called the Hot Wells, and formerly the more populous, is situated at the base of the cliff, and has a mild and genial atmosphere peculiarly adapted to delicate and consumptive constitutions. It first rose to importance from the efficacy of its hot springs, originally noticed in 1480 by William of Worcester... and brought to general celebrity in 1632, when the water was applied externally in cases of cancer and scrofula, and internally in cases of inflammation, dysentery and hemor-rhage. These waters issue from an aperture in the rock, about ten feet above low water mark... they contain sulphuric-acid, but are peculiarly soft and pleasant to the taste and free from any offensive smell.
A Topographical History of England, 1848

BRISTOL'S GLASS INDUSTRY OWED MUCH IN ITS DEVELOPMENT TO THE export of water from the Wells to other parts of Britain and overseas. The business in spa water was so extensive and lucrative that fraudsters issued bottled water claiming it was from Hotwells in order to tap in to the market. As a result the owners of the spa were forced to issue handbills warning the public that only bottles bearing their official seal were the genuine article. *The New Bristol Guide* explained the process for warming the water to spa temperature:

For those who cannot take it at the fountain-head, should place a bottle of the
The Hot-well Water retains its purity in whatever part of the world it is sent to, which occasions a great and continual demand for it abroad. And those who cannot take it at the fountain-head, should place a bottle of the

Water in a pan as deep as the bottle is high, draw the cork, and pour hot, or boiling water up to the neck of the bottle, let it stand so for a few minutes, and it will have nearly the same degree of heat that it had at the spring; thus it will be rendered more agreeable to the taste, prevented from chilling, and its virtues will have greater power of exertion.

The old Pump Room lacked a bath but the facility could be made available as Heath advises:

For those who may be advised to bathe in this salutary Water, for internal or external complaints, a convenient Bath is provided behind the Hotwell House, which can be filled from the Spring, in a short time, by the Pumpers.

At the close of the eighteenth century much work was done to attempt to keep visitors by improving the walks and facilities at the Wells themselves. The Colonnade was built and partly survives to this day and tree-lined parades were laid out in front of St Vincent's Parade:

The town called the Hotwells, has been greatly improved within a few years. The new Colonnade and the extension of the Parade and trees by the side of the River, have added much to the beauty and convenience of the place. Here, and at Clifton above, many handsome piles, mansions and houses have been lately erected... the dwellings below, which generally receive the noble and polite visitants, are, the Hot-well house, the Colonnade, St Vincent's Parade, a range of superb houses fronting the River; Paradise-Row, Dowry Square, and the paved Parade, Chapel Row, Albemarle-Row, Hope Square, Granby Place etc in all of which are good lodging-houses, some of them built in an elegant style.

*

For those who prefer walking after taking the Water, there are a Colonnade in the form of a crescent, with shops, for shelter in rain; and a gravelled parade about 600 feet long, shaded with trees, by the side of the River: so that during its influx and efflux, the company may be amused with the sight of the vessels that pass up and down. They whose strength will permit, frequently sail down the River in boats, sometimes with music, which when echoed by the rocks, has a delightful effect, not only to those on water, but to auditors on land. Companies often sail down as far as Portishead, take cold collations with them, and go ashore and dine in the woods, which are shady and cool, and through their apertures there are views of the Bristol Channel...

*

Here is likewise a CIRCULATING LIBRARY kept by Mr J. Philpott, the lower end of the Parade... books are lent to read by the year, quarter, or month. Under the Colonnade is an extensive and well-conducted SUBSCRIPTION CIRCULATING LIBRARY, kept by Mr Thomas Matthews, consisting of a scarce and valuable collection of Books, let out for the year, season, quarter, month, or by the single volume... Here the daily London and country Newspapers are taken in for subscribers, who are accommodated in a spacious room open from eight in the morning till eight

W Whitehead's *Hymn to the Nymph of Bristol Spring*, 1751, glorifying the waters of Hotwells.

in the evening, Sundays excepted.

There was a rival to the original spring high up on the down at Sion, in Clifton that drew some of the custom away from the traditional Pump Room.

Sion Spring, or Upper Hotwell, next claims our attention. The late Mr Morgan, and attorney of Bristol, built a house for himself on the hill, just above the Hot-well... Mr M. was determined to sink a well... and when they had sunk 246 feet a copious stream gushed in upon them... They not only

At the bookseller's. F Eginton, *The New Bath Guide* of 1807.

'Another good lady of delicate taste/ cries "fine Mr Bookseller bring me some paste/ I'll close up this leaf or my daughter will skim/ the cream of that vile Methodisitical hymn".'

commonly called the Tennis-court House. It issues out of a chasm in a rock (about 20 feet under the surface of the earth) which was opened twelve years ago by the present proprietor sinking a well. A Gentleman of the faculty accidentally tasting it, declared its medicinal properties. It has since been recommended by most of the Physicians of Bristol; and has, undeniably, cured many persons afflicted with various complaints... convenient hot and Cold Baths are prepared with the most excellent Saline Spring, for the reception of those who are advised by the faculty to bathe... There is a neat Pump-room in the house, and a small colonnade before the door.

Unless accredited otherwise all quotations above are from *The New Bristol Guide*.

The Hotwell House as seen from the rocks at Clifton, George Holmes.

found water, but that it was warm... on taste and trial, that the water had the same qualities as that of the lower House. Mr M. erected a fire engine to raise the water, which works every day, built a spacious Pump-room, about 50 feet by 30, which was finished and opened about five years ago; and prepared bathing places for those who wish to try the external as well as internal use of the water... this water does not materially differ from that of the lower well; and the presumption of its being derived from the same source is certainly strong. The temperature of this water... is from 66 to 70 degrees of Fahrenheit's scale…

Sion Spring was not the only rival to the treatment at Hotwells, however as the visitor could experience saline water near the Mardyke on the road to the spa:

SALINE MINERAL SPA WATER, or inimitable chymistry of Nature, is situated below Mardyke, in the street leading from the city to the Hot-well, at the house of T. Davis,

Death at the Wells

I will fly from quackery as a pest

THE DEATH OF GUESTS AT HOTWELLS AND THE SUBSEQUENT FUNERARY requirements were probably just as financially rewarding to local tradesmen as the exercise of entertaining them whilst alive had been. Death was big business in Clifton and Hotwells. Although the waters were recommended for curing consumption, it was generally recognised that they were incapable of saving the truly ill, notwithstanding what the local publicity steadfastly maintained. For the desperate patient or for doctors not wishing to have patients dying whilst under their care, treatment in Hotwells was the only recourse. As a result deaths amongst the visitors was an everyday occurrence.

Such descriptions as the following anecdote from *The Lounger's Commonplace Book* of 1798 perfectly encapsulate the horrors with which the seriously ill had to contend and illustrate how their misfortune was welcomed by the tradespeople of Clifton and Hotwells.

Hotwell's Anecdote
A consumptive patient, on whom sentence had been passed, one of the many thousands who fall a sacrifice to that cruel disease; after exhausting the patience of his physician, and the gally pots of his apothecary, was hurried away to Bristol, according to the customary routine, which succeeds perhaps once, in a million of instances.
The unfortunate gentleman of whom I am speaking, would not suffer lodgings to be taken for him, previous to his arrival but after sitting an hour or two, to recover, from the fatigues of his journey, walking out with his mother, and two sisters, found apartments he liked, and had condition-

ally engaged them. As the party descended from the first floor, the ladies remarked, that the situation was pleasant, the house and furniture in good condition; 'the balustrade, and the wall on the staircase,' said the sick man's mother, 'are only exceptions to the praise I was bestowing.'

'Your observation is just, ma'am,' replied Mrs *****, 'but I have had them repaired so often, that I am tired with the trouble, expense, and dirt; the mischief you see, is occasioned by conveying COFFINS up and down stairs; this circumstance occurs so often, and the undertaker's men are so careless that I really thought it labour in vain to

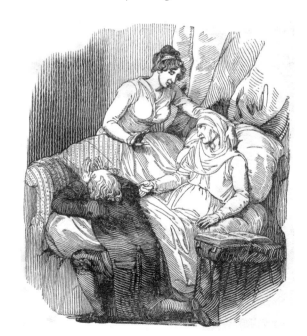

Despaired of!
The New Bath
Guide of 1807.

have it repaired, when perhaps I might have it to do again in another fortnight.'

The trembling valetudinarian hurried out of doors, and could not be prevailed on to enter them again; in less than a month he was carried down stairs himself.

I cannot quit the subject without a word on consumptions; wit, beauty, and accomplishment, are daily and hourly torn from our arms, whilst medical art, and human sagacity, confess their impotence with a sigh; for after all the efforts of the college, and the pompous misrepresentations of

above: Death and the carriage ride

right: Death as a wet nurse

opposite: Death and the gourmand.

All from R Dagley's *Death's Doings*.

confirmed pthisis, or atrophy, in its earlier or later stages, has never been cured.

If a release from life, in this form, is to be my lot, as medical friends tell me is not very improbable, I am resolved on the plan I will pursue, as long as I have reason to guide, and strength to enforce my resolutions.

While any probability of relief remains, from duty and necessary attention to the calls of friendship and affection, I will try every resource which experience, judgement, and qualified professors can point out; but once convinced that my disease is a consumption, I will fly from quackery as a pest, and from the apothecary as an unnecessary append-age; and not possessing a sufficient fortune to carry a shipload of friends with me to Lisbon, I would submit with all possible content of the circumstances of my situation, and moderately indulging in whatever food my stomach would take, pass the short remains of life in the bosom of my family.

impudent empiricism, emptying the pockets, and exasper-ating the disease of the miserable victim, in spite of the splendid parade of quackery, there is no well authenticated instance of that disease, which we call a consumption, being cured, where it was clearly and incontestably proved to be such, by scientific, and disinterested persons.

I will not deny that coughs, that colds, hectic heats, and many alarming complaints, resembling a decline, have been, and may be alleviated, perhaps removed; but a

For death in any form, is far preferable to being dismissed to cough a man's heart out in a solitary gravel-pit, or to being exhausted by a journey to Clifton, with ghastly undertakers, thrusting their cards of funeral performed, into the post-chaise; apothecaries anticipating nitre powders, spermacaeti drafts, silk hat-bands, and long bills; and carpenter's apprentices taking measure of a skeleton as he walks the street, and wondering the gentleman remains so long.

The Narraway Letters

Letters from John Narraway to Thomas Coutts

THESE LETTERS DATING FROM 1798 WERE DISCOVERED BY THE EDITOR during the compilation of the Bristol 1807 exhibition and are now transcribed in full for the first time. They were found in uncatalogued material collected in the nineteenth century purely for autographs. They were written in a clear and elegant hand by the Devonshire-born Bristol businessman John Narraway from his home in Broadmead to the wealthy banker Thomas Coutts with whom he was on friendly terms. Narraway was 54 years old at the time.

John Narraway is a rather shadowy figure known to art historians as the friend of J M W Turner's Devonian father and uncle and host to the young artist in Bristol. He was the possessor of Turner's first watercolour exhibited at the Royal Academy in 1790 and of other early works.

The letters are full of delightful details about Narraway, food and everyday life in contemporary Bristol. The handwriting and content belie the patronising description of Narraway as a bumpkin trader often found in monographs on Turner. A further letter, preserved in the Bristol Record Office, and recently located, dates from the year of his death. It concerns Narraway's disgust at a bear and badger baiting event that was to take place on one of his tenanted properties and the unsavoury elements it would encourage to the area. Narraway's warm and kindly nature shows through in the letters. Subsequent research has allowed me to flesh out the story of John Narraway for the first time.

Born in 1744 to William and Joan Narraway, John claimed to be a Devonian but was christened in Kilkhampton just over the Cornish border. By trade he was a fellmonger or leather dresser and by 1767 an inhabitant of Barnstaple, where in 1773 he married Ann Dart. They subsequently moved to Bristol, where his son John was born in 1774 and a daughter, Susanna, followed in 1777. Narraway established himself in Broadmead and gradually expanded the property until by 1822 it extended back some 400 feet over most of the area now covered by the Galleries west of the Greyhound Inn and included houses, a coach yard and work yard. At the rear flowed the noisome Froom, a useful resource for an industry requiring water and a resource for removing effluents. By 1798 Narraway had a leather mill beyond Bath and regularly sent his cart through that city. Typically he offered its use as a carrier to his friend Mr Coutts and the latter's son-in-law, Lord Guilford, on its empty return journey. By now Broadmead was seemingly reserved for his gluemaking business. That he was very proud of his success shows through the letters. Interestingly Narraway was not admitted as a burgess of Bristol notwithstanding his obvious wealth. A portrait sketch by Turner believed to portray him reading portrays a plump-faced bespectacled man in a powdered wig.

Narraway owned a farm at Horfield that provided the family with fresh provisions and additional income.

The letters contain much fascinating advice as to where to obtain the best foodstuffs and how to treat the mutton and poultry that he sent his friends. Good food and knowing from whence it could be obtained was a passion. Without his letters would we have known that Bristol butter was inferior to that available in Bath or that clotted cream butter would last the winter? Who would also have guessed that laver was so popular in Devonshire or that Minehead was a ready natural source for its importation to Bristol? Narraway is in fact an ideal illustration of the better sort of tradesman whose business acumen and enthusiasm had made Bristol the wealthy city she had become.

When the sixteen-year-old Turner stayed with the Narraways in 1791 and 1792 he was so captivated by the Avon Gorge that the family nicknamed him the 'Prince of the Rocks' because of the excessive time he spent sketching there. A sketchbook and various watercolours survive from this visit. The Narraways collected so many of his works during those and subsequent visits that they gave examples away to friends. A watercolour of Stoke House on the Downs features Turner, John Narraway, John Jnr and Sir Henry Lippincott.

Ann Dart, Narraway's niece, who met Turner in 1798 but heard much of his earlier visits from her cousins, was Ruskin's source of information on the painter and ours for the family, and perhaps for other families of their class in the city. We hear that they were very fond of music, and although they sometimes went out in the evenings (into society and to plays which Turner did not enjoy), they generally stayed at home. Although 'pleasant' to his hosts who treated him as a family member, the artist was entirely absorbed in himself and his art. Generous with drawing anything they requested, including a self-portrait (now in the National Portrait Gallery) he rejected any other social nicety. Miss Dart recalled that 'though so often entertained by my uncle he would never write him a letter, at which my uncle was very vexed. My uncle indeed thought Turner somewhat mean and

An old house on Bristol Back, demolished in 1818. JS Prout after Hugh O'Neill.

ungrateful'. Worse was to follow when in 1798 Turner set out from the Narraways' for a tour of North Wales. Generous as always, Narraway gave him a pony and loaned him a saddle, bridle and cloak, which he never returned. John was deeply hurt

The Fourteen Stars
an ancient inn on the
Countess Slip,
[Counterslip] Bristol,
JS Prout, lithograph.

and branded him 'an ungrateful little scoundrel'. Turner was never welcomed again, and his portrait was relegated to the hall.

Susanna Narraway mindful of the perils of such a journey, gave Turner the 'receipt' for an ointment for cuts made of herbs and unwashed butter that still survives in one sketchbook along with some nautical songs that may have been an attempt to encourage participation in musical evenings in Broadmead.

Narraway continued in business adding '& Son' to the name of the firm in 1819 when he perhaps could no longer continue as sole director. He died on 9 December 1822 aged 79 after a long

and painful illness endured 'with much fortitude and submitted to with exemplary resignation.' He was buried in Temple church-yard on 16 December. *Felix Farley's Bristol Journal* concisely summed up his character in its death notice; 'Mr Narraway will be long remembered and esteemed by many, as a firm friend, as well as a model of that valuable character, the genuine English Tradesman'. Even in his last illness, and less than a month before his death, he had written to the Mayor concerning the bear and badger baiting event.

Whether his long illness had impaired his business acumen or his son was less fortunate, events were to take a turn that fortunately the old man was no longer around to see. On 11 May 1824 John Jnr was declared bankrupt and in the following months auctions advertised the disposal of his property, providing us with details of its location in the city. However, the firm was temporarily saved as it appears in the 1826 *Bristol Directory* as John Narraway & Co. and remains until 1828. In the *Bristol Mercury* of 14 April 1832 the Council advertised an auction of the lease of the Broadmead property which was due to expire in September 1833 and described the extent and current usage of the various buildings.

By this time, and probably before, the family had moved to St James' Square. John Jnr. died there after a short illness on 23 February, 1837, aged 63, and joined his father in Temple church-yard on 6 March. Susanna died early in January 1856 aged 78 leaving the bulk of her estate and the family paintings to her unmarried cousin and companion Ann Dart. She had been listed in the census as a lady fundholder at 8 St James' Square, so all of the family's wealth had not been lost. Unless she shared the house with another genteel spinster companion, it is possible that she took in at least one lady boarder, or friend as the *Mercury* for 3

October, 1840 records the death of Martha Wheeler 'at Miss Narraway's, St James' Square'.

Ann Dart sold Turner's paintings to various collectors and it was from her in 1860 that Ruskin purchased his sketchbook and miniature, and heard what we know of the youth's visits to the Narraways and afforded us information about the family. An article in the *Bristol Mercury* of 21 April, 1860 in the 'Conversazione of the Bristol and Clifton Graphic Society', concerning the acquisition of the Turner memorabilia, described Narraway as 'keeping a small shop in Broadmead' which hardly did the old man justice.

Bristol 2 Jany 1798

Dear Sir

I should have acknowledged the receipt of your favour of the 30th Ult; yesterday, but I was obliged to attend a parish meeting at a little Parish [Horfield] about 2 miles from the City, at which place I have a small Farm & being the only Overseer I could not well avoid it—I am sorry the Mutton at Lord Guilfords did not prove to be so good as that which you last had in London, but it is very easily accounted for, In the first place it not being intended for you, when I bought it, I went the cheapest way to work, viz, by stripping the Suet, this by the length of time in keeping, robbed the Mutton of every thing that would have preserved it, therefore it did not eat generous (I mean rich and full of moisture) but you may be assured it was a Sheep of the same kind and not more than one year old, bred by a farmer Shapland & killed by one Widgery a Butcher— The Turkey I am glad met Lord Guilfords approbation, but it was not one of your lot (you have 4 yet in store) for that,

The grimy lost grandeur of The Pithay and old clothes shops. JS Prout, lithograph.

like the Mutton, was not intended for you when I purchased it, but on my return, seeing it so fine in its grain, I thought I could not bestow it better, your not being at

Bath, as I expected, I thought Lord Guilford then to be next of kin—I did not rob myself neither by so doing, for I had one that same Sunday for dinner which weighed when out of its feathers 11lb oz, that I bought for 4/6—Lord Guilford's cost me 2/6 these things here and in Bath are at a shameful price, which to me, if I had ever so much money, would do away all the goodness of it, I could not enjoy it—Woodcocks are scarce indeed, but come a little hard weather I will remember; that was a fine bird the postmaster at Barum gave me (but these things should never be over kept) I therefore desired Lord Guilford to have it drest the Saturday;

With respect to Butter we look upon it there is no better in this Country than that which is carried into Bath Market but it is very probable your servants don't know where to find it. If you will only speak to Doctr Sole, and tell him that I will thank him if he will be so good as to ask our good Landlady at the Christopher to spare you 2 half pounds of her best butter (which will be just for a taste) and if you like that for her to take you in Market days, what you may want the business is done, She knows all the honest Dairy Women about Bath, and many roguish ones too. I'll answer for her—but anything which that house can asist you with, mention but my name and you can depend upon every attention being shewn you—I have been in Bristol about 25 years and I dont believe I ever eat 2 lb of Bristol Butter in all my life. I always stock myself with Devonshire Butter every Autumn, sufficient to last the family till Spring—that is scal'd cream butter, made from Clouted Cream (I fear you will not understand my Devon-

A worker in a fellmonger's yard, W H Pyne, 1805. Pyne believed few places as picturesque as fellmongers' yards and considered they afforded 'many excellent subjects for the pencil.'

shire Language) but I will get up from thence a little pot fresh made just for Miss Coutts to taste—Does Miss Coutts like Laver? A sea weed, do you know what I mean? The Rocks on the Sea Coast in Devon are famous for it, the most healthy vegetable perhaps in all the world.

As I do not know what stay you mean to make in Bath you will be pleasd to let me know how I shall order these Turkeys up from the Country, whether one or two at a time & when. And I have now to make you and Lord Guilford the offer of a Roasting Pig each, in about 3 weeks hence or at whatever age you will be pleased to have them, and of which I shall beg your acceptance, and that you may not think you are depriving me, I will give you some account of my Stock—about 10 days since I killed a nice little porker 35lb—to day I sold 3 about 38 to 40 lb at 8/ a peace, in about 2 or 3 weeks hence I shall have 6 more of the same farrow fit to kill—on Friday last I had a young Sow brought me 5 and on Sunday last I had another brought me 8. I fear I shall weary you out by reading so much of my Devonshire explanations

I am Dear Sir your most obedient &
Very Hble Servant
J. Narraway
[addressed to 'Thomas Coutts Esq re', sealed]

Bristol 10 Feby 1798
Dear Sir
    Time would not permit me to put in two or three lines with the Mutton yesterday Morng – but on receipt of your note respecting the Bread I repaired to my own Baker here (for it will take some time to procure that article from the West), and desired him to make me two sixpenny loaves, my own way – no Sugar, no Superfine, to be well baked,

and one of them to be made of Red wheat, the other to be white, and to be from the flour of 1796, (last years will not do), he did so, and sent them to me, and yesterday morn'g I put them up in a small basket by themselves—

However, in the afternoon I saw my Baker and he told me his Barm – (some places they call it yeast), was not so good as he could have wished it, but that another time it would be better and he would make any alteration I would point out – will you therefore be so good as to make your remarks. In that respecting the Butter you were perfectly right, because I know now where to apply again, but the last was beautiful butter for the time of year, it only wanted a little more working there was too much buttermilk left in it – there was none in the first, or second – and had Mrs N have been well you should have seen none in the third; I had written to Minehead yesterday morng before I received your favour of the 8th for a doz pots of Laver, and had also ordered a few leaves of the weed to be gathered for Lady Guilford, and to be instantly thrown into a bucket of Salt water & to be brought up on the Ships Deck, so that by the next Minehead vessel I hope to receive it.—The Baskets etc came all in very good time, but I must tell you I always keep one Mutton basket behind—that is going down the Country while the other is going to Bath—please to say if I shall order such another little pan of butter as the first was, and this frosty weather I hope will produce a brace of road Woodcocks, but the season I fear is far gone.

I remain Dear Sir
Your most obedient Very Hble Servt.

PS. The Quarter of Mutton yesterday was a little Picture – pray be so good as to see it before its dressed, and will you excuse my freedom if I point out to you that this Mutton be always hung up horizontal – your servant will see where it has been hung in by the flapp.

Addressed to Thomas Coutts Esq.,
Bristol 21 April
8 o ck at night
Dear Sir

My Cart will go through Bath to the Leather mill on Monday morning next, and if you will be so good as to order the baskets and what Laver pots &c. you have to return, to be looked up in readyness at about twelve or one a clock at noon, my man shall call as he returns and take them up; I have also further to inform you that the cart returns empty, if therefore Lord Guilford or yourself have any thing you wish to have taken to Clifton, or the Wells, the Cart and Horses are at your service, And should it so happen that you should take one trip more down to Bristol, before you go for London, and that you would come into Broadmead you would now see the whole process of Gluemaking. I am now just about the heighth of my glory, the whole premises in full work from end to end, every inch of ground covered, and any day before 12 or 1 o ck the whole process is in full works, the sight would be highly entertaining to Miss Coutts and Lady Guilford I am sure, and if you have never seen any thing of the kind yourself I think you would be much pleased, and should Mrs Coutts be of the party, she will now find every part of the yard neat, dry and clean,

I am with the greatest respect –
Dear Sir your most obedient &
Very Hble servant—
J. Narraway

PS. I am just returned from Horfield, I had been up to pay my man and I have now got my Garden made & laid out in squares, and raild out in a proper manner and I will assure you it looks fine, such a day as this has been, would have been the day for strangers to see the prospects of Horfield and should the French drive you out of London do you please to come down to me.

Addressed to Thomas Coutts Esq.,
London Thirteenth Oct.1798
Mr Coutts Esq
Cheltenham
Mr Trotter
Dear Sir,

I received your favour of the 9th yesterday & Note the Contents, and by way of diverting Mrs & Miss Coutts, if you should in form them that I have stopped your Bread, no doubt but they will laugh: – no more will now come on till you let me know you are again in London.

Inclosed I send you the Book, and I am very careful to set every thing down for you, and your Ten Pounds is now all gone, and you are sevenpence halfpenny in my debt to the end of it.

This Sir pays every thing to the 2nd Inst.

I hope you are all in good health as it leaves them belonging to me together with

Dear Sir, Your most Obedient Very Hble Servt.

J. Narraway

Broadmead

Thursday Eveg 11th Oct 1798

P.S. I must beg you will be so good as to make a little bit of an apology for me to Mr Trotter when you see him, for my freedom in requesting him to put this under cover for you, I have no knowledge of Mr Trotter neither can I see his name upon the list of the Ho of Co but I presumed that if his name would frank a letter from London to Bristol, it would from Bristol to London, I hope I have not been guilty of a blunder by so doing, but to trouble you with a sevenpenny letter about a sixpenny loaf would be a backward way in going to Market.

Tomorrow Morng I go for Devon

[end of the letter]

Broad Mead

Wednesday Nov 13th 1822

To James George esq

The Right Worshipful the Mayor

Mr Narraway presents his respectful compliments to the Mayor and requests permission to inform him of a public exhibition about to take place this afternoon of a bear and badger bait for which purpose a loft has been privately let by one of J Narraway's tenants and seats are erected in the yard he now holds under the Corporation in Broad Mead.

As the above intended disgraceful scene which JN has endeavoured to prevent but hitherto without effect will be the means of bringing together a collection of the lowest characters to the great annoyance of the neighbourhood and particularly those who rent workshops in the above premises. He hopes his Worship will not think it an intrusion if he requests his interference in the business.

A waterman to a hackney coach stand, WH Pyne, 1805. Around his neck he wears a brass licence badge stamped with his number. Similar badges were worn by porters on Bristol docks to prove they were licensed to work. Watermen had to feed and water horses and open doors for passengers.

A gallon of stingo for each man

The New River and other Harbour Improvements

Some merchants of Bristol have for many years had it in contemplation to keep the water up, and the vessels constantly afloat in both Rivers, by damming the Avon, at the Redcliff above Hot-wells. Several plans for this purpose have been proposed, and one is now adopted. And if this scheme can be executed, without any inconvenient delay in the passage of ships and boats, by lock or ice in winter, or danger of muddy sediments that might tend to fill up the channels, it will be the most important and desirable improvement. The plenitude of the rivers will afford safe riding for the ships, render the maritime parts of the Town extremely pleasant, and facilitate the passage of boats and barges up the River towards Keynsham and Bath. The objections of stench and infection are utterly nugatory.
New Bristol Guide 1804

NOTWITHSTANDING WHAT THE OFFICIAL PROPAGANDA CLAIMED, THE Bristol docks in the early 1800s were quite unsatisfactory for their purpose. Apart from the hazards of sailing down the Avon, once a ship had arrived at the port it was subject to the colossal change in the tide experienced in this part of Britain. James Malcolm commented on how ridiculous it was that at low tide the ships were ten feet below the level of the wharves and grounded on mud, but it was not until the early years of the nineteenth century that anything was done to improve the situation. Most local accounts of the docks saw very little amiss, as for example W. Sheppard in his *New Bristol Guide* of 1804:

The KAY of Bristol is upwards of a mile in extant, or circuit, reaching from St Giles'- bridge down to the mouth of the Froom, and up the Avon to Bristol-bridge; being one uninterrupted spacious wharf of hewn stone, having sufficient depth of water before it for ships of the greatest burden and fully laden to come up close to the walls, and discharge their cargoes. It has different names, as the Head of the Kay, Tontine –Kay, Broad-Kay, Gibb, Mud-Dock, the Grove, and the Back. At this Kay lie safely, on a soft bed of mud, a considerable number of ships at all times of the year, which makes a pleasing appearance; and the large quantities of different merchandise seen on the wharfs, prove the very great trade of the port of Bristol. – N.B. the French write Quai, from the non-usage of K. The word Kay is derived from Welsh-Gallic and Irish, signifies to enclose, or fence: hence Cahir, Caer, a walled place, town. etc.

On the western side of the Mud-Dock is the great Crane, erected on fourteen pillars cased with iron, by the ingenious Mr Padmore; a curious piece of mechanism, and worthy of observation. Cranes of the same internal construction are erected in proper situations for loading and unloading, which are all numbered, for more readily finding the subjacent vessels.

Various schemes had been proposed previously but not acted upon. Early in 1802 a plan to build a floating harbour was put before the Corporation and the Merchant Venturers who passed it to William Jessop an engineer to design. Jessop had previously suggested building a floating harbour by constructing a dam at Rownham. He now suggested a plan to excavate a new cut from Prince's Street to Rownham and to make the existing river channel into a new floating dock. This idea would have cost only £150,000 and would have given ships the option of docking in the new harbour or of taking berths in the old river channel at Welsh Back and The Grove as previously. The plan was rejected by the promoters because they felt that they would lose income from the traditional river berths and wanted as many ships as possible to be made to pay. Jessop was asked to alter the plan and extend the cut to Netham. In 1803 an application was made to Parliament for powers to make a new course for the river from Rownham, near Hotwells, to Totterdown, and to convert the existing river for the distance of two and a half miles into a wet dock with entrance locks and basin. The Corporation levied an annual rate on the fixed property of the city and imposed a standard tax on ships entering the port. The opposition from householders and merchants was considerable especially as the new company was for the financial benefit of individuals and the council had passed the measure by only one vote. The Act was obtained in 1803. A company was formed called the Bristol Dock Company, consisting of the Corporation, the Merchant's company and private subscribers to the sum of £250,000. It was estimated that the cost would be £300,000.

The construction works involved damming up the river at Rownham to create a floating harbour stretching back as far as Totterdown. Also a huge excavation would slice through the existing meadows and cut off Bedminster from the city at the bottom of Redcliffe Hill in its course to Totterdown. Along this the tidal waters of the Avon would flow. Construction work on

The corruption of the Froom.
The Man in the Moon, (a radical pamphletist) illuminates a web of corruption holding official documents.
A kicking ass frees a bundle marked 'Dock Company' and the deity of the Froom holds his nose at the stench. His usual water urns are replaced with slop buckets and dead cats float by. A sailor vomits in the waters behind.

this commenced on 1 May 1804 at 5.00 am when the first sod was cut at Wapping in a field near to Mr Teast's shipbuilding yard. This was the usual time that labourers started their day's work. All 105 workmen then present were given a shilling to toast the success of the undertaking. The Dock Company had decided this and reimbursed Mr Jessop five guineas. From that date the tax on the city came into operation. It should be pointed out that there is no truth in the tradition that French prisoners of war were used to cut the new river course. Indeed *Felix Farley's Bristol*

The view towards the Drawbridge and St Augustine the Less from near St Stephen's Church. W H Bartlett

Journal of 14 February, 1807 records a strike amongst the English and Irish labourers:

Last week a refractory disposition showed itself among the labourers, principally the diggers, on the New Cut, in this city; and on Friday a body of them refused to work. Their pretended grievance was, an undue exaction on the part of the contractor, respecting the hour of breakfast. Their example was followed by the whole line of diggers, about 400 in number, and threats were advanced of stoning all workmen of every denomination who persisted in working until their supposed grievance was redressed. In consequence of this, about 800 workmen suspended their labour,

and as one motive of discontent is too frequently made subservient to another, the rioters required an advance of wages; but their demands in both cases were so unreasonable and ill-judged, that the contractor, much to his credit, resisted in refusing to comply with them; and the men, after losing three quarters of a day, returned to their labour.

As the work progressed on the New Cut a remarkable discovery was made as the *Bristol Journal* for 25 July reported:

In excavating the new canal, near the Redclift-house, the workmen have discovered a great number of oak trees, about 15 feet below the surface of the earth. Some of them are as much as three feet in diameter; on being exposed to the atmosphere, the outside peels off and moulders away, but the heart is so pure and sound, that several of the pieces have been manufactured into spokes and tables, which in appearance are not unlike faint-coloured mahogany.

The trees were all orientated in one direction as though felled by a hurricane. By chance on 7 November of that year the same newspaper could report a similar modern event as Bristol was struck by the first of two tremendous November gales that caused great devastation in the area and damaged ships in the harbour. The effect on the trees of Ashton Court bore comparison with those recently excavated:

On Monday night this city and neighbourhood were visited by a tremendous storm of wind with rain and hail; and though many instances of its effects are visible, yet none so remarkable have been observed as those in the park of Sir

Hugh Smyth, Bart. at Ashton Court. It there assumed the appearance of an hurricane, and took a direction from that beautiful gothic structure, the upper lodge, and pursuing its course towards the mansion, left behind it a shocking scene of devastation; more than 100 trees are rooted up or torn to pieces by its violence. The duration was short, but the mischief it occasioned will be long regretted by those who have ever witnessed the sylvan beauties of the park previous to this visitation.

Because the New Cut had severed the village of Bedminster (and with it the road to Bath) from the city, a new bridge was needed. The foundations were laid by John Scandrett Harford in 1805. It was to be an up-to-date all-iron structure. However, the art of building such bridges was still relatively new and on 20 February 1806 the structure suddenly collapsed as it neared completion. Two workmen were killed in the collapse. Not realising that the design was at fault the bridge was rebuilt exactly as before, but would collapse again years later with more fatalities on 20 March 1855 when struck by a coke barge. It opened for carriages on 15 July 1807.

On 27 August the *Bristol Gazette* published an advertisement for the sale of horses and 'rail-road waggons' used in the excavation work as one of the contractors was nearing the end of his contract with the company. It is interesting to see how the spoil was removed from the site:

BRISTOL DOCKS, 21st August, 1807. To Waggon Masters, Brewers and Others.
EIGHTY Good Working GELDINGS For SALE by AUCTION.

The view to the Drawbridge and St Stephen's Church from St Augustine the Less churchyard. J and H Storer.

The Horses are now employed in excavating the said Docks, and will be sold by Mr JOHN SADLER, at his REPOSITORY, on WEDNESDAY the 2d day of September next. They are from four to eight years old; all in good condition; and the best lot ever offered for public sale in the country. The Contractor having nearly completed his contract under the Bristol Dock Company, does therefore give this early notice, in order that any persons who may wish to become purchasers, may see these Geldings employed on the said Works.

Further information may be known by applying to WILLIAM EVANS, head horsekeeper, at the Stables, near the Star Inn, Bedminster.

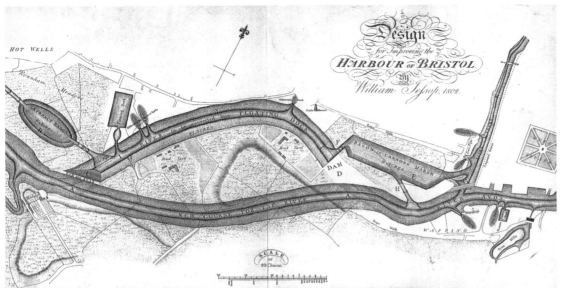

William Jessop's early plan for the Floating Harbour and New River, 1802

BRISTOL DOCKS, 26th Aug. 1807.
For SALE, in One or separate Lots, SIXTY RAIL-ROAD WAGGONS, which have been used in the Excavation of the Bristol Docks; they have all been built within one year, the greater part within eight months, and of the best materials; the Tennants are put in with Adam's Paint, for their preservation. The wheels are of the best grey Metal, and the Arms are sufficiently strong to carry a Weight of about Four Tons: they are all turned, and the weight of the work of the Carriage and Bed is about 130lb. Their construction is such that any one part may be separated from the rest, without there being a necessity for taking the whole to pieces. They may be tipt by one man with ease, and will hold 28 Bushels of Sand each. They will be found useful to any Concern, where Waggons are necessary, either for the purpose of Excavation, Conveyance of Coal, or Lime Stone; for such purposes they will be found to answer every object, and will be sold at a cheap rate, especially if any Person or Concern will treat for the whole together.

For the Dock Company things were definitely not going well, however, and it soon became obvious that Jessop's airy estimates were vastly below what the scheme would in fact cost and that another £300,000 would be needed.

The extra expenditure had arisen from various causes. So called 'casualties' caused by collapsing banks, quicksands etc entailed an extra £35,000. Trim Mills (Bathurst Basin) cost £49,700 instead of £19,500. The Feeder canal and its locks, estimated at £3,700, cost £21,000. The purchase of land and compensation estimated at £88,000 actually cost £140,000. Huge miscalculations in the Cumberland Basin's costs were made and this finally was priced at over £118,000. The making of the new cut was also hugely underestimated. Because of the underestimating of the lock and basin at Rownham it was found necessary to contract the excavated area by a third. The directors promoted another bill to empower them to raise new capital on the security of hugely increased charges on shipping and cargo, without informing the city as to what they intended. This would have meant that the coasting trade, which had always been free of such duties on goods was no longer exempt. The Corporation itself had not been informed about the Bill and the latter was already making some progress in Parliament before the citizens became aware of its intentions. 'A citizen' was prompted to write to the *Bristol Journal* on 19 September.

CITIZENS of BRISTOL, When will your contention with the Dock Directors have an end? – When will they cease to persecute you with new Dock bills, and let the town be quiet?- Again you are called upon to resist the imposition of Taxes unprecedented, oppressive, and unjust. The moment the principle was lost yet do they provoke another contest. But again defend yourselves- your case is just, and your victory certain.

The Corporation and other coastal ports also petitioned Parliament and the scheme was finally rejected in the Commons by 88 votes against 55. Another Bill in 1808 passed unopposed and this enabled the company to erect a toll bridge at Prince Street and a caisson, resulting in the raising of £500,000 capital.

The New River became known as the New Cut even before it had been finished. It was not until January 1809 that the river was diverted into its new bed and April before the first ship entered the Bathurst basin. The work was certified as completed on 1 May that year. To celebrate the completion all of the thousand workmen then employed on the project were treated to a dinner in one of the fields opposite the Mardyke. Two oxen were roasted whole, supplemented by potatoes and six hundred-weight of plum pudding. A gallon of strong beer was provided for each man, which led to the inevitable arguments and confrontations between the English and Irish labourers employed. These had never enjoyed cordial relationships. The Irishmen tried to hijack a cart loaded with more 'stingo' (strong beer), and having

been routed by their foe, withdrew to their base in Marsh Street. They returned armed with shillelaghs. Anxious for a fight the drunken English followed behind and the two armies met on the field of Prince's Street. The Bristol police force being totally inadequate to deal with the situation, the press gang was called upon, and they carted off the opposing ring leaders.

The Cumberland basin (named after the Duke of Cumberland) functioned well until the increased size of steamers and the awkward angle of entry from the river necessitated the building of a new entrance lock in 1873. The building of the Floating Harbour and the New Cut was a phenomenal piece of engineering for the period. It finally removed one of the great problems of the port, namely the grounding of vessels at low tide that in some cases resulted in damage. Only Bristol-built vessels were constructed to deal with this problem, giving rise to the phrase 'Shipside and Bristol Fashion'.

The improvements gave Bristol the most modern docks in the country for a time. However, as the century progressed, the increase in the tonnage of shipping gradually made them difficult to use. Added to this were the exorbitant dock dues. These facts, combined with the dangerous approach up the Avon, gradually drove away the passenger trade that had once been so lucrative. The failure to act on the plan to develop Sea Mills harbour for passenger traffic was yet another lost opportunity, squashed by Corporation lethargy and mercantile vested interest. Not until the bold venture of the new dock at Avonmouth in 1868 did Bristol have such a stimulus in her docks again.

The full story is told in *Bristol's Floating Harbour, the first 200 years* by Peter Malpass and Andy King and published in the bicentenary year.

The compleat accommodation of the Nobility: Clifton

Probably the best account of Clifton around 1807 is that
contained in W. Sheppard's *New Bristol Guide* of 1804

CLIFTON is, indubitably, one of the most pleasant, healthy, and elegant villages in the kingdom. Its air is so remarkably pure, salubrious, and restorative, that it has been long ago, and by various authors, styled the MONTPELIER of England. It commands a pleasing prospect over the western part of the City; and of the Avon, which, when full, and vessels are sailing up or down, add much to the beauty of the view. On the opposite shore, the agreeable, well cultivated, and wholesome part of Somersetshire, completes the landscape. This rises gradually for five miles, from the River to the top of Dundry-hill, on which is a lofty tower that serves as a barometer; it being generally overhung with clouds, or enveloped with mists, before rain; and when clearly seen, it indicates fair weather. As the delightful situation of Clifton has, long since, induced many opulent persons and families to make it their principal residence, the continually new accessions of inhabitants have occasioned the hill to be almost covered with elegant piles of buildings and separate mansions, such as a few villages can shew.

The principal buildings for the reception of those who prefer this elevated situation, where the houses are so airy and pleasant, and command fine prospects of the circumjacent hills and country, are – Sion Row and Glocester Place, on Clifton Down; the Prince of Wales's Crescent, above the Well-house. There are on this hill two noble piles of freestone, opposite and perfectly similar, at the distance of 150 feet from each other, which enclose a spacious Parade. These are called the MALL, and are the beauty of Clifton. There are also Rodney Place; Boyce's Buildings;

Richmond Buildings, an extensive pile; York Buildings; Bell Vue, &c. &c. Two noble Crescents, the upper of brick ornamented with stone, called the Royal York Crescent; and the lower of freestone; yet remain unfinished: The former of these is now purchased by Government, to be converted into Barracks for the Soldiery. This caused much alarm among the landlords and inhabitants of Clifton and the Wells, some of whom were deputed to remonstrate against the measure; but it had no effect. Whether it will turn to the advantage or disadvantage of this place of fashionable resort, time will evince. However we cannot help thinking that a more remote situation would be preferable.

At the entrance of Clifton Down is a good house that belonged to the late Sir William Draper, who erected, at the western part of the garden, before the front, an obelisk of freestone, with a short Latin inscription on its base to the late Earl of Chatham: and on the eastern side a cenotaph with Latin verses; and an English inscription to the memory of those departed warriors who fell in various battles and sieges in the East Indies; at Madras, Arcot, Pondicherry, and Manilla; with the names of officers and list of the battles.

Opposite to Clifton Church is the house of *Gabriel Goldney*, Esq. Celebrated for the curious grotto composed of a vast variety of rare and costly shells brought from various parts of the world. The interstices are enriched with *Bristol* and other stones; different kinds of spar, mundic, metallic ores, fossils, and petrefactions. It is floored with Mosaic brick; at the upper end in a cavity is the statue of a river-god leaning upon an urn, out of

left: Grisaille watercolour by Nathan Cooper Branwhite of the Bath Hotel. This range of buildings lay between Sion Row and Gloucester Row. In 1828-9 the façade of the hotel was altered and raised one storey.

right: Grisaille watercolour of a lost gazebo at Goldney House, Clifton.

which issues a stream of water; this runs murmuring over rough stones, partly, into the hollow of a large escallop or oyster-shell, which weighs near to 300lb. from the brim of which it falls in gentle rills into a reservoir, in which are gold and silver fishes. There is a representation of a lion's den, in which are figures of a lion and lioness, well executed. From the grotto is a subterraneous passage to one of the finest terrace walks in England: from whence are rich and delightful prospects. The gardens are extensive and in excellent order. Here are supplied with water, by a fire-engine, fountains, and a large canal abounding with gold and silver fishes. The avenues are decorated with statues, and bordered with lofty trees which afford cooling shades in the hottest times in summer.

A little to the north-east of this is a capital mansion, built by *Paul Fisher*, Esq. formerly a merchant of Bristol. It was designed by Mr *Ware*, in whose book of architecture are its plan and elevation.

The set of public Rooms at *Clifton* are entitled YORK HOUSE, *Hotel and Tavern*: this has an elegant ballroom with a good organ;

and commands a picturesque view of Leigh Woods and the Downs. The whole building is a complete Hotel, handsomely fitted up, and extremely well calculated for parties who arrive here, or make excursions for a few days to this delightful spot. It is kept by *John Warne*, and is situated in *Glocester Place*.

Mr *J. Philpott* has opened a Circulating Library, in *Glocester-Row*, and has laid in an elegant and very extensive assortment of Stationary, Perfumery, Hardwares, Toys, Jewellery, &c. &c.

Here is also a Circulating Library, in *Sion Place*; where the Miss *Prust's* have made their selections with much taste and judgment:– and for the compleat accommodation of the Nobility and Gentry resorting to, and resident on, Clifton, they have added an extensive assortment of Foreign and English Perfumery, Jewellery, Hardwares, Toys, and Stationary of all sorts.

May prosperity ever await: opulence and corruption

May prosperity ever await,
May the paths of her life, ne'er be rough;
May her joys as her virtues be great,
And den she'll have pleasure enough.
The Goldfinch for 1803

NOTWITHSTANDING THE PROBLEMS ENGENDERED BY THE NAPOLEONIC blockade and the war, Bristol's elite in 1807 had great private wealth. Even in the middle of the previous century Bristol had been known as the 'Opulent City'. Probably the best way of appreciating what material things a wealthy household in the city would have at its disposal is to study the notices in the press advertising the auction details of the property of those either leaving the city or of unfortunates who suddenly found that the Fates had turned against them and that they were bankrupt. These are fascinating social documents and give one a very clear idea of what was then fashionable in the way of furnishings. Likewise the various failed businesses in the city such as that of Mr Vaughan, a cabinet maker of Charles Street, illustrate what was available for purchase in the shops. Apart from an auction announced in *Felix Farley's Bristol Journal* of 6 June advertising the sale of contents at a house in Somerset Street, one of the best listings of contents is that of the unfortunate sugar refiner William Gravenor's house on the upper side of Berkeley Square. This appeared in the same newspaper on 7 November 1807. Gravenor had no doubt been ruined by the sugar glut caused through raising the import duty and subsequent fall in demand from consumers. The houses were less than twenty years old so the contents may also have been relatively new and fashionable as well. Mahogany seems to be the favoured wood in all the sales of furniture. It was obviously in great demand as *The Bristol Gazette* of 25 June informed the public that:

> JOHN PHILLIPS, CABINET-MAKER, No. 7, Beaufort Court, and No. 13, Montague Street, has just been commissioned to work up 5000 Pounds worth of prime seasoned Mahogany, and to sell the Goods at very reduced Prices. Persons of respectability, either Housekeepers or Brokers, may have from Six to Twelve Months Credit.

The furnishings of Gravenor's house comprised 'mahogany fluted, four-post, field, and other bedsteads, with dimity furniture, and window curtains to match; prime bordered goose-feather and mill-puff beds, mattresses, blankets, and counterpanes; a very handsome suit of drawing room furniture, consisting of three dyed calico window-curtains; ten painted black and gold elbow-chairs, with cushions and sofa to match; two large pier glasses, two satin-wood card-tables, and a large Brussels carpet. The remaining furniture includes mahogany tables and chairs, Scotch and Venetian floor and stair carpets; a set of blue and white Staffordshire table-ware; kitchen-furniture, and a variety of other useful articles.' The advertisement indirectly informs us that the three windows of the first-floor drawing room had single side curtains rather than pairs.

Mr Vaughan's household furniture and stock in hand at the time of his bankruptcy and advertised again in the *Bristol Journal* on 26 December, comprised 'four-post and other bedsteads, millpuff beds, blankets, sheets, and quilts; mahogany and other chairs; mahogany circular, card, Pembroke, and dressing tables; mahogany chests of drawers; pier and swing glasses; carpets; and kitchen furniture, with many other articles'. Added to the above was much mahogany together with beech and deal for making lesser furniture.

In November of that year the newspapers were advertising the publication of George Smith's now famous *Collection of Designs for Household Furniture and Interior Decoration*. This volume with its 158 aquatint plates and their descriptions was available from Mr Browne at Tolzey, Bristol. The book was expensive and sold for £7 17s 6d hand-coloured or £4 14s 6d uncoloured. It is a marvellous illustration of high fashion in interior design of the period. Smith styled himself 'Upholder Extraordinary' to the Prince of Wales and his book covers everything from designs for curtains to jardinières. Greco-Roman and Egyptian styles predominate, but patriotic British Gothick also makes a romantic appearance. That the Egyptian style was taking a hold on fashionable Bristol that year is illustrated by an advertisement placed by Elizabeth Ring in the *Bristol Mirror* on 18 April that stresses the availability of 'Egyptian antique shades'.

REPOSITORY FOR WEDGWOOD's WARE, CHINA, GLASS, BRONZE LUSTRES, &C.
No.9, BRIDGE-STREET, BRISTOL. ELIZABETH RING, RESPECTFULLY informs her Friends and the Public in

The English after Dinner, by a French ex-prisoner-of-war. A collection of Frights take tea, served by a black servant. Whilst the ladies indulged in tea and gossip the men had their own pursuits (as may be seen in the companion plate in the colour section of this book).

general, of her removal from her late residence, No.14, Bath-Street, where she has just opened an extensive collection of the above Articles, both useful and ornamental, with the addition of the so much admired EGYPTIAN ANTIQUE SHADES, LAMPS, &c. the whole carefully selected from the first manufacturers in the kingdom; and hopes her endeavours to give satisfaction, will meet a continuance of that distinguished preference which she gratefully acknowledges to have received for many years past.

Elizabeth Ring's trade card, showing the front of her shop when at 8 High Street.

Elizabeth Ring was the widow of Joseph Ring, a potter in Temple Street. He was killed by the collapse of a warehouse in 1788, leaving his widow with nine children. Determined to succeed as a 'Chinaman', she made her china shop the most fashionable in Bristol for ceramic wares. Elizabeth died in 1816 and in her will she ensured that her daughters Elizabeth and Sophia, 'shall have a stock, capital, share and right etc in the trade or business of an earthenware & china dealer, now carried on by me at 6 High Street, Bristol.'

The best houses were now expected to have a garden and a good water supply. The latter could either be a rain-water cistern, or preferably a spring water pump that could draw on a hopefully unpolluted local source. Those with both at their disposal were advertised as having 'both kinds of water'. Water closets were in use but could cause problems if only joined to a cesspit and not to a drain.

For those able to afford them, country villas, sometimes as second homes, had begun to spring up in the vicinity of the city. There were plenty of new architectural volumes available packed with ground plans and designs available in the booksellers to inspire. John Plaw's *Rural Architecture or Designs from the Simple Cottage to the Decorated Villa* went into several editions. The first decade of the nineteenth century was particularly fruitful for such architectural design books catering for a wish to escape to country life, but still retain a comfortable city life-style. Other authors such as Edward Gyfford (the architect used by Nelson and Emma at Paradise Merton) and Thomas Dearn joined the growing catalogue of authors many of whose works were published by the Architectural Library in London.

Any Bristolians or visitors wanting to have a likeness taken to add to their houses' furnishings, had a choice of resident or travelling portrait artists. Many artists travelled around the country to different resorts and spas looking for new sitters. William Armfield Hobday (1771-1831) settled in Bristol around 1802. He lived in Clifton for the following fourteen years and painted many of the notables in the city. George Keman, who described himself as 'miniature painter to His Royal Highness the Duke of Cumberland', was typical of one of the seasonal portraitists who came to Bristol each year. 1807 was his ninth visit and he invited sitters to apply as usual at Mr Haas' confectionery shop on St Augustine's Back, where perhaps he lodged. On 10 October that year an advertisement in the *Bristol Mirror and Journal* advertised a revolutionary new machine for taking likenesses. It may have been similar to the Orthocyclic Glyptograph later used in Clifton in the 1830s by William West. This produced an engraved image of the sitter in basso relief.

LIKENESSES, GRATIS,Taken, (at Mr Knowlton's, No. 17, Clare-street,) by the NEW PATENT MACHINE, from LONDON
The first twelve persons of respectibility, well-known in Bristol, who will apply to Mr HERVEY, (Proprietor of this singular Machine), and have no objection to exhibiting their Likenesses publicly, shall receive them gratis, finished in the same manner as those charged Half-a-Guinea. It is

no exaggeration to assert, that they are the strongest Likenesses in the world; the Machine touching the Face cannot deviate from correctness. It is hoped, that the smallness of the Price will not deter the Nobility and Gentry from calling on the Proprietor; it merely requires that these resemblences should be seen to have their value appreciated; the short time required for accomplishing each, enables him to afford them so low a rate. These Likenesses are taken in colors, at Half-a-Guinea each, at one sitting of half-an-hour; in black, by the same Machine, at Half-a-Crown each, in one minute. A share of the profits of this Machine, is dedicated to the establishment of the new Benevolent Institution. Having had extensive practice in Minatures, Mr HERVEY paints them also, in the usual style, and will remain a short time in Bristol, at Mr KNOWLTON's No. 17, CLARE-STREET

The drawing of the National Lottery tickets at Coopers Hall, London. WH Pyne, 1805. Lotteries started in England in 1569. In 1807 two wheels were used and guarded by the Life Guards. Tickets were chosen by boys from Christ's Hospital.

Other artists working in Bristol at the time included George Holmes (1776-1861), who specialised in local landscapes to sell to visitors and Edward Bird (1772-1819), the portrait, landscape and historical painter who was arguable the most influential. Bird came to Bristol in 1797 and set up an evening drawing school for young gentlemen in Temple Back, near the Passing Ship ferry. This was the first such school of its kind in the city that we know of. His fees were very modest. The surprising address was partly accounted for by the fact that during the day Bird was employed in painting tea trays at the Japanning factory in Temple Back in his first years in the city. Bird had previously served as an apprentice to a tea-tray maker in Birmingham. According to Braikenridge (volume 23, page 95), Bird also painted inn signs at this early period. He states that one of his Japanned 'tea waiters' that was

offered for sale in a shop window in the city attracted a buyer in the shape of the merchant and art lover Benjamin Baugh of Portland Square. So taken was he with the tray that he sought out the artist and commisioned him to do a series of pictures for his drawing room on the subject of 'The Poacher'. These were so admired that his reputation locally was assured. Bird painted many local landscapes and portraits, some of which were engraved and later exhibited. He exhibited at the Royal Academy from 1809 and his work was so admired that Princess Charlotte granted him the title of 'Historical Painter to Princess Charlotte'. From 1803 Bird lived at 3 Portland Street, Kingsdown but by the time of his death he had removed to 8 Kings Parade, near to what is now Apsley Road. He advertised himself as a 'Drawing Master'. Financially, however, he never prospered. On his death 300 admirers followed the procession down Whiteladies Road to the

left:
How to dress your turtle from Lady Elizabeth Warburton's *The Experienced English Housekeeper*, 1782
With the numbers of turtles that were brought to Bristol alone over the decades of the turtle craze, it is remarkable that the species is not now extinct in the wild.

below left:
Auction and bankruptcy notices are an excellent research tool for discovering the contents of Bristol houses and shops. This one is from *Felix Farley's Bristol Journal* of 6 June 1807.

Cathedral where he was interred in the Cloister floor near the steps from the south transept.

The pleasures of the table were considerable in 1807 if one could afford it. Several excellent cookery books were available, but perhaps the most influential was Richard Briggs' *The English Art of Cookery, according to the present practice; being a Complete guide to all Housekeepers.* First published in 1788 it went into many editions. Richard Briggs was for many years at the Globe Tavern, Fleet Street and at other inns in the capital. His work seems to have been based on earlier cookery books but he considerably expanded these adding quantities, cooking times and a wider range of foods such as fish and vegetables. Although writing mostly about English food he also includes German, Spanish, Italian, Dutch, French, Jewish and West Indian recipes. A feature is a month-by-month two-course menu guide. His book was primarily aimed at house-keepers and was so successful that it was republished in America under the title *The New Art of Cookery.* Amongst the myriad delights within were recipes such as Pigeons in Pimlico, Yorkshire Christmas Pie and Grateful Pudding. Briggs also included sections on marketing, food for the sick, provisions for seafarers as well as wine making and brewing.

Bristol, quite naturally for a port, was well supplied with wine merchants. Polglase, Ring and Harry were a typical firm and advertised in the *Bristol Mirror* on 13 June:

GENUINE WINES
CONSISTING of prime and superior Old Port Sherry, Madeira, Tenerife, Lisbon, Calcavella, Bucellas, Mountain, &c. imported by POLGLASE, RING, and HARRY, and on Sale at their Wine Vaults, in NARROW WINE-STREET, Bristol, in Pipes and Bottles, on the most reasonable terms. Cognac Brandy, Hollands Geneva, and Jamaica Rum.

For those requiring more local tipples, Bristol had plenty of breweries. A new one was the Clifton Genuine Beer Company which was established by Henry Hunt in December, 1806, at Jacob's Wells. Hunt advertised in the January newspapers that his strong beer or porter would not be ready until March. He claimed that his products would be free from any ingredients beyond the BEST MALT and HOPS, and that he was determined 'to vend no other Beer, but what is brewed wholly with Malt and Hops'. Henry Hunt (1773-1835) was a man ahead of his time. Later known as 'Orator Hunt' (a soubriquet coined by Robert Southey) he was a champion of the people. Tall, athletic and classically handsome with a stentorian voice and habitually seen with a white top hat, he later became notorious for giving a speech in which he demanded annual elections for Parliament and universal suffrage. This went down very well with women and a song praising him survives in the *Bush Scrapbook* in the Bristol Reference Library collection.

SONG, *Written By a Young Lady*
(to the tune of 'Praise my soul the King of Heaven')

Sons of Freedom! See Bristolians!
See brave HUNT distinguish'd rise!
See the Laurel that adorns him,
Claims its kindred with the skies.
CHORUS.
Come, then, hail him, come, then, hail him
Joyful see HUNT take the prize.

See the needy, see the naked,
See the sick, and see the lame!
See distress from every quarter
Blow the trumpet of his fame!
CHORUS.
Come, then, &c. &c.
Shout fair Freedom's Champion's name:

Freedom! O, thou ancient Goddess,
Crown with Peace our fertile land!
See HUNT chosen to support us;
He'll ne'er touch a bribe in hand.
CHORUS.
Come, then, &c. &c.

Hunt shall all our fears beguile.

Free Electors, brave Bristolians,
Let my Muse her tribute pay;
And in grateful Song applaud ye;
Merit does your voices sway.
CHORUS.
Come, then, &c. &c.
Freedom's Cause will ne'er give way.

In 1807 Hunt established the Bristol Patriotic and Constitutional Association. He wanted to end parliamentary abuse and also to stop soldiers being flogged. To the Corporation 'mafia' and those content with parliamentary corruption he was an anathema. His opponents accused him in broadsheets of openly living in adultery (which was perfectly true) and warned against him in a satirical poem entitled 'THE HUNT!';

See Bristol's fair queens advance hand in hand;
Stretched wide are his arms to gain them he thinks
But Virtue *draws back and* Industry *shrinks.*

He deserves to be better known in Bristol, and certainly recognised with a blue plaque. On 5 May 1807 he caused a riot at the Guildhall when he put forward the name of another candidate against the two sitting members. His nomination was rejected and the mob pelted the Tory nominee Mr Bathurst with mud and sticks and he was forced to leave his carriage and flee. Hunt stopped an attack on Bathurst's hotel by promising the rioters two butts of beer at his brewery, but they later came back and smashed the windows of the Council House and the neighbouring hotel.

The British had their own customs at the dinner table and also after dinner when the men shared the port and the ladies enjoyed tea and scandal in the drawing room. Foreigners were horrified by the antics of Englishmen who seemed to drink for the sake of it. They were particularly shocked by the tradition of toasting each guest as he openly used the chamber pots concealed in the sideboard. In 1814 a French ex-prisoner of war produced two witty caricatures as prints entitled 'The English after Dinner'. The women are portrayed as frumpish and badly dressed and are served tea by a black servant. The men are shown as almost totally drunk. A young man seeking the chamber pot has not been quick enough. A rain soaked landscape hangs on the wall as over familiarity, stupor and depression find the guests.

Apart from private dinners the Bristol elite had plenty of official functions to attend such as the 'sumptuous banquet' that took place at the Merchants' Hall on 6 October as part of a visit by the Prince of Wales and his brother the Duke of Sussex to the city. The Prince arrived in Bristol in a closed carriage so none of the thousands lining the route actually saw him. That did not go down well with the citizens. In the evening he attended a ball at the Gloucester Hotel in Hotwells.

Another Corporation dinner took place on 25 June 1807 at the opening of a new hotel at College Place. This was in a house which for many years had belonged to Alderman Noble. It was on a site in College Place later occupied by the building now known as Brunel House but originally called The Royal Western Hotel. The latter replaced the 1807 hotel in 1839 and was designed to accommodate GWR passengers who were transferring to Brunel's steamships. In 1807 the original building was called Reeve's Hotel and Tavern and the proprietor, John Reeve, had been butler to the Mayors of Bristol for many years. He later became famous as a caterer.

By all accounts the Corporation was corrupt. There is much criticism aimed at the members throughout the early years of the century. Reeve himself was later given a sinecure position and was one of several friends who received a salary for doing nothing. At the opening dinner the Mayor presided over twenty-two guests, mostly aldermen and common councillors. The truth concerning the Bacchanalian abilities of a score of Englishmen survives in the bill for that night's entertainment: Dinners at 25s., £27 10s; 12 bottles of sherry at 5s 6d., £3.6s.; 12 bottles of port, at 5s, £3; 12 bottles of hock, at 10s 6d., £6.6s; 20 bottles of claret, at 11s., £11; with six bottles of champagne paid for by the mayor. The total came to sixty-two bottles shared between twenty-two guests. Not surprisingly, John Reeve made a fortune of £20,000 before retiring.

Later the hotel was managed by Henry Perry and used for guests wishing to embark from the Floating Harbour.

Reeve advertised in the local press and on 5 September announced the arrival of 'a quantity of fine LIVELY TURTLE, of all sizes; which will be dressed every day during the season, and potted up to be sent to any part of the kingdom, in large or small quantities'. A similar announcement appeared in the *Gazette* for 20 June, from the proprietor of the Bush Tavern, the splendid and premier coaching inn opposite the Corn Exchange where many travellers stayed.

J. TOWNSEND,
BUSH TAVERN,
BRISTOL, respectfully informs his Friends and the Public, that he has just received a quantity of fine lively TURTLE of all sizes for sale, and to be dressed every WEDNESDAY

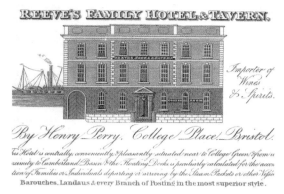

Card for Reeve's Hotel, College Place in the 1820s when it benefitted from the steam boat trade and was owned by Henry Perry. During John Reeve's time he had 'fine LIVELY turtles' dressed every day. The Great Western Hotel was later here.

and SATURDAY during the season; to be sold in any quantity, and potted up to be sent to any part of the kingdom.

An oil painting by Samuel Jackson, *The Avon at Hotwells* in the City Art Gallery (K4), features a boatload of unfortunate turtles about to be unloaded at the quayside. Indeed, considering the craving for turtle in Bristol alone, over so many years, it is a wonder that the species was not wiped out.

A Christmas bill of fare from the Bush Tavern dated 1800 survives in the Bristol Reference Library's collection. It lists everything from bustard, 'land tortoise' and sturgeon to Paraguay pies, swan, peahens and even cuckoo, '42 Hares, 87 wild ducks, 149 snipes, 121 larks etc, etc.' Travellers of 1807 arriving at a modern inn would find a very meagre choice nowadays. John Weeks the proprietor of the Bush Tavern was brother to Philip Weeks who kept the famous Lamplighter's Hall Inn and Tavern on the river at Shirehampton. Philip's advertisement in the *Bristol Mercury* for 25 June suggests that the hostelry could compete in its range of fare, especially fish:

WEEKS'S HOTEL And Lamplighter's Hall Inn and Tavern. P. WEEKS, truly sensible of the gratitude he owes to a generous Public, begs leave to return them his thanks for the very flattering and increasing encouragement he has experienced since opening the above House. He continues to dress DINNERS for Parties on the most liberal Plan. TEAS, COFFEES, &c. as cheap as at any House in the United Kingdom.

Ladies and gentlemen going Passengers to any part of Ireland, or elsewhere, provided with Sea Stock of every description.

He wishes to inform Ladies and Gentlemen living in the Neighbourhood, that he has a constant Supply of fresh Fish, of every description, in the highest perfection.

PLEASURE BOATS of any Size, with comfortable Accommodations, provided to go to any Part of the Bristol Channel, at Six Hour's Notice.

Bristol Reference Library holds a scrapbook (B28209) belonging to John Weeks of the Bush who was famous for his turtle dinners. It is a wonderful collection of manuscript and printed items from the seventeenth century onwards and includes much Napoleonic ephemera and also many snippets of information about Henry Hunt whom one assumes he supported.

In concluding a chapter of self indulgence in Bristol, one cannot do better than quote Byron from *English Bards and Scottish Reviews*:

Too much in turtle Bristol's sons delight,
Too much o'er bowls of rack prolong the night.

Most fashionable and frequented: College Green

crowded with young men devoid of the least principle of modesty

There are several other open places in Bristol that are not termed Squares, the principal of which is COLLEGE GREEN. This is on a fine, pleasant, and healthy elevation, and there is an ascent to it every way. Its plan is nearly triangular: on the southern side are the Cathedral, St Augustine's Parish Church, and the beautiful ancient Gate of the Monastery: and, on the northern, the church of St Mark, commonly called the Mayor's Chapel. This contains some good modern houses of stone and brick, before which, and all around the Green, are foot-ways paved with smooth stones, and a street for carriages, in some parts very spacious. The Green is enclosed with rails, within which, a gravelled walk, quite shaded with lime-trees, bounds the whole area. There are two broader walks between stately elms that pervade the whole, in form of a cross: the principal is from East to West, and the other leads from North to South, opposite to the door of the Cathedral. This, on all accounts, is the pleasantest, and, next after Queen's Square, the largest open place in Bristol. An officer is paid annually for rolling and keeping it in repair; and there are a few lamps lighted in the walks by night. This is the principal public walk of Bristol; and is most frequented in the Summer, on Sunday evenings, as St James's Park in London.

New Bristol Guide 1804

College Green, Thomas H Shepherd.

THE COLLEGE GREEN OF 1807 BORE VERY LITTLE RESEMBLANCE TO THE space we know today. At the time it was still more obviously a plateau raised up above the surrounding streets that had sprung up to the west in the previous century on the site of the Bishop's Park and was separated from the slopes of Brandon Hill behind by a dry river valley. The road from Hotwells, now called St George's Road, approached it along this valley and then climbed up steeply to meet the Green at Frog Lane. This situation continued even after Park Street (named after the lost Bishop's Park) was built occasioning great difficulty for horse-drawn vehicles attempting to make the ascent. There are stories of loitering boys who for a few coppers would aid the progress of a carriage at this point by pushing it. The building of the bridge to link the bottom of Park Street with the Green in 1871 eased the situation but masked the actual geography of the plateau. The same thing had happened at the south-western corner of the Green next to the historic abbey gateway in 1869. Previously a wing of the Deanery had spread northwards from the gateway. This was demolished and a viaduct constructed to make another route (now called Deanery Road) from the Hotwells Road up to the Green and the Cathedral. Buck's prospect of this part of the city that was printed in 1734 shows the great drop that existed behind the demolished wing of the Deanery. What was a low two-storeyed building facing College Green was tall when viewed from the park behind.

Originally, College Green had been the burial ground of the Augustinian canons. It had been enclosed in the twelfth century to become the precincts of St Augustine's Abbey, which became the Cathedral at the dissolution of the monasteries. It was at first known as St Augustine's Green. A chapel dedicated to St Jordan (with an open-air pulpit) existed on the spot throughout the Middle Ages and until at least 1673. Jordan was said to have accompanied St Augustine at his meeting with British Christians by the Severn in 603 and his image and shrine were objects of pilgrimage in the abbey. The Green was also the burial place for the Gaunt's Hospital, now St Mark's Chapel. At the beginning of the eighteenth century the cathedral laid out the walks on the raised area of the Green. Until the building of the Council House in the 1940s and early '50s this area of the Green was six feet higher than the surroundings and was approached by steps. It was lowered to its present level and the old avenues of trees felled at the insistence of the architect of the new building to improve the

The Cathedral and College Green, H Storer 1814. This interesting view of the Cathedral shows the main entrance in the north transept and the houses and gardens on the site of the nave. Soldiers stroll amongst the Bristolians.

proportions of his building when viewed from the east.

At some time after 1733 the 40-foot-high civic High Cross was moved from its historic position at the crossroads in the centre of the city to the centre of the walks laid out on the Green. It does not appear on the Buck engraving of 1734. Unfortunately its new position in the centre of the walks interfered with fashionable promenading of two or more abreast and after a campaign it was finally taken down and stored in the cathedral. In 1768 Cutts Barton the new Dean allowed his friend Henry Hoare to have it for the gardens of Stourhead. In Bristol, it survived only in the form of engravings and in replica gingerbread versions in the

A detail from Nathaniel Buck's panorama of Bristol, 1734. The heavily buttressed wall in the centre illustrates the great drop in ground level between College Green and the park behind. The Library now occupies the site of the Deanery and Canon's House.

eighteenth-century city.

The Green soon became *the* place to parade in the city and this was still the case in 1807 to the detriment of other places. Regimental bands played every day to add to the atmosphere:

> A precedent writer concerning Bristol has very justly recommended the exercise of walking to people of leisure there. In fair weather, the walks at Bath and London, sufficiently and daily show the high opinion entertained of pedestrian exercises by the ladies and gentlemen of those places. Nothing tends more to the improvement of health, strength, and spirits, than exercise in the open air. And it is remarkable, that more of the convenient walks in Bristol

(excepting College-green on a Sunday) are, like the Exchange, almost unfrequented and useless.
New Bristol Guide 1804

The Green became the most fashionable and frequented Parade in the city where people went to see and to be seen and to do and to be undone. It was not without hazards however:

> The College-Green (and indeed most public Walks in the city) is crowded with young men devoid themselves of the least principle of modesty, who arm in arm form a phalanx of impudence in defiance of any one. If they meet the married woman or the single, they treat her with no more respect than if they meet the prostitute; they rudely insult her.
> *The Observer* 1794

The Orange Girl

The imprudent young man could meet his match – as does the young lawyer in James Kemp's poem of a flirtation started on the Green with a beautiful orange girl. This is part of it:

The busy Captains cry: The Girls in all directions fly.

Love and Law or the Orange Girl

The Lisbon Fleet had hove in sight,
With swelling sails and streamers bright;
The Sailors had their native bay,
And heap their treasures on the Quay;
With turtle for the City dinner,
And genuine wine to glut each sinner:
Fraught with rich juice was every lime:
The lemons too were large and prime.
The Orange Girls, replete with charms,
Flock'd round with baskets on their arms.
The Tars well-pleased such girls to see,
Each takes a fair-one on his knee,
To give her from his private store,
And hug, and kiss her o'er and o'er.
Avast! The busy Captains cry;-
The Girls in all directions fly.
'Sweet Oranges!' they call aloud,
And sell to all the gaping croud,
Dispers'd, through different streets they go,
Stopping to chat with all they know.

But one, more lovely than the rest,
Inspired our Lawyer's gentle breast;

He met her tramping through the Green,
The sweetest Girl he's ever seen!
First, bade her lay her basket down,
Then gave her from his purse a Crown.
'Your Oranges are fine to view,
'I'll have but one, this one will do:
'But step into another walk,
'Apart between the trees we'll talk.'

'You Gentlemen are very good,
'But much I fear you will be rude:
'To stay with me is very wrong,
'Let me request you, go along.'

'I never yet, I sear by Jove!
'Proved faithless to the Girl I love.'
On this her seeming anger rose,
And thus her feign'd resentment shows.
'Nay Sir, with you I dare not stay,
'So take your money back I pray:
'five shilling for an Orange give!
'I'll tell your Wife on't as I live.'

At every word he quak'd with fear,
Thinking some Stander-by would hear
Afraid to stay, yet how to leave her,
Puzzled for once an old Deceiver.
Raising her basket to her side,
'Sweet Oranges!' again she cried;
'Good Morrow, Sir,' then turned to say –
He stole with conscious shame away.

But doom'd once more the Girl to meet,
He pass'd her in Old Market Street:
To speak again seem'd half inclin'd,
She turn'd, and trotted close behind.
Homeward, with speed, his way he took,
Ashamed to cast a backward look.
Arrived he knock'd, the Damsel nigh –
'Pray won't you Sir an orange buy?'

Bristol Now

an ancient Town surrounded by a modern, partly well built and partly ill built

AS A CONTRAST TO THE ACCOUNTS OF VISITORS THE FOLLOWING BY
W Sheppard from his *New Bristol Guide* of 1804 shows a balanced view of what Bristolians thought of their city.

Most of the streets are well paved on each side with flat stones for foot-passengers, and have also smooth cross-ways from one side of the street to another. Some of the foot-ways are not yet flagged, but; like the carriage-ways; covered with that irregular and execrable *Pitching* (as they term it) which is a disgrace to the City, and should be for ever abolished. The streets between the foot-ways ought to be paved with blocks of hewn stone, fastened together with a cement of lime and sand.

*

It is not our business to puff concerning the Town, but to endeavour truly to describe it.

Many of the houses in the ancient streets have been newly fronted and modernized, and some entirely rebuilt, but yet continue irregular. And many parts of Bristol are so antique, as to enable us to form an idea of what the whole was about two or three centuries ago. The great house on St Augustine's back, now Colston's School; a spacious old mansion in Small-street, with a large bow-window (which probably received Queen Elizabeth and King Charles I); the north-east corner of High-street; some houses in Baldwin, Wine, Broad, and Maryport-streets; the Pithay, St James's-back, Lewin's-mead, on the Broad-Weir, Temple-street, and many other places, may help us to judge what

appearance the City had in former times. But within the last century Bristol is so increased, that it is almost surrounded by modern streets and houses. And therefore to give a proper decription and idea of this place – *It is an ancient Town surrounded by a modern, and is partly well built and partly ill built.* The antique and internal parts of the Town are confessedly irregular, consisting principally of ancient houses constructed of wood, faced with plaster, and covered with red pantiles; most of them have sharp tops, and some of three stories or more, projecting and hanging one over another; these are intermixed with old fronts modernized, some good houses of brick, and here and there of freestone, with level tops to the fronts, and cornices of stone, some higher, some lower, composing remarkable specimens of irregularity, but in several places more pleasing than in others.

Some of the most ancient streets have latterly been widened and improved, and several have been totally rebuilt, viz. Bridge-street,

Remains of St Ewen's Church on the corner of Broad Street. An act was passed to demolish it to create room for a new council house – which then took 30 years to build. JS Prout.

all of freestone, the houses four stories high, and elegantly finished; (the pile of buildings next to the river is the noblest in town); Clare-street, Union and Bath-streets, of brick, ornamented with stone, and some others. Bristol has done much, and expanded vast, incredible sums in improving an old, irregular, narrow, confined and ugly Town. The reader, who is strange to Bristol, may scarcely give credit to the information, that since the commencement of this century, several hundred thousand pounds have been expended for buildings and improvements.

The modern and external parts of Bristol are more regularly, decently, handsomely, or elegantly built of brick, and some entirely of freestone; and now, all other sorts of buildings and fronts of wood are prohibited by Act of Parliament. The narrow streets of Bristol have been much observed by strangers, and complained of by the inhabitants; but most of the inconvenient places have been somewhat widened. And though the inner parts of Bristol are still rather close, yet there are many spacious and pleasant streets in the external parts. The Old-market and West-street are much about the width of Holborn and St Giles's, or Whitechapel. Prince's-street, King-street, the Kay, St Augustine's-back, Park-street, St Michael's-hill, Stoke's-croft, the Hay-market, Redcliffe-hill, and many other places without the old City, are spacious and airy. Park-street is, principally, and many other streets and squares are built of freestone; and there are a great number of streets and buildings well constructed, which are fit for genteel families, let at easy rent, and, with the other conveniences peculiar to Bristol, such as plenty of coals, good air

and water, moderated price of provisions (comparatively with some other populous places), attract families to settle here, and to occupy many of the new houses that are continually, in a greater or less degree, erecting by the builders of this City.

The entrance to St Bartholomew's Hospital at the bottom of Christmas Steps. JS Prout.
The medieval sculpture that once sat in the niche but has now been moved inside, is here shown as complete.

The Black Presence

The ardour for the trade to Africa for men and women, our fellow-creatures and equals, is much abated among the humane and benevolent Merchants of Bristol. In 1787 there were but thirty ships employed in this melancholy traffic; while the people of Liverpool in their indiscriminate rage for commerce, and for getting money at all events, have nearly engrossed this trade, incredibly exceeded London and Bristol in it, employ many thousand tons of shipping for the purpose of buying and enslaving God's rational creatures; and are the venders (horresco referens) of the souls and bodies of men and women to almost all the West India Islands!!!
New Bristol Guide, 1804

AS ONE OF THE MOST COSMOPOLITAN CITIES IN THE COUNTRY, BRISTOL had always been used to seeing black faces belonging either to slaves, servants or sailors since the sixteenth century if not before. The situation in the eighteenth century was far more complicated than is generally thought to be the case in modern times. There were certainly black servants in the city and the newspapers of the eighteenth century often had advertisements declaring that one had absconded. However they are not referred to as slaves. The language used is generally the same form as that used for absconding apprentices. Only occasionally are they referred to as somebody's property as is the case of Thomas Shampaine who ran away from the house of Samuel Pye, the Clifton surgeon in 1743. An interesting illustration of how black people could be treated is the court case noted in *Samuel Farley's Bristol Journal* of 12 February, 1737.

A white woman, Sarah Green, was committed to Newgate prison in the city for attempting to extort money from Richard Cornwall 'a Christian Negro Servant to Capt. Day, in College Green' by pretending that he had given her a child. Cornwall asked first to see the child before he would pay and she had borrowed one and blacked it up. His answer was to call 'for a wet Napkin, and rubbing the Child's face, found it of a fair Complexion, quite different to his Specy'. The interesting fact about this story is that Cornwall could rely on the legal system in just the same way as a white person, and that the white woman was punished. Perhaps the difference was that he was Christian as well as being (presumably) a free man.

Against this rather jolly story is that related by Hannah More later in the century in a letter to Horace Walpole concerning a hunt in Bristol one Sunday morning for a runaway black girl:

I cannot forbear telling you that at my city of Bristol, during church-time, the congregations were surprised last Sunday with the bell of the public crier in the streets. It was so unusual a sound on that day, that the people were alarmed in the churches. They found that the bellman was crying a reward of a guinea to anybody who would produce a poor negro girl who had run away because she would not return to one of those trafficking islands, whither her master was resolved to send her. To my great grief and indignation, the poor trembling wretch was dragged out from a hole at the top of a house, where she had hid herself, and forced on board ship. Alas I did not know until too late, or I would have run the risk of buying her, and made you, and the rest of my humane, I had almost said Human friends, help me out if the cost had been considerable.

The Bristol Reference library has the log book of a 150-ton Bristol slaving vessel *The Black Prince.* The book covers the years 1762 to 1764 and recounts a slaving voyage to the Gold Coast of Africa, starting in April 1762 and the commencement of a second voyage in September 1764. The ship was owned by James Laroche and Company and captained by William Miller. The *Black Prince* spent eight months purchasing slaves off the coast of West Africa. When it arrived at Antigua on 7 May 1763, after a voyage lasting two months, only 394 of the original 438 slaves were still alive.

Also in volume 20 of the Jefferies Collection of manuscripts held by the library are some details of the Chepstow and Spring Garden slave estates in Jamaica. These include the names of slaves. When an estate was mortgaged, details of all property belonging to it was required, including the names of the slaves bonded to it. The returns give the slaves' names, colour, whether negro or mulatto (mixed race), age, and state whether they were African or Creole (that is born in Africa or in the West Indies of African decent). Even infants of less than a year old were listed. Interestingly some of the slaves listed still have their African names.

A trade card from the 1790s for the gun-maker William Heard of Redcliffe Street encapsulates the triangular trade with Africa. It shows a British sportsman and an African. The latter has thrown down his traditional weapons and is the proud possessor of a Bristol firearm that would give him dominance over other tribes and over animals. So desirous were the chiefs for the new

Bristol Gazette 24 January 1788

THE Citizens of BRISTOL are requested to attend at the *Guild-Hall*, Monday next the 28th inst. at 11 o'clock, for the purpose of determining on such measures as may be thought necessary, respecting the SLAVE TRADE.

'A negro with a ship fastened to his hat': *Joseph Johnson* by JT Smith. Black sailors wounded in the Merchant Navy were not entitled to relief. Some took to wearing ships on their hats, singing and making the ship 'sail'. Smith's books offer fascinating insights into black street inhabitants.

The root of much evil. The trade card of a Bristol gunmaker c. 1795. African chiefs would happily sell their countrymen into slavery in order to get such European luxuries that would give them domination over other tribes.

weapons that they traded gold, ivory and fellow Africans for them. The merchant ship in the background then continues its journey to the West Indies, before returning with a new cargo to Bristol.

Henry Barth in *Travels & Discoveries in North & Central Africa: being a Journal of an Expedition undertaken under the auspices of HB.M.'s Government in the year 1849-1855* (1857) mentions in a discussion on the slave trade, with an African 'Vizier':

From this point of our discourse there was an easy transition to that of the abolition of slavery; and here my late lamented friend Mr Overweg made a most eloquent speech on this important question. The vizier could not bring forward any other argument in his defence, than that the slave-trade furnished them with the means of buying muskets; and, lamentable as it is, this is certainly the correct view of the subject, for even on the west coast the slave trade originated in the cupidity of the natives in purchasing the arms of Europeans. Such is the history of civilization! If the poor natives of Africa had never become acquainted with this destructive implement of European ingenuity, the slave-trade would have never reached those gigantic proportions which it has attained. For at first the natives of Africa wanted firearms as the surest means of securing their independence of, and superiority over, their neighbours; but in the further course of affairs, these instruments of destruction became necessary, because they enabled them to hunt down less favoured tribes, and, with a supply of slaves so obtained, to procure for themselves those luxuries of European civilization with which they had likewise become acquainted. This is the great debt which the European owes to the poor African, that after having caused, or at least increased, this nefarious system on his first bringing the natives of those regions into contact with his state of civilization, which has had scarcely any but a demoralizing effect, he ought now also to make them acquainted with the beneficial effects of that state of society. Entering, therefore, into the views of our hosts, I told them that their country produced many other things which they might exchange for firearms, without being forced to lay waste the whole of the neighbouring countries, and to bring misery and distress upon so many thousands.

Barth was different from the explorers of the colonial age, because he was interested in the history and culture of the African peoples, rather than the possibilities to exploit them. He meticulously documented his observations and his own journal has become an invaluable source for the study of nineteenth-century Sudanic Africa. After studying Arabic in London he set out on his travels in 1845. He acted for the British Foreign Office in 1850. He was one of the greatest of the European explorers of Africa, for although not the first Western visitor who paid attention to the local oral traditions, he was the first who seriously considered its methodology and usability for historical research. Barth was the first truly scholarly traveller in West Africa.

Of the export of British goods to Africa the *Bristol Gazette* of 7 February 1788 reported from the London meeting of the Society for the Abolition of the Slave Trade:

It must be acknowledged, that the amount of British manufactures exported to the coasts of Africa, for the purposes of this commerce, is considerable; but there is room to apprehend, that the demand for these would be much greater, if, in the place of it, was substituted an amicable intercourse, which, instead of spreading distress and devestation amongst the unoffending inhabitants; would introduce the blessings of peace and civilization.

The Society also spoke out for the common seamen engaged on the ships and remarked 'that the lives of a very considerable proportion of those engaged in this trade, are annually sacrificed to the nature of the service, and the extreme severity of their treatment.'

Whilst the lot of black slaves in the Indies was often brutish and unpardonably harsh, the condition of house servants or slaves in Bristol depended much on the humanity of their master

Bankruptcy notice of George Baillie and a list of his West Indian estates. *Felix Farley's Bristol Journal*, 17 January 1807.

CEORGE BAILLIE & Co's Bankruptcy.
County of PERTH and Town of STIRLING, in Scotland.
TO BE SOLD,
At GARRAWAY's, the *latter end of February* next (unless previously disposed of by private contract) by order of the Assignees of GEO. BAILLIE & JOHN JAFFRAY,

A Freehold ESTATE, belonging to the Bankrupt JOHN JAFFRAY, situate in the county of Perth, in Scotland; and also a Freehold HOUSE belonging to the said John Jaffray, situate at Stirling, in Scotland; and which estate and premises, by a resolution of the Creditors of the said George Baillie & John Jaffray, the Assignees are at liberty to sell for bills accepted by the house of George Baillie & Co. now remaining unpaid and proved against their estate.

☞ For further particulars apply to
DENNETTS & GREAVES, Solicitors to the Assignees.

GEORGE BAILLIE & Co.'s Bankruptcy.
St. VINCENT's & BERBICE.
TO BE SOLD,
At GARRAWAY's, the *latter end of February* next (unless previously disposed of by private contract) by order of the Assignees of GEO. BAILLIE & JOHN JAFFRAY,

THE several ESTATES belonging to the Bankrupt GEORGE BAILLIE, situate in the Island of St. Vincent, in the West-Indies, known by the names of SION HILL ESTATE, CARAPAN ESTATE, and CARRIERE ESTATE; and also a Moiety of another ESTATE, situate in the colony of Berbice, in the West Indies, called the INVERNESS ESTATE, and a certain Proportion of another ESTATE, in the same Colony, called the CANAYE LOT; together with all the Slaves, Plantations, Stores, and other Live and Dead Stock, in or upon the said several estates; and which estates, by a resolution of the Creditors of the said George Baillie and John Jaffray, the Assignees are at liberty to sell for bills accepted by the house of George Baillie & Co. now remaining unpaid and proved against their estate.

☞ For further particulars apply to
DENNETTS & GREAVES, Solicitors to the Assignees.

or mistress, as it did for all servants. Although such a state could hardly be termed ideal one must bear in mind that, apart from the denial of liberty to those who were *property,* and not the master of their own destiny, the average life of the poorer Bristolian was brutish and harsh in the extreme. Press gangs could also drag free Englishmen into slavery for the good of the country and likewise James Malcolm was appalled at the conditions endured by those who toiled like slaves in the city's kilns and foundries

> Laſt Thurſday one Sarah Elliot was committed to Newgate, for endeavouring to extort Money from one Richard Cornwall a Chriſtian Negro, Servant to Capt. Day, in College Green, under Pretence that ſhe had a Child by him, and which was then alive at Berkley, in Gloucesterſhire; the Black inſiſted on ſeeing the Child before he would condeſcend to her Demand, and told her, that if 'twas his Child, he ſhou'd know by the Colour of the Skin. The Woman artfully to deceive the Fellow, procur'd a borrow'd Child, with its Skin ſmutted over; but he calling for a wet Napkin, and rubbing the Child's Face, found it of a fair Complexion, quite different to his Specy.

Blacking up a baby. *Samuel Farley's Bristol Journal.* 12 February, 1737.

with barely any leisure time to humanise them. The Age of Reason – for all its veneer of elegance – was under the surface nasty and brutish for a great many, and this must be borne in mind when considering the horrors of slavery. Perhaps the most remarkable thing is that sufficient people began to be revolted about the idea of denying a fellow human being his or her liberty and spoke out against it.

By the 1780s the distaste for the West Indies slave trade had started to grow apace amongst informed people in Bristol and elsewhere. In an article in *The Times* of 8 January 1785 entitled 'Negro Trade', the writer criticises the United States and praises the current humanity of Britain. 'On this occasion I rejoice to recommend to them the example of my own country. In Britain, a negro becomes a freeman the moment he sets foot on British ground'. This was a reference to the James Somerset case of 1771 when Granville Sharp successfully prevented the man from being

sent from the country against his will, although as far back as 1705 in Smith *v* Brown and Cooper, Chief Justice Holt had stated: 'as soon as a negro comes into England, he becomes free; one may be a villein in England, but not a slave'. Unfortunately this rule was not always adhered to as can be seen by the above case related by Hannah More.

In Bristol, More, Ann Yearsley, Coleridge, Southey and Lovell were amongst the educated and thinking literati and youth who dared speak out against it. Newspaper reports of the murder of a lady by a former black servant of the Duchess of Manchester in February 1787 resulted in several wealthy households dismissing their 'Blackmoor Servants', which suggests that by this period most had been freed in line with the 1771 ruling. Certainly black sailors and soldiers appear in engravings of the armed forces at this period suggesting other career opportunities were available. Charles P Moritz in his *Travels in England* in 1782 relates sharing the roof of the Leicester stage with a 'blackamoor' who was an independent and seasoned traveller. Moritz disregarded his advice on outside travel to his cost. By the early 1790s Bristol guidebooks were apologising for the city's past involvement in the trade and stressing how much greater the association of London and Liverpool was with it. John T Smith's *Cries of London* mentions the novel abilities of British black street enter-tainers and hawkers who by their innovations made 'a great deal of money.'

A sad little story concerns the death at Hotwells on 16 August 1806, of Samuel Thompson, aged 20 who was a black servant of William Thompson Esq., of Bath and Jamaica. It was recounted in *Felix Farley's Bristol Journal* of 23 August. The previous Saturday the boy had been swimming in the river Avon opposite St Vincent's Rocks and was seized with the cramp and drowned. His body was not found until the next day. William Thompson was distraught as Samuel had been a loved member of the family since his seventh birthday and was much cared for. He raised a monument to him 'as a testimony of the regard his Master bears him… He died lamented by his Master and all who knew him'.

The passing of the Abolition of the Slave Trade Bill in 1807 still did not wipe out slavery in the colonies. This had to wait until 1838 and the passage of the Slavery Abolition Act of 1833, but from 1807 the practice was officially despised. In 1819 the British West Africa Squadron (Royal Navy) was set up to suppress slave trading and by 1865 had rescued nearly 150,000 people from foreign slave traders. With these good works in mind and the knowledge that many people in Bristol were quite free from prejudice, one is shocked to discover a letter in the City Record Office dating from 1812, advising the Mayor of the continual harrassment of a black doorman by a mob. The anonymous correspondent no doubt lived nearby and feared for his own property should the mob learn of his involvement.

Bristol, Nov 27th 1812

To the Right Worshipful the Mayor,

Sir, I feel it a duty incumbent on me, as a man & a Christian, to apply to you for protection, on behalf of the Proprietor of the Mechanical Exhibition, Corn Street; to whom I understand you have granted licence to exhibit: I also learn from unquestionable authority, that a set of men and boys – men did I say... I would not so far degrade the character and dignity of man, in associating such a barbarous herd among the class of men for they are unworthy the appellation and ought to be extirpated from Society, therefore must in justice observe that a set of

SLAVE TRADE.

THE Meeting of the Citizens of Bristol at the Guildhall on Monday last, pursuant to an Advertisement from the Mayor, was very fully attended, many respectable Merchants of this city were present.

As the Mayor was confined to his house by illness, Joseph Harford, Esq; was voted to the chair.

The business of the meeting being opened by the Chairman, the following resolutions were then offered, which passed without any opposition.

Resolved,

That the Trade in Slaves, giving occasion to great violence and bloodshed, in reducing them to slavery in Africa for the purpose of supplying the West India markets; and afterwards to great oppression and the loss of innumerable lives, is inconsistent with humanity and justice, and abhorrent from the benevolent spirit of the religion we profess.

That an application be made to Parliament for effectuating the abolition of the Slave Trade, in such manner as to their wisdom shall seem fit; humbly expressing our hope, that so benevolent a measure, whilst it reflects a lustre on our national character, will at the same time (by the prudence of their provisions) be rendered not inconsistent with the soundest policy.

The following petition being thereon read, the same was approved without opposition.

Bristol Gazette 31 January, 1788

miscreants and uncivilized barbarians, make a practice almost invariably every evening, to convene together, at the entrance of the Exhibition, evidently for the very purpose, of wantonly abusing and sporting with the feelings, of a poor harmless and inoffensive Black, employed by the Proprietor of the Exhibition, and who is stationed at the entrance. And indeed I can with truth assert, that I have myself witnessed, the most atrocious insults offered this man, and not content with reviling and abusing him, in language *the most scurrilous and shocking to the ears of humanity*, but the *Savages* (for I can call them no better) *in the most cruel and malicious manner*, must have recourse, to pushing one another violently against him, merely for their own *barbarous amusement*, for I am well convinced, if any of these villainous wretches were interrogated as to their motives for such conduct, they could not give any justifiable answer, but would at once stand self convicted: and in addition to their infamous conduct, have actually thrown stones at a transparent lamp, which was suspended at the Entrance leading to the Exhibition Room, and which was no later than two evenings ago, dashed to the ground, and a window also broke, belonging to Mr Harris the stationer contiguous thereto. In consequence of which outrages, I now beg leave to appeal to your discretion, (as a man of feeling and humanity), the propriety and necessity of adopting such measures, as shall in future, best prevent a recurrence and continuance of the like *abominable and unpardonable proceedings*. And as we have peace officers, I should presume they cannot be better employed than in supporting the laws of humanity and protecting those, whom you have particularly patronized, from insult and injury.

I am sir, Your most obed & hble servt

Anonymous

It may be of course that, as the exhibition was about new machines that could ultimately put people out of their traditional work, then the mob's anger may have risen from this. However, one is left with the fear that this was not the case and that it was a nasty example of the Bristol public at its most unpleasant.

Fights, beasts and theatre

During these Fairs... For the juvenile and puerile throngs, and those who are fond of delicacies, a rich profusion of confectionary wares, sweatmeats, comfits and all sorts of pastry, are exposed for sale in rows. For the amusement of the populace there are not wanting flying-coaches, exhibitions of wild beasts and birds, wax-work, wire-dancing, tumbling, balancing, puppets, Punch and his wife Joan, sea-fights, conjuration, magic and mummery of all sorts, recommended by merry-andrews, buffoons, drums, trumpets, French-horns, fiddles, rattles and vociferation. The shops and standings for these Fairs are built and covered with wood. At St James's they are disposed into streets and rows, and are generally a month in preparing.
New Bristol Guide, 1804

FOR THE RESIDENT AND VISITOR TO BRISTOL IN 1807 THE CITY COULD offer a wide range of diversions from the cultural to the sordid and the elegant to the brutal. Some, like the fairs and concerts, were seasonal and regular, whilst others were occasioned by the visits of travelling entertainments such as the menageries or wild beast shows. Travelling exhibitions of curiosities, antiquities and art works were regularly shown at venues within the city. Often the more salubrious inns would hire out a room for the purpose. Sarah Biffin, the miniature painter who was born without arms or legs, exhibited at 'a commodious room in Avon–street, Great Gardens' in February, 1807. Sporting events included boxing and horse racing, cock-fighting, badger and bear baiting. Of course in many cases, just as in later times, local families and individuals made their own entertainments at home. We know from the example of the Narraway family of Broadmead that musical evenings at home were popular and the norm. Institutions such as the Prince Street Assembly Rooms refused admission to local residents unless they became subscribers and really relied on the patronage of visitors to keep going. The winter concerts featured such entertainment as Miss Randles the seven-year-old Welsh infant prodigy, who had a brief blaze of glory after playing the pianoforte before the Royal Family and earning the patronage of the Prince of Wales. The Rooms' closure, albeit temporary, in 1810, showed the folly of relying on this casual clientele. When the rooms reopened after refurbishment they had slipped down the social scale to become a small local version of the capital's Astley's Amphitheatre, but were probably more likely to raise an interest with the local Bristolian. Matthews' 1815 *Guide to Bristol* could state: 'The edifice has lately undergone various internal alterations, and may most properly be called a Theatre. Equestrian and Pantomimic exercises are generally here exhibited.' The Equestrian Theatre in Limekiln Lane (now St Georges Road) had been built in 1791 to display exhibitions of horsemanship. It is described as being of considerable length and breadth with the eastern end fitted up semicircularly for spectators. It quite possibly survives as the ruined horse bazaar building next to Brunel House, although there the western end is apsidal. More equestrian entertainment could be found at The Amphitheatre, Great Gardens, on the site of Temple Meads as the *Bristol Mirror* of 14 March 1807 proclaimed:

Banisters Troop Of Equestrians performing here at the Amphitheatre by permission of the Right Worshipful the Mayor, and at the particular Request of many respectable Inhabitants of the City of Bristol.

Bristol Mirror, 28 February 1807.

TEMPLE FAIR.

MR. POLITO, the celebrated Collector of Living Curiosities, most respectfully informs the Ladies and Gentlemen of this City, and the Public, that he has now brought forward the brightest and most beautiful Assemblage of FOREIGN ANIMALS and BIRDS ever seen in Europe; exhibited in *Six large and commodious Caravans,* built for that purpose, of a superior plan and magnitude, and all united; which forms one of the grandest and most extensive views of the Wonderful Productions of Nature ever beheld;
Consisting of the most rare and uncommon
LIVING BIRDS and BEASTS,
from the remotest parts of the habitable World; among which are,
A NOBLE LION,
From Senegal, in Africa, landed at Liverpool March 24, 1806.
This astonishing animal has limbs superior in size and strength to any horse or ox; he is of the finest and largest kind in the known world, and absolutely the only Male Lion that travels in his Majesty's Dominions. To the astonishment of every beholder, this majestic animal shews a great affection to his companion, a fine Pointer Bitch, which has remained with him since he was taken from his dam.—She suckled him till he was able to eat flesh, and his attachment to her is such, that he suffers her to rule quite over him.
A Beautiful LIONESS,
From the Tower of London.
A Striped BENGAL TYGER,

131

THE LAST NIGHT BUT TWO OF BANNISTERS
TROOP of EQUESTRIANS PERFORMING HERE.
AT THE AMPHITHEATRE, IN THE GREAT-GARDENS,
ON MONDAY next, and Two following Evenings, will be
brought forward the greatest Variety of New Performances
ever exhibited in this City; consisting of HORSEMAN-
SHIP, TIGHT AND SLACK ROPE DANCING, JUMPING
OVER MEN ON HORSEBACK. STILL VAULTING,
Wonderful Performance on the Double Rope, MISS
BANNISTER on the Slack Wire, and a great Variety of
other new Performances never before attempted.
*** For further particulars see the Hand-bills.
The Amphitheatre will be kept well aired, with patent
Stoves.
Doors to be opened at Six, and to begin precisely at Seven.
Boxes, 3s. Pit, 2s. Gal.1s.

The *Bristol and Hotwell Guide* of 1805 concisely summed up the
main places of literature and amusement in the city:

The THEATRE is in King-street, of which we need not say
more, than that late Mr Garrick, on accurate survey,
pronounced it to be, in his opinion, the most complete in
Europe of its dimensions: it was opened on Friday, May 30,
1766, with the comedy of the Conscious Lovers, and farce
of the Citizen; on which occasion Mr Garrick wrote a
prologue and epilogue; the prologue was spoken by Mr
Powell, and the epilogue by Mr Arthur; the scenes were
painted by the late Mr French; they are executed in a
masterly style, and all the decorations are in elegant taste.

The theatre offered weekly Monday performances, with actors
from the Bath theatre and these were said to be hardly inferior to
those of London. The *New Bristol Guide* believed the performances educational and a school for elocution as a standard of
pronunciation; and a means of diminishing and gradually
annihilating improprieties and inelegancies of provincial speech.
On Monday, March 30 and the following Monday in 1807 the
famous Mrs Siddons appeared as Elvira in the tragedy, *Pizarro*.
The 1805 guide continues:

The ASSEMBLY ROOM is on the west side of Prince's-
street. The front is built with freestone, and consists of a
rustic basement, which supports four double columns of
the Corinthian order, over which is a pediment; on the
frieze is inscribed CURAS CITHARA TOLLIT (Music
dispels Care). You ascend to the Ball-room by a flight of
steps; it is large, lofty, and handsome, and the windows
being judiciously placed at a proper height, the company
cannot be overlooked from without; from the ceiling are
pendent three beautiful glass lustres; the middle one is very
large and brilliant; the orchestra is fitted up with great taste,
and contains a capital organ. Behind the Ball-room is the
Drawing-room, and underneath that, the Coffee-room.
There are Assemblies here every Thursday fortnight, during
the winter season, also on the King and Queen's birth days,
and at other times on particular occasions. The Assemblies
are conducted by a committee of gentlemen, principal
inhabitants of the city, who have appointed Joseph Smith,
Esq. Master of the Ceremonies; who has a ball annually.

Here are also public concerts during the winter, under the

conduct of a committee of gentlemen, who take care to engage the best vocal and instrumental performers. The subscribers pay two guineas each and are entitled to two tickets for the admission of ladies. Gentlemen living in Bristol, or its vicinity, are not admitted, unless they become subscribers. Non-residents pay five shillings for their admission.

The CITY LIBRARY, in King-street, is a handsome free-stone building. It contains a valuable collection of books, which is perpetually increasing, in consequence of donations and annual subscriptions made thereto. A Librarian is appointed to attend at a fixed salary, who, by the institution must be a clergyman. But on account of the great increase of the Library since its commencement, the business of conducting it has been found too much for one to superintend, there-fore a sub-librarian has been appointed to assist in executing that office. The Rev Mr Catcott, late Vicar of Temple, in this City, having bequeathed to this Library his whole museum of minerals, fossils, and natural curiosities, with a valuable collection of books, a new wing of freestone is added for their reception. The subscriptions are, four guineas at entrance, besides a guinea in hand, and a guinea annually. Hours of attendance, eleven till two, six till nine (Saturdays excepted).

A provincial fair, WH Pyne, 1805. The craze for handbell ringing at this period is said by Pyne to have originated with the unnamed subject of this picture who invented an ingenious set that were attached to his body. The Scaramouch behind accompanies his tune on a saltbox.

The philosophical apparatus which was lodged in the Library, has lately been removed to St Augustine's Place, where a Society is formed, called the BRISTOL PHILO-SOPHICAL and LITERARY SOCIETY.
Bristol and Hotwell Guide, 1805

St James' Fair, Braikenridge Collection. This drawing shows the style of booths and amusements available from rides to Wild Beast shows. In the centre a Recruiting Sergeant enlists a drunken man and on the left a blind beggar with pigeons on his head and shoulders seeks largesse.

Balls and country dances were of course very popular although not without danger to one's partner as *The Miseries of Human Life* warned: 'Entering into the figure of a country dance with so much spirit as to force your leg and foot through the muslin drapery of your fair partner.'

The local press gave a full account of any balls of note:

On Friday last, at the Mansion-House, a ball was given by the lady of our worthy Chief Magistrate, which was attended by a brilliant assemblage of the beauty and fashion of the city and neighbourhood. A temporary awning, leading to the Mansion, was brilliantly illuminated with variegated lamps, continuing through the hall, staircase, &c. to the ball-room, which was superbly lighted. Great taste was displayed in the coloured lamps extending from the ball-room to the drawing-room, where the company first assembled. Mr Butler Claxton and Miss Wagner opened the ball. There were present, His Grace of Beaufort, Lord Arthur Somerset, Sir John and Lady Durbin, Lady F. Belford, Lady Mary Sotheby, &c. The supper consisted of every delicacy of the season; the three rooms in which it was laid, displayed the taste and liberality of the elegant hostess. The company did not part till four o'clock in the morning.

Felix Farley's Bristol Journal, 10 January 1807

The fairs that provided so much enjoyable basic entertainment to the ordinary Bristolian and scandalised others were not without their semi-cultural side or their hoped-for genteel visitors. In the *Bristol Gazette* for 3 September, 1807, the 30-year-old Giovanni Belzoni, the great future Egyptologist, may be found advertising a display of 'two different Philosophical Experiments in HYDRAULICS and HYDROSTATICS, on FIRE, AIR, and WATER; also an entirely new experiment in Optics called PHANTAS-COPIA'. Belzoni's entertainment was held 'in a commodious Booth in St James's Church Yard,' and concluded with him carrying a pyramid of seven men without using his arms. Wealthier spectators could avoid the crowds by using the pit door or could have private displays in the morning by arrangement. Equally the Temple Fair could boast a visit that year from

GANTER's UNIVERSAL MUSEUM comprising the greatest variety of the CURIOSITIES of NATURE and ART, ever seen; which will be exhibited from Ten in the Morning till Nine in the Evening, during the Fair, in a large Room, in the centre of TOWER-STREET, near Avon-street, Great Gardens. Among which are, NINE CURIOUS PIECES of MACHINERY; also, Curious MODELS, in IVORY and RICE PASTE; SCULPTURE; MEDALS; ANTIQUITIES, &c. FOREIGN BIRDS and INSECTS, of all Descriptions, FISHES, QUADRUPEDS, REPTILES, &c.&c.

In short, the Proprietors are bold to assert, that such an exhibition was never before offered to the Public. It consists of nearly 2000 Natural and Artificial Curiosities.

Admission, One Shilling.

A List of Curiosities may be had at the Museum.

Bristol Gazette, 5 March 1807

George Weare Braikenridge commented on the Bristol fairs in his collection of *Bristoliana* now in the Reference Library and included a child-like drawing of the booths, merry-go-rounds and round-abouts at St James' Fair. Amongst the figures dotted about are a recruiting sergeant, his assistant and their drunken prey.

Bristol has long been famed for its Fairs, which however are not so considerable and well frequented as formerly. Of late years since travelling on commercial affairs has become so general fewer persons find it worth while to attend them, and by this new mode of transacting business; it is in a great degree rendered unnecessary for the great manufacturers to attend at Fairs twice a year as was the prevailing custom formerly. They have in consequence dwindled away very considerably and are now principally attended by manufacturers in small ways of business who wish to convert their stock of goods into ready money. Amongst these many come from as far as Yorkshire with both coarse & fine cloths, rugs, blankets etc. Carpets from Kidderminster, Woollen & Cotton Stockings, the latter from

Tewkesbury, Hardware from Birmingham, Sheffield, Wolsal & Wolverhampton are also to be found in quantities for sale, with Earthenware from Staffordshire &c &c. The two first days of the Fair, the street at the bottom of St James's Church Yard called the Horse Fair, with Broad Mead & several of the adjoining streets are filled with Horned Cattle & Horses which are brought for sale, many of them from a considerable distance. More tanned Leather continues to be sold at Leather Hall on the Back during the Fairs, than at any other Fair in England. A large quantity of Ticking for Beds is also brought to the Tick Hall adjoining the Back Hall. For the juvenile throngs Play Toys are displayed in abundance in the Rows of Standings with a profusion of confectionary wares, Sweetmeats, Comfits &c. For the amusement of the Populace, there is no deficiency in Flying Coaches, Ups & downs &c with exhibitions of wild beasts & birds, Equestrian Performers, Wax Work, wire dancers, tumblers, puppets, Punch & his Wife, Sea fights, conjuration hocus pocus, magic & mummery of all sorts, recommended by Conjurors, Merry Andrews, Buffoons, Drums, Trumpets, French Horns, Fiddlers, Rattles & Vociferation. The Shops & Standings are Built of, and covered with Planks, kept from Fair to Fair for the purpose; disposed in Streets & Rows and are generally a Month in preparing and although the Fairs both of St James & Temple are charter'd only for nine days, they are both generally protracted for a fortnight. Many laudable endeavours have lately been used to get these Fairs suppressed altogether as they are so productive of vice & ruin to many but considerable profit being derived by the Parishes of St James & Temple from the erection of the

Rows of Standings which together with Houses situated in the Fairs rent at a high rate for the time, all attempts to put them down, have hitherto proved of no avail. Temple Fair was formerly held on the 25th January St Pauls day & thence called St Pauls Fair & St James's Fair on the 25th July being St James's day; but the days in January being so short & the Weather so bad in general, the Winter Fair was removed to the 1st of March and the Summer Fair to the 1st of September on which days they now continue to be held. *Braikenridge*

In WH Pyne's great work of 1808 *The Costume of Great Britain*, plate 45 is entitled *The Round-about* and is accompanied by a useful if censorious account of the machines. Unless they were artistically arranged or placed into picturesque groupings, Pyne could not be said to be an admirer of the lower orders. One suspects that he would not have been in favour of candy floss:

Amongst the many modes of amusement conducted by the low dissolute people who live by attending statues, fairs, &c. may be included that of the round-about, which is a machine addressed to the boys and girls who frequent these noisy scenes. The proprietor charges a halfpenny for each passenger, and some of these vehicles will hold sixty children, who ride for about a minute and a half, being whirled about by miserable straggling boys who receive a few halfpence for pushing it swiftly round, by running within the cross bars that connect it together. There is a great variety of round-abouts, some going horizontally, others vertically, raising people seated in chairs a frightful height: there are also swings of a curious construction, the whole of which in motion together, amidst the other noisy amusements of a fair, produce a scene of the utmost bustle and confusion.

An immense sum is annually expended in this country, in the indulgence of low amusements at statues, fairs &c. Indeed as many carts, wagons, chaises, caravans and horses, are employed in transporting from one fair to another, strolling players, harlequins, pantaloons, punches, scaramouches, tumblers, salt-box musicians, wild beasts, giants, dwarfs, monsters, learned horses, learned pigs, fire eaters, stone eaters, fortune tellers, conjurers and fools, as would be sufficient to convey a considerable part of the camp equipage of his Majesty's land forces.

The Round-About, W H Pyne, 1805. The rides were propelled by 'miserable straggling boys' who would push them around for a few halfpennies.

Cold baths and swimming for the health-concious ladies and gentlemen were available at Rennison's Baths off Stokes Croft, near the turnpike leading to the Gloucester Road. It was a safer and more pleasant alternative to swimming in the Avon. In May 1807 the baths were cleaned and the bathing houses put in good order. A male and female attendant were always present to avoid accidents. The baths were fed by a local spring and had a large swimming lake as well as covered pools.

In the eighteenth century Bristol produced a number of legendary bare-knuckle fighters who became nationally renowned. Some of them fought at 'The Hatchet' in Frogmore Street where there was a boxing ring: including Benjamin Brain, Jem Belcher and Henry Pearce.

John Gully (1783-1863) was a renowned prizefighter who was born at The Crown Inn (now the Rose and Crown) at Wick near Bristol. Although at the age of 21 he found himself in prison for debt, his talent for fighting was soon noticed. He entered a bout with the famous 'Bristol Game-Chicken' Henry Pearce (the reigning champion) and although Gully lost he so impressed the onlookers that he had all his debts paid. He was then trained as a

JAMES BELCHER.

top:
Tom Cribb by De Wild, 1811. Cribb wears a cravat pin in the shape of two pugilists.

below:
James Belsher (Belcher).

rival to Pearce but the 'Game-Chicken' retired through ill health in 1805. Gully then became his successor, but retired from prize fighting in 1808. He went on to become a successful racehorse owner, MP and landowner. He died in County Durham and was buried in Pontefract.

Henry Pearce, 'The Bristol Game-Chicken', was another bare-knuckle fighter born in Bristol and the protégé of famous Bristol fighter Jem Belcher. He was called the 'game-chicken' as he signed himself 'Hen'. Pearce went on to become undisputed champion and his bouts with Gully were legendary, although the two became friends. After his retirement, he returned to Bristol and allegedly saved a woman from a burning building in 1807 and also rescued a woman from being attacked in the street. He died in 1809 of tuberculosis.

Sic transit gloria mundi
Our bruising friends in the Metropolis will learn with deepest regret that their favourite Game Chicken, that pink of pugilism, has not only refused the challenge given to him by GULLEY, and paid the forfeit of twenty-five Guineas, but that there is little likelihood, owing to his impaired state of health, of his ever again contending for fistic honours. It may be a question for the casuists in these matters whether the Chicken can still retain the title of Champion of England, after having refused a challenge. By the Laws of chivalry, we think he can not.
Bristol Mercury, 5 October 1807

Probably the most famous of the pugilists born in the Bristol area was Tom Cribb, who (contrary to local myth) has nothing to do with Cribbs Causeway.

Cribb (1781-1848) was born at Hanham. He moved to London at the age of thirteen and from that time had little to do with Bristol. He worked as a bellhanger then became a porter and was afterwards a sailor. From the fact of his having worked as a coal porter he became known as the Black Diamond. He won his first public contest against George Maddox at Wood Green on 7 January 1805 and won three more that same year. In 1807 he was taken up by Captain Robert Barclay Allardice who trained him. After successful bouts against Jem Belcher and Bob Gregson (that were assiduously reported in the Bristol press) he was challenged and was victorious over Tom Molineaux, although not without some nefarious assistance by his supporters. Challenged again he this time fractured Molineaux's jaw. After this he was fêted and became, firstly, an unsuccessful coal merchant and then a publican. Lured into gambling he lost his public house and finished his days living with his son, a baker.

There were plenty in 1807 as nowadays too who wished to avoid such events. One of the horrors catalogued in *The Miseries of Human Life* included 'being met and blockaded on the road, by innumerable gangs of the Carrion and Offal of the human species, as they are swarming home, in savage jollity, from a bull-baiting, a boxing-match, an execution & &.'

Horse racing on the Downs and rowing matches on the river occurred occasionally. In June 1807 a race took place that attracted great crowds.

On Tuesday evening, about a quarter past eight o'clock, a rowing match from the Hotwells to the Gib-slip, between a new gigg, built on a new construction, with four oars, and a wherry, with two pair of sculls, the property of Mr James, of Wapping. The wherry at the start was allowed 200 yards, and preserved the distance nearly the whole way. The race was performed in eleven minutes. The banks of the river were lined with thousands of spectators.
Bristol Mirror, 27 June 1807

Seasonal celebrations were greatly looked forward to by the ordinary Bristolian as a break from everyday routine. Guy Fawkes night was a particularly popular event, both for its anti-Catholic sentiments and for the mayhem that it could cause. Fireworks in the wrong hands were then just as dangerous as they are now and the newspapers chronicle a list of accidents and fatalities in the city. The habit of also firing loaded guns to make noise only added to the problem and on such occasions Bristol must have rather resembled the wild west.

We understand that a young man was fined one guinea, by the magistrates, which was given to the Infirmary, for firing off a squib in the street, by which a lady had her gown considerably burnt, and narrowly escaped being herself materially injured.
Bristol Mirror and Journal, 31 October 1807

COUNCIL-HOUSE, BRISTOL, 2d November, 1807. WHEREAS much mischief has been done, and more is apprehended from the practice of throwing, casting, and firing Squibs, Crackers, Serpents, Rockets, and other Fire-works, and also the firing of Guns and Pistols in the Public Streets: the Mayor and Aldermen of this city, in order to prevent and deter persons from such practices, and from the making, vending, and selling Fire-Works, Do hereby give Notice, That by the Laws in being, all persons guilty of any of the offences aforesaid, are punishable by Fine and Imprisonment; and that the said Laws will be strictly carried into execution, for which purpose orders are issued to the several Constables and other Peace Officers of this city, to apprehend and bring before the Magistrates such persons as may be found committing any of the offences aforesaid, in order to their being dealt with according to the said Laws. WORRALL.
Bristol Mirror, 7 November 1807

Thursday last, being the anniversary of the Gunpowder plot, was observed in this city by the accustomed rejoicings – flags were displayed on the public buildings and shipping; successive bell-ringing; and the corporation, with the several Trading companies, attended divine Service at the Cathedral.
We wish it was in our power to add that the festivities of the evening passed off in as harmless and peaceable a manner; but it falls to our lot to relate one of the most atrocious acts of wantonness and cruelty, which has ever appeared in the columns of our Journal. The repeated complaints of attack upon the peaceable inhabitants of this city, from squibs,

The Halfpenny Showman, WH Pyne. Such showmen travelled the country carrying their displays on their backs. These were peepshows with moveable figures and scenes occasionally powered by clockwork. The flap at the top allowed daylight to illuminate the display.

crackers, &c. and of which we complained in our last, did at length arrest the attention of the magistracy; and hand-bills and advertisements appeared in the course of the week, which we flattered ourselves, were symptoms of a vigorous and determined interference on the part of the police, to put a stop to such disgraceful, and as it now appears, fatal conduct, of the rabble of this place; and we fully expected to have had the pleasure to relate the conviction of every offender, could we have believed such an one was to be found after such notice, who would have had the hardihood to pursue such nefarious practices. Our vigilant peace-officers, however, have let them all escape, though hundreds of pistols, squibs and crackers assailed the ears of every passenger the whole of the evening; — and we have in consequence to relate the loss of an innocent fellow-creature, who has been cut off in the prime of life, by the wanton aggression of one of these barbarians! A young woman, of the name of Sarah Osborne (niece, we hear, of Mr Webb, cooper, of Simms's Alley) was purchasing some oysters or herrings at a shop in the Horse-Fair, when one of these gentry fired a musket or pistol so heavily laden with bullet, that it penetrated the doors both of the front and back of the watch house opposite to where the young lady was standing, passed through her head, and a pane of glass, and lodged in the wall of the house.—The young creature immediately fell, and received from the bye-standers the most prompt and humane assistance they could afford. She was speedily conveyed to the Infirmary, where we are concerned to add all medical and surgical assistance was unavailing, and she expired in great agony at about 6 o'clock yesterday morning. – The Jury have not yet

set upon the body. Sorry are we to hear that no clue has yet been found by which to discover the perpetrator of this crime.
Felix Farley's Bristol Journal, 7 November 1807

CAUTION RESPECTING FIRE-WOKS [sic]
Thursday evening, a fire broke out in the stables of Mrs Belloger, of Woodstock, which entirely consumed the same, and a quantity of hay and straw. The fire was occasioned by some boys throwing squibs, one of which went directly into the hay-loft. The magistrates of Woodstock have in consequence resolved to enforce rigidly the statute of 10th William III. which lays a penalty of 5l. upon the vender of the squibs, and of 20s. on the persons using them.
Bristol Mirror, 7 November 1807

WHEREAS, on the Evening of the Fifth day of November instant, some Person did maliciously fire a Gun or Pistol in St James's Church-Yard, in this City, whereby one SARAH OSBORNE, who was standing in the Street called the Horse-Fair, was killed. The MAGISTRATES of this City hereby offer a Reward of FIFTY GUINEAS, to any Person who will give information against the Person who fired the said Gun or Pistol, so that he may be brought to Justice for the said Offence. WORRALL, Town Clerk.
Bristol Mirror, 14 November 1807

For the reasonably polite Bristolians who found their greatest entertainment in sitting in one of the numerous taverns or coffee houses of the city

Guy Fawkes Night, W H Pyne. 5 November was celebrated with great gusto in 1807 and still had a strong anti-Catholic content.

It is the custom here for all Parlour and creditable visitants of Public-houses to drink out of Plate; Tankards and Pint Cans as they are termed. Therefore as the Public-houses, and their frequenters, are very numerous, perhaps there is not a City in England so rich in silver as Bristol.
The Bristol Guide, 1815

The Rude Conduct of Idle Boys: a year of crime

Gates are barr'd, a vain resistance;
Females shriek, but no assistance;
Silence, silence, or you meet your fate;
Silence or you meet your fate –
Your keys, your jewels, cash and plate!
The Old Bath Songster

PROBABLY LIKE MOST CITIES OF THE AGE, BRISTOL IN 1807 SEEMS FROM the newspaper reports to have been a place where crime was rife. Many crimes like stealing lead from buildings, shop-lifting and dangerous driving are still plaguing the city today. Others like failure to sweep the pavements in front of one's premises or highway robbery are either defunct or mercifully outmoded. The idea that the present century is more violent than those preceding it is quite erroneous as only a casual glance through old newspapers will prove. Murders in the eighteenth century were more common, but still happened in the nineteenth with great frequency. The ease with which one now hears the news from the entire country gives a false impression of how violent life is nowadays.

Loutish and brutal behaviour was just as common 200 years ago as it is now. Bristol in 1807 was full of great wealth and opulence, but that was a magnet to poverty and felony. The rough mining area of Kingswood was of great annoyance to the citizens of Bristol and the surrounding areas, and a great many crimes were laid at the doors of the wretched inhabitants of both sexes. The Cock Road gang were a notorious group of thieves and ruffians that terrorised the area around Bitton, Hanham and Kingswood from the late 1720s until the 1830s. Cock Road and the immediate neighbourhood became a no-go area for law-abiding citizens and the lawlessness of the locality was reported at national level. The gang largely centred on the Caines family who have been dubbed the 'Kingswood mafia' as they demanded extortion money, fenced stolen goods as well as committed murder and highway robbery. They felt themselves above the law, but a number of them were transported and some even executed. The *New Bristol Guide* of 1804 explains the measures in place to combat crime and safeguard the inhabitants within the city:

This City is divided into twelve Wards… Every ward has one Chief Constable, and twelve others; a Night-Constable, and a proper number of Watchmen under him; so that the whole *posse comitatus* is numerous, and, in general, sufficient to keep the peace. There are for the several Wards watch and round houses, standard boxes; Scavengers, and Lamplighters. The Guardhouse for Soldiers is in Wine-street. The number of nightly Watchmen is said to be upwards of 140.

At the eastern end of Wine-street is Newgate, the City Jail for Debtors and Malefactors. The gate, which has been lately taken down, was, before there was a passage through the Castle, one of the principal entrances into the city. It was very strong, and a port cullis for its defence, as appeared by the grooves on the top of the arch on each side of the gateway. The Prison has been enlarged and improved by a late Act of Parliament, and a spacious Fives-court

The Pillory, W H Pyne.
Typically, an hour in the pillory was punishment for embezzlement of state property, perjury and swindling. Those convicted of crimes against authority were generally not molested by the crowd.

added to it, so that it is much more healthy and convenient than before. Here is a decent Chapel with galleries, in which the Ordinary, appointed by the Corporation, performs divine service. Both the Prisons of this City were judiciously placed close by the river Froom, which supplies them with air, and receives and washes away the filth of these populous Colleges: Newgate generally containing from 80 to 100 debtors and malefactors; male and female. The Corporation have lately obtained an Act of Parliament for building and supporting a new Jail, on Howard's plan, to be erected on the loftiest part of the site of the old Castle, which is undoubtedly the most eligible spot in Bristol for a Prison. This bill enforcing a perpetual tax has occasioned a contest between the Citizens and Magistrates: the Citizens are willing to pay a temporary tax for building the Prison, but not to be obliged to pay for ever towards its support: especially as the corporation have hitherto supported it out of the City-stock; and as taxes are already numerous and heavy.

Bridewell, the other City-prison, has two gates, and within them two opposite fronts of the buildings, which are for the commitment, confinement, and correction of offenders.

Those parts of the Town not under the government of the Magistrates of Bristol, and which are large and populous, both in the counties of Glocester and Somerset, are governed as the out part of London are, by Justices of both the counties; and have Constables, Bailiffs, and Criers, for the different districts. A spacious strong Prison of stone, on the Howardian plan, has been lately completed for the suburbs of Bristol in Glocestershire. It has 70 separate Cells, a Chapel, a Hall for the Justices in its front, which extends about 150 feet high. It contains upwards of 200 tons of iron, and cost 9000L. This stands at the end of a street called *Glocester-street,* and as it is without the place where Lawford's-Gate stood, it is named *Lawford's-Gate Bridewell.* Here, and in another part of these suburbs, are held weekly Courts; as there are for the suburbs of Bedminster in Somerset, which have also a Bridewell, though but little used as offenders are quickly sent to Shepton-Mallet Jail. London was first lighted with lamps in the reign of King Charles II. The Act for lighting Bristol was not procured till the latter part of the reign of King William III. This Act obliges citizens to hang out their own lamps: subsequently, public lamps were lighted for half the year only, but for many years past have been lighted every night in the year. Some of the principal and most frequented streets and places in Bristol have a tolerable number of lamps, though some are confessedly wanted all over the town.

According to the acts of Parliament for the Police, the streets should be cleaned, punctually, twice a week, the footways swept every morning, and mastiff-dogs muzzled.

*

The watchmen of Bristol amount to about 150, and are so stationed in watch-houses, and centry boxes, in every Ward, that persons may, in general, pass securely at any time of the night. The Mayor and Aldermen are ready at the Council-House, on complaint, to redress grievances, rectify abuses, and fine offenders.

New Bristol Guide, 1804

In 1806 a bill for amending previous local Acts relating to the sewerage, cleansing, paving and lighting of the city received Royal assent, much to the annoyance of the public who could see the corporation extending its powers at their expense.

Wednesday morning last, about four o'clock, the house of Mr. Westwood, in Southwell-street, Kingsdown, was burglariously entered by some villain; but very fortunately his intention of robbing the house was frustrated, by the servant hearing a noise in the house and giving the alarm to her master, when the robber made a precipitate retreat, and in the hurry of his departure dropt a table-cloth, which was the only article he had got in his possession, under a wall, over which he jumped to make his escape.—The house of Mrs. Norris, St. Michael's-hill, has also, we understand, been robbed during the past week.

Felix Farley's Bristol Journal 10 October 1807.

Bristol from the Avon, Thomas H Shepherd
The construction of the floating harbour was an amazing feat of engineering and gave Bristol the most modern docks in Britain. This coloured engraving from the late 1820s shows the area by Bristol Bridge full of small traders. A ferry transports passengers across the water in the foreground.

above: *A Trader in Bristol Harbour,* JA Atkinson, 1808
'What can be more absurd than to assert that the harbour is one of the deepest, safest and most convenient in England, when ships and small craft are seen up to their wales in mud, ten feet below the quays?"

left: Bristol from the Docks, William Westall
A smoke-free Sunday morning on the Avon. Sundays were the one day when the city was not shrouded in smoke from the many kilns and industrial chimneys. The view is taken from near the Mardyke. Houses clustered along the Hotwells Road can be seen to the left of the picture, whilst the cone of a glassworks vies with the cathedral tower near to the centre.

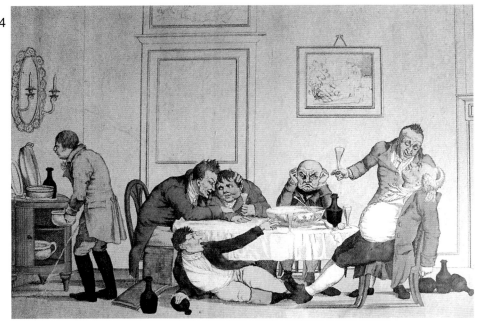

4

The English After Dinner
In 1807 the English of all classes were notorious amongst foreigners for the amount of alcohol they consumed. It was said that English men drank for the sake of it. *L'Après-Dinée des Anglais* was one of a series of satirical prints about the English produced in Paris by a former French prisoner of war. The gentlemen have left the ladies to their tea. Depression, lust and stupor reign whilst a young man is caught short before he can aim at the chamber pot. Open use of such conveniences and the toasting of the user by the rest of the company horrified foreign visitors. At a dinner held at Reeve's Hotel in 1807, 22 Bristol councillors and aldermen consumed 62 bottles of assorted wines.

6

5

The Miseries Of Human Life; or the Groans of Timothy Testy, and Samuel Sensitive, with a few supplementary sighs from Mrs Testy.
'Sunt lacrymae rerum' – 'here are tears for the things of the world' – says one of the characters in Pyne's coloured frontispiece from James Beresford's review of calamities. It is a typical 1806 drawing room with the furniture placed around the borders of the room. Paintings labelled 'Fortitude', 'Temperance' and 'Mountain of Misery' ornament the walls; volumes entitled *The Art of Tormenting* and *Much ado about nothing* are abandoned on the carpet. Irascible Timothy Testy and the depressed Samuel Sensitive wear less fashionable clothes than their younger companion and still use hair powder.

7

left:
The Bill-Sticker, W H Pyne, 1805
Printed handbills made town criers obsolete. News could pass round a city in a day and around the country in a week. The biggest posters were produced by the national lotteries of the day.

left:
Woman Churning Butter
W H Pyne, 1805
The barrel churn was an eighteenth-century invention for producing considerable quantities of butter. In very large dairies barrel churns were turned by horses. In 1806 50,000 tons of butter were consumed in London alone. Narraway considered Bristol butter very inferior and during the winter used clotted cream butter, made by pouring cream into brass pans which were left to stand for eight hours. It was then gently heated until the cream began to shrivel, and then skimmed at a consistency close to butter.

The Garden at The Red Maids' School, Denmark Street, Bristol
oil on canvas, early-nineteenth century.
A rare portrayal of a city garden that would have been old-fashioned by 1807. By that time the fashionable formal garden often had railed and squared beds as John Narraway had installed at his farm in Horfield and as survives in one of a series of contemporary watercolours of the gardens attached to the Pole family's house in St James' Square, and now in the Bristol City Art Gallery. The geometric and box-hedged flower beds portrayed at the school are set in a gravelled courtyard and may even be coeval with the seventeenth-century building behind. The tower of the Lord Mayor's Chapel and the back of one of the still surviving Georgian houses facing College Green may be seen to the left of the picture. Another version of this painting survives at the Red Maids' School.

ANECDOTES, NAVAL & MILITARY.

Anecdotes, Naval & Military
An early-nineteenth-century print of two much-battered war veterans, a sailor and soldier, in a tavern. With all of the conflicts of the previous century and with the country still at war, ex-servicemen must have been a common sight in the city. The pair sit on a bench discussing old times and campaigns in a room decorated with paintings of naval and land battles. A supply of clay pipes on the side table suggests that these were supplied to the patrons. Bristol was remarkable for the number of silver tankards and cans in its inns. Whether these veterans are used to drinking from silver or pewter cannot be determined, although the sailor's is obviously engraved.

A View from Trinity College, Cambridge, The Bishop of Bristol, William Lort Mansel
A print by Robert Dighton, 1810
In 1807 John Luxmoore was given the Bishopric of Bristol. He was succeeded after only a year by Mansel, who spent much of his time in Cambridge between 1808 and 1820 rather than in Bristol. Dighton's caricature says much about what he thought of the Bishop.

Traditional costume of a Bristol orange seller, WB Wilcocks
This hand-coloured lithograph shows the eighteenth-century costume for fruit sellers that was to remain in Bristol into the reign of Victoria. Women wearing the straw hat and red-hooded country cloak appear in many of the pictures featured in this book. Bristol was renowned for its fruit, both local and imported, and orange girls would meet the ships to procure newly imported produce.
The poem 'Love and Law' tells how they would then speed off to make sales on the promenades and streets crying 'Sweet Oranges'. The hat she wears was almost certainly one of the local ones made by Bristol's thriving straw-plaiting industry.

12

13

14

Old Bristol in colour, Edward (Evacustes) A Phipson
Although painted a century after 1807, Phipson's watercolours show the colours of the old plaster and timber buildings of an earlier time.

top left: Old Market Street
left: Broad Weir
above: St Mary-le-Port Street with the Brewers' Guild house.

15

The Year (1740) a Ladys full dress of Bombazeen — The Year (1807) a Ladys undress of Bum-be-seen.

THE FASHIONS OF THE DAY or Time Past and Time Present.

Woodward del.   W. Sculp.

Respectfully Dedicated to the Fashionable Editors of La Belle Assemblée — Le Beau Monde No 3c — Published Nov 2d 1807 by Walker No 7 Cornhill

Fashionable Morning & Evening Dress as worn in October 1807

Printed and Published by John Bell, Southampton Street, Strand, for No 32 f La Belle assemblee Nov 1 1807.

16

The Fashions of the Day, or Time Past and Time Present, George Woodward, 2 November 1807

The Grecian styles introduced after Emma Hamilton took London by storm with her classically-inspired dress in 1793, were to persist in fashion for over twenty years. The introduction of her undergarment 'the pad' that was worn below the breasts caused much scandal and amusement as it gave the wearer the appearance of being pregnant. The styles of 1807 with clinging and often revealing muslin dresses, low décolletage, and worn in an age that had not yet properly invented drawers drew much comment from caricaturists and writers in the newspapers. This cartoon mocks the fashion plates to be found in the women's journals of the age.

Fashionable Morning and Evening Dress Worn in October 1807

This plate from the women's journal *La Belle Assemblée* was published in November 1807 (the same month as Woodward's fashion caricature). It illustrates the sort of garments that he was making fun of. The lady in evening dress wears a splendid hair ornament decorated with ball terminals.

17

LIEUT. COL. GORE.

18

19

MONOPOLIZERS caught in thier own TRAP or a COMPANION to the FARMERS TOAST.

above left: Lieut Col Gore, SF Downman of Bath, 1804
In Bristol on 18 February 1797 the Royal Bristol Volunteers Regiment was founded by a number of merchants and tradesmen, to guard the 2000 French prisoners-of-war held at Stapleton should the militia be posted to active service. William Gore was one of two Lieutenant Colonels. The artist also issued the likeness as a coloured engraving. Gore is commemorated by a decayed monument in the north transept of Bristol Cathedral.

left: The uniform and colours of the 1797 Bristol Volunteers Regiment in a watercolour from the Library's Braikenridge collection. The image was used by the Bristol Pottery at that time. The uniform may also be found on the elegant life-size figures of Tyley's superb monument to William Gore in Bristol Cathedral.

Monopolisers Caught in their own trap, caricature by Charles Williams, May 1801
The period of the Napoleonic wars coincided with a series of bad harvests. John Narraway mentions the poor flour resulting from the harvest of 1797. By 1807 British farmers had a virtual monopoly of domestic markets because all trade with Europe was ended. Scarcity and bad harvests caused a rapid rise in prices, with much suffering and corn riots across the country. In this print four farmers who have been hoarding their wheat in hope of still higher prices, are horrified to be told by the Mayor that he has set the Assize of Bread (which adjusted the weight and price of bread to the price of wheat) at half its previous amount. In Bristol, bakers and brewers were fined for adulterating their products with bulking ingredients.

The Bush Tavern, Corn Street, Bristol in the Old Coaching Days, chromolithograph by William Lewis after J H Maggs

The Bush Inn or Tavern, here seen in a later painting, was one of the most famous coaching inns in the country. It was opposite the Corn Exchange where Lloyds bank now stands. Many travellers stayed there when visiting the city, until its demolition in 1854. Its Coach Office could book the traveller on to a dozen daily services to all parts of the country. Six services to Bath ran every day on the half hour. The area must have been full of excitement, bustle and frustration. The main Post Office stood opposite, awaiting the mail coaches. In 1807 the Bush was run by the irrepressible John Weeks, who had appeared on its balcony dressed as a sailor (accompanied by the band of the Oxford Militia) to toast a peace treaty with France in 1801. It incorporated Jack's Coffee House. The Bush offered a huge range of dishes for the traveller to try including the inevitable turtle. The Society of Ships' Captains met here every autumn and processed to the Cathedral.

21

The Royal Mail
WH Pyne, 1805
The introduction of specially designed mail coaches for a postal service was a relatively recent wonder in 1807. Inn keepers, by law, had to ensure that parcels of letters were ready as the coach would not wait. The service more than halved the time letters had previously taken to reach destinations. The coachman and armed guard wore royal livery.

The Lamp Lighter,
WH Pyne, 1805
Bristol had street lighting. The lamps were of clear glass and burned cotton wicks in good quality oil. They were trimmed each morning and cleaned as necessary. The same men lit them at night. Malcolm mentions that in Bristol, the globes were protected from the public by nets or cages.

23

22

The Stage Waggon
WH Pyne, 1805
Luggage, furniture and the occasional passenger were transported by the stage waggon. Freight had to be carefully balanced to avoid accidents. The roller wheels not only spread the weight of the huge loads carried but also flattened any ruts in the road. As a result the vehicle paid lower tolls on turnpike roads. These were the articulated lorries of the day and excited much admiration.

The Dustman, WH Pyne, 1805
Dustmen rang a handbell to announce their arrival. As money could be made from 'elements of the dust' both scavengers, who cleaned the streets, and the dustman had to pay the Corporation for a contract to cart away rubbish. This would then be sorted by men and women 'of the lowest order' and sold on.

24

25   *The Arrival of the London Mail*, Robert Cruikshank
This engraving from 1825 captures some of the excitement engendered by the arrival of the London Mail coach at the Post Office in
Corn Street, Bristol. The same scene would have been repeated to a lesser extent as the other coaches from various parts of the
Kingdom arrived throughout the day.
The Post Office stood next to the Exchange and spread down the narrow alley (Exchange Avenue) to its west. The Post Office had been
there since the middle of the eighteenth century, but following its transfer to Small Street in 1865 the building became a tea warehouse.
The postal delivery from London arrived around noon on every day apart from Sunday and Monday, and returned at 4 pm.
Postal deliveries were made to all parts of the city and suburbs three times a day from the principal post office.
Local mail was sent at a penny for the city and two pence for the suburbs.

26

View of the Avon towards the Severn, JMW Turner, c.1792
A lost watercolour once owned by John Narraway and sold by his niece, Ann Dart, around 1860 to the Turner collector WG Rawlinson. The view is taken from the top of the great ravine above the bend in the river and beyond the wall that John Wallis erected along the cliff edge in 1746 to prevent fatalities. For his good works the name of Wallis' Wall was oddly, (and somewhat churlishly), changed to Sea Walls by later Bristolians. Figures believed to be the Narraways clamber over the rocks. The teenage Turner was entranced by this scenery and spent so much time sketching it that his hosts called him 'The Prince of the Rocks'.

27

Bristol Diamonds
'it is rare to see a chimney not decorated with pieces of spar. Specimens have been dug of the weight of half a hundred.'
Bristol Diamonds were actually quartz, but quite remarkable in their clarity and hardness. They were made into jewellery or used as mantelpiece or grotto ornaments. Goldney Grotto in Clifton has a fine, but weathered, display of them. This example in red haematite from St Vincent's Rocks survived the bombing of World War II which destroyed much of the city's outstanding geological and palaeontological collection.

opposite:
Rownham Ferry, Rolinda Sharples, oil on canvas, 1820-22
Rownham Ferry is arguably Rolinda Sharples' most delightful painting, but unfortunately not one that is in the city's collection and one whose present whereabouts is unknown. It encapsulates the fun of being on holiday and residing in Clifton and Hotwells. It is crammed with humour and information for the social and local historian.

left:
'The mountain almost opposite to the Hot Well is transcendently beautiful.' An early-nineteenth-century watercolour of the Avon Gorge from the Somerset side of the river. The little building was the New Pump Room that tapped the copious hot spring nearby. Established around 1730, it had never prospered because of difficulty of access and the lack of a carriage road. By 1795 it was practically abandoned and finally became quarry workers' cottages. A (dry) wall fountain now marks the spot on the Portway. Artist unknown.

left:
'The Assembly-Room was originally built, very early in this century, and was then one of the principal Rooms in the kingdom.' A detail from *A view of Hotwells and the Avon Gorge* c.1730 and now in the Bristol Art Gallery (K4646). The imposing Assembly Rooms with its frontage enhanced by a Paradise or garden was to become the Gloucester Hotel. Later in the century the towering bay-fronted block would be built to the rear and right of the old building in the back gardens seen in this painting.
Artist unknown.

A late-eighteenth-century sailor's horn or bone beaker decorated with scrimshaw work and with an attached small silver panel inscribed *H.M.* The scrimshaw work on this important and rare item shows a ship and two African heads. One has an elaborate top-knot hairstyle. Around the rim is: AFRICAS * BRISTOL * LIVERPOOL.

The Portrait Studio, Thomas Rowlandson
One of the most popular souvenirs to take home from a holiday at a spa was a portrait. The *Bristol Directory* for 1807 listed seven portrait and miniature artists who could oblige the willing sitter in achieving this aim. Added to this there were peripatetic portraitists who spent their lives following the Season around the country, and who would advertise their arrival in the local press.
This plate comes from the rare first strike of Rowlandson's *The Comforts of Bath*, published in 1798. The activities illustrated in the series of twelve plates were common to Hotwells and Clifton.

34 *Edward Rolle Clayfield*, William Armfield Hobday, 1803
Edward Clayfield, (1767-1825) was a sugar and wine merchant of Host Street, Bristol. In 1795 he married Frances, the eldest daughter of James Ireland, also a sugar merchant, of Brislington Hall – an estate of 664 acres in the village of Brislington. The family continued to reside at Brislington Hall until 1923. This portrait shows Edward aged 36. He wears his hair powdered, which may have been to show his wealth in view of Pitt the Younger's wartime tax on hair powder.
The painter William Armfield Hobday (1771-1831) arrived in Bristol about the time that this portrait was commissioned. He lived in Clifton for the next 14 years painting visitors and residents alike. He regularly advertised in the local press his 'Portrait Room' at 20 Small Street.

above:
'The village of Westbury, through which the road passes, is extremely pleasantly situated, and many families of fortune reside here.'
Villas near Westbury-on-Trym in an early-nineteenth-century watercolour. The long wooded ridge behind the houses suggests that this view shows the road from the Downs to the village, Henbury, and the New and Old Passages beyond. By 1807 Westbury-super-Trym, as it had often previously been called, was the home to many wealthy Bristol families, who had built houses and villas in and around the village.

above left:
Long Ashton, William West, oil on canvas. This rather stolid painting in the City Art Gallery (K1543) dates from the 1820s but shows a temporary market in the village of Long Ashton peopled by traders, farmers, pedlars and visitors from Bristol. On the remains of the market cross (now in the churchyard) a Bristol orange woman declaims her wares to two ladies. The village was a favourite destination for visitors from Hotwells in search of cream teas.

left:
Donkeys on the Downs, Charles Branwhite, 1846, oil on canvas
This painting by Branwhite in the City Art Gallery (K1295) shows two donkeys and their attendant waiting for customers on Durdham Down. The London-based James Malcolm was amazed to see a lady of quality riding a donkey here in June 1805. This is, so far, the earliest record of their use for pleasure at any resort in Britain, although by 1806 they were the latest craze at Brighton.

Sentence of Death: reporting crime

REPORTS IN THE LOCAL NEWSPAPERS OF NEW CRIMES AND COURT proceedings give us a good indication of the day-to-day felonies that were committed in the city. The following are typical, taken from the press throughout 1807:

CONVICTED

At our General Quarter-Sessions on Monday and Tuesday last, the following prisoners were tried & sentenced, viz,- Wm. Knight, for stealing a can, Richard Bird, flour, Thos. Cocum & Tho. Burton, a hat, Peter Williams, knives and forks, Henry Gibbons, cotton braces, Elizabeth Powell, glass, to be transported for 7 years; Rd. Collins, stealing sugar, 12 months in Bridewell; John Hudd, stealing flour, Edward Phillips, a watch, John Denny, carpenter's tools, Ann Lewis, calico, and Mary Jenkins, wearing apparel, 6 months in Bridewell; Isaac Rose, stealing deal plank, and Ann Jenkins, wearing apparel, 3 months imprisonment; Thos. Beavan, stealing sugar, and Job Russell, copper, were acquitted.
Felix Farley's Bristol Journal 17 January 1807

FORGERY

Caution – Several forged five-guinea Glocester bills, of the bank of Merrott and John Merrott Stephens, have appeared in Bristol and its neighbourhood; they are easily distinguished by the want of both stamp and water-mark.
Felix Farley's Bristol Journal 17 January 1807

BROTHEL KEEPING

At our Quarter-sessions last week, a bill of indictment was preferred by the Society for the Prevention and Suppression of

> During the very thick fogs which have covered this city for several days, three men walked into the river; one on Saturday night, on the Back, who was killed on the spot; the other two on Tuesday evening, one broke his leg, and the other was considerably bruised.
> On Monday last, during the time the workmen

Felix Farley's Bristol Journal 26 December 1807.

Vice, and a true bill was found by the Grand Jury against a man and his wife, for keeping a house of ill-fame, in Marlborough-street, both of whom have been committed to Newgate to answer the same.
Felix Farley's Bristol Journal 24 January 1807

ASSAULT

A lady of respectability was passing down Terril-street, in this city, on Thursday se'enight, she was assaulted by three boys, who spoiled her pelisse, and otherwise violently insulted her. The same lady had her pocket picked of her handkerchief in the Market-place on Saturday. The rude conduct of idle boys towards unprotected females in our streets, demands the immediate attention of the police officers.
Felix Farley's Bristol Journal 31 January 1807

LEAD STEALING

On the night of Thursday se'nnight, or early on Friday morning, some person or persons stole from the roof of the conduit adjoining St John's church, in this city, and from the roof of a monumental building in St John's church-yard, considerable quantities of sheet lead, and succeeded in carrying the same clear off. A reward has been offered for the offenders.
Bristol Mirror 7 February 1807

Wednesday last upwards of forty persons were convicted before the Magistrates of this city, in a penalty of 5s. each and costs, for not sweeping the pavement before their houses, under the act of the 28th Geo. III. which enacts, "That the " respective occupier and occupiers of all houses " and other buildings, and the churchwarden and " churchwardens of the respective churches, and " all and every persons and person having the " care of meeting-houses for religious worship, " and all and every keepers and keeper of halls, " and other public buildings and places within " the city of Bristol and liberties, shall well and " sufficiently scrape, sweep and cleanse the raised " footway or pavement, before his, her or their " respective houses, churches, meeting-houses, " halls, buildings, walls and premises, on every " day (Sundays excepted) between the hours of " eight and ten of the clock in the morning, upon " pain of forfeiting for every neglect the sum of " five shillings."

Henry Hicks, alias Locking, who escaped lately from justice, was a few days since apprehended at Milford, and Tuesday lodged in Newgate in this city.

Failure to sweep the pavement in front of one's property was an offence and resulted in a fine. Felix Farley's Bristol Journal 19 December 1807.

SHOPLIFTING AND LEAD STEALING

Much praise, we understand, is due to T. Evans, keeper of Bridewell, and Robert Harman, night-constable of Trinity Ward, for their exertions in apprehending a notorious set of thieves, who have for some months past infested this city, in shop-lifting, cutting off lead-pipes, &c.

Bristol Gazette 12 February 1807

PAVEMENT ABUSE

Eight persons have been convicted and fined before the Magistrates this week, for not sweeping the footway before their doors;

one person was fined 10s for laying ashes in the streets; and another person 10s. for running a truck on the footway.

Felix Farley's Bristol Journal 14 February 1807

DANGEROUS DRIVING

Friday last two waggoners belonging to Messrs. Castle, were fined by the magistrates at Failand's Inn, 20s. each, for driving their horses so furiously through Bedminster, as to endanger the lives of the passengers.

Bristol Mirror 7 March 1807

VANDALISM AND LIVESTOCK ABUSE

HENBURY ASSOCIATION FOR the Protection of Persons and Property.

WHEREAS, late last Night or early this Morning, some evil-disposed Person or Persons did commit several wanton and malicious Depredations on the Premises of Mr WM. TURNER, at HILL-END-HOUSE, in this Parish, by breaking and removing several Gates and Fences round the said Premises, and by driving upwards of 30 Sheep and Lambs from an adjoining Field into his Garden, and penning them therein, to the great injury thereof; also by removing several Hurdles surrounding a Plantation belonging to Mr THOMAS WILMOT, in the same parish. Whoever will give information, so that the Offender or Offenders may be apprehended shall receive a Reward of TWO GUINEAS, on application to EDW. SAMPSON, Esq. Solicitor to the said Association. In addition to the above, WM. TURNER offers a Reward of TWENTY GUINEAS, to be paid on conviction of the Person or Persons concerned, on application to the said Mr SAMPSON.

An Accomplice making a discovery shall be entitled to the above

Reward, and every means used to obtain a Pardon. Henbury, 14th April, 1807.
Bristol Gazette 16 April 1807

POULTRY THEFT
Tuesday morning between the hours of four and five o'clock, the premises of Mr Thomas Bratt, of Dove-street, in the out-parish of Saint James, were feloniously entered by a man, about five feet five inches high, who was discovered in the act of stealing and carrying away poultry from the fowl-house behind the dwelling-house.
Felix Farley's Bristol Journal 25 April 1807

INDELIBLE INK TO COMBAT PILFERING [Advertisement]
Pilfering is become so notorious, that it behoves all Seminaries, Families, Travellers and others, to adopt those measures which may most contribute to prevent or detect it. In the articles of Linen, Apparel, Silk and Cotton Stockings, table and bed Linen & this cannot be better effected than by marking such property with INDELIBLE INK, as prepared by J.Clarke, Chemist, Birmingham, the reputation of which has been established many years. – Sold by his appointment at Mr Talbot's, druggist; J.M. Gutch, Harris and Bryan, and at Mrs Shiercliff, stationer, in this city… at 2s.6d., 3s.6d and 4s. per case.
Felix Farley's Bristol Journal 18 July 1807

CONVICTED
At the general quarter-sessions on Monday, the following prisoners were tried, and received sentence, as under:
Wm. Bayley, for stealing shoes, Ann Whittington, for stealing linen from the dwelling-house of her mistress, at Bath, and James

Comer, stealing sugar from the floating-dock, to be transported for seven years; Job Bennett, stealing a bridle from his employer, confined six months in Bridewell, and privately whipt; David Johns, for assaulting and beating a Royal Bristol Volunteer, to be confined three months in Newgate, and pay a fine of 10l; Harriet Bray, stealing a silver watch, acquitted; and against John Howard, for receiving tobacco, knowing it to be stolen, no true bill was found.
Felix Farley's Bristol Journal 18 July 1807

HIGHWAY ROBBERY
At Glocester, John Harris, for stopping Mr B. Butt, of Westbury-upon-Trym, upon the highway near Bristol, and robbing him of his watch &c.; and Hester Haviland, for stealing wearing apparel from the dwelling-house of W. Smith in Painswick; received sentence of death… Hester Haviland is reprieved; but John Harris, whose crime was attended with acts of cruelty, and an attempt to murder Mr Butt, is left for execution.
Felix Farley's Bristol Journal 25 July 1807

SHOPLIFTING
A deaf and dumb man was detected a few days since in stealing a pair of gloves in a shop in Swansea, which he artfully threw into a dark passage, to prevent discovery. He was, however, afterwards suffered to depart, from pity for his infirmities.
Bristol Gazette 30 July 1807

HORSE STEALING
The Kingswood Diamond, or a Cut right and left.
About a week ago two gentlemen near Taunton lost each a valuable horse from the pasture in the neighbourhood. After

much trouble they traced them in the direction of Bristol, and suspecting that they might have strayed towards Kingswood, they hastened thither, and in their search found one of them grazing on Cock-road Common. The gentlemen seized the horse; as it was late in the evening, they did not think it prudent to bring it through the country, but led it to a neighbouring inn, secured it in the stable, and bespoke supper and beds for the night. In the morning they discovered that the stable-door had been forced, and not only the stolen horse carried off, but the two others which they had used in the pursuit, with saddles and bridles all together! Neither the horses nor the audacious felons have since been heard of, and the gentlemen returning home were congratulated by their friends, that they had not lost their boots and spurs.
Felix Farley's Bristol Journal 26 September 1807

BURGLARY
Robbery at Kingswood Hill
On Saturday morning, about one o'clock, the house of Mr Fussell, of Kingswood Hill, in the parish of Bitton, was broken open, and seventeen pounds, in Cash and Bills, with a silver watch, and half a dozen silver tea-spoons, one ditto table-spoon; one ditto punch-ladle, taken there from. The robbers have not yet been apprehended.
Bristol Mercury 5 October 1807

ACID ATTACK
TEN GUINEAS REWARD ('BLACK ACT')
WHEREAS, at sundry different times, at distant intervals, and lastly, in the dusk of the Evening of TUESDAY the 6th instant, some atrocious Ruffian did attempt to force himself into the House of a Gentleman in this City; and, on being refused admit-

tance by the Maid Servant, did assault, wound, and endeavour to maim her, by striking and throwing some corrosive and destructive Liquid upon her arms, face, neck and breast; Whoever will give any information (through the means of the Printer hereof) which shall lead to the detection, apprehension, and conviction of the said Ruffian, shall recieve TEN GUINEAS reward. And whereas by some words and threats dropped by the said Ruffian, there is reason to suspect that he has accomplices in his malevolent and nefarious designs; whoever will discover any person or persons instigating, aiding, abetting, or being party to or privy to the same, shall also receive the above offered Reward. The said Ruffian is a man about or rather above the middle size, near 40 years of age; was dressed on said 6th inst. in a light coloured coat, with velvet collar of same colour, round hat, and boots with clean tops; and has altogether the appearance of a gentleman's servant.
Felix Farley's Bristol Journal 10 October 1807

UNWELCOME CALLERS
CAUTION – As the winter is approaching, we would caution the servants of families which may be absent from home, as well as others, against admitting strangers within the street door, under pretense of speaking with their masters or mistresses. A few days ago two men called at the house of J. Savery, Esq. in Bedford Place, and finding that Mr Savery was from home, they desired to see Mrs Savery.- They were shown into the parlour, where Mrs S. and family were sitting, and informed her they called upon Mr S. respecting a house which he had to let at Bath. Mrs S. knowing this to be an untruth, took the alarm, and rung the bell with some precipitation; She informed them that Mr S. was at the next door, and ordered the servant to call him. The men were confused, and began to retire, hoping she was convinced it was not an excuse

which they had made for calling. Mrs S. followed them into the passage, and as they were retreating towards the door, one of them attempted to to lay hold of it, with the intention of shutting out the servant, who had gone for Mr S. when Mrs S. with much presence of mind, threw the door wide open, and very fortunately got rid of her unwelcome visitors. One of the fellows has lost an eye. They were of tall stature, and shabbily dressed. The same men, the following evening, attempted to enter a house at Kingsdown, in the absence of the family; but the servant maid very prudently spoke to them from the window, instead of opening the door, and they were again unsuccessful in their attempt. They wished her to permit them to write a note. A short sliding chain and bolt to the Street-door is a very excellent safe-guard.
Bristol Mercury 2 November 1807

TEENAGE BURGLARY GANG

James Porter stands committed to take his trial at Glocester, for breaking into the dwelling-house of Lydia Peuchy, in the out-parish of St Philip, with intention to rob the same. He was apprehended in the shop, with some goods in his possession, at five o'clock, on Tuesday morning, by the night watchman. He has confessed his intention to rob the shop, and has impeached 6 others as his accomplices, four of whom are in custody: They are all under 20 years of age. He also confesses that, in company with two others, he some time since broke into a dwelling-house in Wilder-street, from whence they carried off some articles without discovery.
Felix Farley's Bristol Journal 7 November 1807

BRISTOL TRAFFIC – WHAT POLICING?

Is not the Police of Bristol very deficient, and would it not be attended with considerable advantage, if some of the most useful

Newgate Prison, Hugh O'Neill. The back premises of the Keepers compartments in Newgate Prison. Described in 1775 as 'white without and foul within', Newgate was abandoned by 1820 for the new prison on the New Cut.

and prominent City Laws were placed at the corners of a few of the principal streets, and on some of the public buildings? Scarcely a day passes, but one sees waggons and carts driven at full speed through the streets, trucks wheeled on the pavement, and the excellent regulations of the city transgressed, to the damage and annoyance of the inhabitants. By such a plan, these laws would be generally known, and the fines and punishments avoided.

Letter to *Bristol Gazette* 12 November 1807 from W.N.

FORGERY

A forgery of the £2 notes of the Old City Bank of Messrs. Elton Edwards & Co. of this city, has this week been discovered to have been committed; it is so well executed as to deceive those best acquainted with the notes issued by this house. On a careful comparison of the arms on the forged notes, it will be found that they are not so much shaded as the others, and that the ship on the former wants her fore-top-mast stay; the engraver's name on the bad notes is also much larger than on the others. We understand that the forgery extends only to the £2. notes issued by this house.

Felix Farley's Bristol Journal 21 November 1807

INFANTICIDE

Sunday last, as some boys were throwing stones down a well behind the unfinished houses in Great George Street, near Brandon-hill, their attention was arrested by the appearance of something resembling a human form; which, on a further search, turned out to be the body of a female child, apparently about 6 weeks old. On being taken out of the well, it was conveyed to St Peters Hospital, where an inquest was afterwards held, and a verdict returned of – Wilful murder against some person or persons unknown.

Felix Farley's Bristol Journal 21 November 1807

THEFT OF TOOLS

On Monday last, during the time the workmen were at dinner, some person or persons stole from the top of the new warehouses, erecting in Nelson-street, belonging to Alderman Morgan, four handsaws, a large iron sledge, and sundry other tools belonging to the workmen.

Felix Farley's Bristol Journal 26 December 1807

After such a list it is good to record that there were honest citizens and visitors within the city still as the following advertisement proves:

FOUND, BETWEEN the New-passage and Bristol, a POCKET BOOK containing CASH NOTES.

Whoever can give a proper description of it, may have the same, by applying to Mr TURNER, White-Hart Inn, Broad-Street, Bristol.

Felix Farley's Bristol Journal 4 July 1807

Shut up the public houses: religion

Methodism is so prevalent in Bristol, that there are no less than nine Chapels for the followers of the Doctrines and discipline of the late Rev Messrs, Whitfield and Wesley: most of which are large, and all of them crouded at times of meeting. Some of the Clergy of the Church patronize and promulge these Doctrines; and none else are so popular and well attended as the numerous Congregations of St James's, St Maryport, and St Werburgh, fully prove. Sermons are not only preached in the Town, within doors, but frequently in Summer, given gratis in the streets, by inspired and vociferous Orators, who voluntarily expose themselves for the good of the Public.

There is something remarkable in the observation of the Sabbath here. At nine o'clock in the morning, the Tenor bells of all the Parish Churches are risen, rung for a knell for half an hour, and fallen; then the Bells in each Tower are chimed for some time, which, from about 20 Churches, make a very solemn jingling; these are succeeded by small Bells, which toll the people into Church. The same commences at Two in the Afternoon. Just after the beginning of Divine Service, the Constables of each Ward go about their respective Districts, to rid and shut up the Public-houses.

The Bristol Guide, Bristoliensis. 1815

… It has too often been our melancholy task to record the awful Visitations of Providence on Sabbath-breakers: A new instance occurred last Sunday week. A youth of the age of 14 years, fell from a high wall, which he had ascended to take a bird's nest, on that sacred day, when he ought to have been better employed, and

St John's Church, Broad Street and St John's Conduit by Edward Bird. In January 1807 thieves stole lead from the roof. Until the passage to the left of the picture was cut, many pedestrians were killed by vehicles in the gateway.

151

Charles Calvert, Esq.
There has been a good deal of rioting at Bristol
and Liverpool. At the former place, Mess. Bathurst
and Baillie were elected without opposition, and
chaired, but they were so annoyed by the cries of
" No Popery," that they were obliged to descend,
and take shelter in the nearest house. A similar spirit having been manifested at Liverpool, Mr Roscoe
resolved to decline the contest, but his friends de-

fractured his skull in so shocking a manner, that he expired at the Infirmary on Thursday last, after four days of severe suffering, to the great distress of his afflicted parents...
Bristol Gazette, 4 June 1807

DISINTERESTED PIETY, A gentleman who employs a great number of hands in a manufactory in the West of England, in order to encourage his work people in a due attendance at Church, on a late Fast-day, told them, that 'if they went to church, they should receive their wages for that day, in the same manner as if they had been at work.' Upon which a deputation was appointed to acquaint their employer, that 'if he would pay them for over hours, they would attend likewise at the Methodist chapel in the evening!'
Bristol Mirror, 22 August 1807

above left:
Better Late than Never. From *Trusler's Proverbs Exemplified*, 1790.

left:
The Aberdeen Journal 20 May 1807
'rioting at Bristol and Liverpool'
Anti-Catholic prejudice was still very strong in Britain especially amongst the lower classes. Although the establishment had softened and passed the Roman Catholic Relief Act of 1791, strong resentment would persist amongst some sections of the populace for many years following.

Fashion: from Bombazeen to Bum-be-seen

Vauxhall Fashions, August 1806 from *La Belle Assemblée*.

It has been frequently observed, that formerly, the Ladies of Bristol were noted for homeliness of person, and an ungraceful appearance. It is difficult to account for such a native and universal ugliness and deformity as have heretofore been their characteristics. These attributions might possibly be, as many other local reflections and stigmas are, utterly groundless, but whether so or not, at present the contrary is absolutely the case. Many of the Fair Sex here are truly fair, and England cannot produce finer and more beautiful woman than the city of Bristol.
The Bristol Guide, Bristoliensis 1815

THE WRITER OF THE SHORT STORY *ONE HOUR AFTER MARRIAGE* (see page 63) in the 1770 volume of the *Town and Country Magazine* who refers to Bristol as the 'very fag end of fashion' was no doubt a Londoner. His main victim was the Bristol male, but by the early years of the next century things had changed. James Malcolm found the male inhabitants equal in style to those of the Capitol.

His impression of the women of Bristol and their sense of fashion was less flattering and he considered that they lacked even the style of London servants.

In 1807 the classically inspired styles based on the Grecian model were still high fashion. Generally the introduction of this classical style 'imitating the drapery of pictures and statues' has been attributed in histories of fashion to Lady Charlotte Campbell in 1793.

However, in 2005 whilst preparing an exhibition for the Reference Library entitled 'Divine Emma, Lady Hamilton a Tribute in Words and Pictures' I came across a hitherto unrecorded article

How to measure a gentleman. John Biss' instructions to servants ordering their master's new clothes from abroad.

'Walking and full dresses for the summer months.'

French laces, veils and handkerchiefs, and a great variety of fans: Mr Simeon's immense stock of goods must be sold off immediately.

A positive and valuable SALE of French LACES, &c.
AT AND UNDER PRIME COST.

MR. SIMEON, respectfully informs the public, that his whole immense Stock of Fashionable Goods must be sold off immediately, *at* and *under* prime cost, declining the retail trade; and as the premises are to be cleared in a very short time, the Sale will be totally unreserved.

Mr. S. having lately imported and purchased all the under-mentioned articles, they are warranted perfectly fresh, good, and fashionable:—Mechlen, Valenciennes, Lisle, Normandy, and other FRENCH LACES; VEILS and HANDKERCHIEFS, black and white, in great variety; durable Cotton Laces and Edgings, warranted to wear well; Silk and Cotton Veils, Handkerchiefs, &c. UMBRELLAS, on an improved plan, of every description; and a great variety of Fans.

⁂ *The House and Shop to be Let, and entered on immediately.*

French Lace Warehouse, and Bristol Umbrella Manufactory, 56, Wine street.

in *The Times* for 3 May 1793 that gave its true origin and that stated that Emma had promoted it before it became fashionable in England. In fashion she was an early exponent if not the originator of high waisted classical Greek dress so typical of the late Georgian era. It was developed from the simple 'antique' way in which Sir William had dressed her on her arrival in Naples. 'Sir William and his Lady are passionately fond of Grecian models, and she has attempted to introduce the dress and manners of those people, but in vain...'

Emma – who as Mrs Hart, *The Times* of 31 August 1791 had called 'The most accomplished and fascinating woman in England' – was also the inventor of the pad. This notorious item of underclothing was placed below the breasts and gave a new high waisted 'Grecian' outline to the female figure but also suggested pregnancy in the minds of others. It secured the popularity of the Grecian style: 'Lady Hamilton had no followers until she rased the pad, which is in imitation of the Grecian Venus, who is described by painters with a remarkable high zone.' Not surprisingly this led to a farce at Covent Garden called 'The Pad' and a bevy of satirical cartoons. Amusingly the high waist of the Greek fashions were to disguise her pregnancies later in life. Emma's ex-lover Greville, writing after her London visit said that the Court was full of bad imitations of her Grecian dress.

It is quite likely that these bad imitations percolated down to provincial dressmakers. The essence of the style was simplicity and those same women of the court circle who had adopted Emma's style and gradually adapted it were later to criticise her everyday dress as being tasteless and overloaded. It had no doubt been forgotten that the simple classical styles they so admired had originated with her. Malcolm's criticism of Bristol women's style may well have stemmed from just this sort of love of expensive finery and show.

Women's journals such as *The Lady's Monthly Museum* or *Polite Repository Of Amusement and Instruction*, contained amongst other things hand-coloured fashion plates to alert the women of Britain to whatever important innovation was expected in their dress that season. They are of course now a major research tool.

Newspapers also included fashions for the month:

FASHIONS FOR OCTOBER, 1807
English Costume
LADY'S DRESS. A round gown with a short train, ornamented at the feet with flutings of muslin or needle-work; a long sleeve rucked, with full top; frock back, and lapelled bosom cut low and trimmed with scalloped lace. A chapeau à la bocage of imperial chip or sarsnet, ornamented with a wreath of ivy or jonquille; a single sprig of the same in front of the bosom in lieu of a brooch. A shawl of Chinese silk, thrown negligently over the shoulders. Hair in a single band across the forehead, relieved by loose curls in front and at the sides. Hoop earrings of amber or cornelian. Straw-coloured kid gloves and shoes.

CHILD'S DRESS. A frock and trousers of fine cambric, bordered at the bottom in rich fancy Vandyke; French back, and bosom cut very low, and ornamented with the same; Circassian sleeve very short. The Moorish boot, or high pomposa, of bright yellow kid, laced with purple. Sash to correspond, tied in short bows and ends behind.
Bristol Mirror, 3 October 1807

The Bristol newspapers joined in the general disbelief at the state of women's costume in the country:

> Much is said about the scanty drapery of the Fair Sex, when it is well known that Sin and Dress began their career at the same time:
> When Eve first put her cov'ring on,
> Her Robe of Innocence was gone!
> *Felix Farley's Bristol Journal*, 21 November 1807

A coloured engraving called *The Fashion of the Day or Time Past and Time Present* drawn by Woodward and Published in London in the same month contrasted modern dress with that of the 1740s. 'The year (1740) a Ladys full dress of Bombazeen – The year (1807) a Ladys undress of Bum-be-seen.'

A fake 'lost and found' advertisement from Clara Candid appeared in *Felix Farley's Bristol Journal* on 27 June 1807:

> Lost or stolen from the subscriber, some time in December last, a *Maiden's Modesty*. It was first missed in Mr _ _ 's Ball-room, where a number of ladies were rifled of that jewel by a certain personage, well known by the name of *fashion*, long suspected of being an arrant *Thief*, and even a *Murderer*; although he is a favourite with genteel company. With her *modesty* the subscriber also lost her *shawl* and *handkerchief*, and the bosom of her gown, which had been plundered of its sleeves the season before. Since the loss of this valuable article, the loser has suffered some decay of *health*, a considerable degree of *scandal*, a great increase of male esteem, and probably some waste or want of *prudence* and *virtue*; all of which she can but attribute to

that insidious and seductive villain, *Fashion*, who has often times before imposed upon her the great hardships, and oppressed her with the greatest rigour. Though the caitiff stole the modesty of many others about the same time, and very strict search has been made ever since to recover the property, but little of it has been obtained; and we are threatened with the ruin or loss of everything valuable about us, if the ravages of the monster are not prevented. It is hoped, therefore, that every lover of good order will interest himself in the detection and arrest of this public disturber, before he corrupts both the manners of the risen and rising generations. On my part, as an incitement of vigilance in apprehending the villain, I promise to whomsoever shall return the stolen and missing goods to me, the uncovered bosom, the *loud laugh*, the *shameless countenance*, & the impudent demeanour I have been obliged to exhibit ever since the loss of my proper apparel, with a few colds, aches, stitches, & c, I have taken in my new dress, as a reward for trouble; with the hearty and sincere thanks of their beguiled friend and humble servant, CLARA CANDID

The local press was also full of advertisements for beauty aids for local ladies including on 9 May one in *Felix Farley's Bristol Journal* for Bagazet's Oriental Depilatory, for removing SUPERFLUOUS HAIRS from the Face, Neck, Arms etc. It was reported to have been introduced to Britain from Turkey by the famous oriental traveller Lady Mary Wortley Montague in the mid-eighteenth century, and in 1807 was still imported from there. It was claimed to be used by the Turks to keep their moustaches trimmed.

All other aspects of feminine attire and essentials were available in the city's shops. Bristol was well known for its straw hat manufacturing and supply. Paramount amongst such retailers was Miss Hopton, chip and straw hat manufacturer of 41 Bridge Street and Oxford Street, London. Miss Hopton claimed to be the supplier to Queen Charlotte and the Royal Princesses. Tortoiseshell, ivory and horn combs could be had from Mr Tully at 24 Maryport Street together with tooth, nail and hair brushes, whilst Mr Simeon at the Bristol Parasol Manufactory at 56 Wine Street could always be relied upon to have secured the best fringes and silks from London.

Men were less well served than women by fashion plates and advice, unless pictured accompanying them in the illustrations, but occasionally received guidance in the journals. A particularly rare survival in the library's collection is a watercolour drawing and hand-written instructions from about 1807 on how to measure a gentleman for a suit of clothes. This was produced by the Bristol tailor John Biss of 32 Corn Street (B22763). The manuscript was intended for engraving and distribution abroad so that 'by the above plan a Gentleman may be measured by his servant with the greatest accuracy' and clothes despatched 'in the best and most fashionable style and on moderate terms.' It was indeed an early form of clothing by mail order.

The *Bristol Mirror* of 4 April did proffer information as to the fashionable colours for coats in that season:

GENTLEMEN'S DRESSES.——Blue coats, with black velvet collars, are quite the rage. Velvet collars are now not only general on blue coats, but on olive and dark green coats, which are likewise becoming extremely prevalent; these are however, the only colours on which the velvet collars are used for evening coats; the blue coat has, of course, a flat gilt button (of which is termed the standard colour, gold,) but all other evening coats have covered buttons. The morning dress is fluctuating; scarlet waist-coats are on the increase; and we doubt not, will obtain some preference during the present month. Coats, breeches, and pantaloons, seem to continue much the same; indeed the severity of the weather rends a great coat more and more necessary, which does the opportunity of displaying any particular taste in the close coat. Olive brown great coats are still the most in favour, and the silk skirt-lining is generally adopted. Velvet collars and lappel facings do not, however, keep pace with the silk skirts.

A catalogue of the trials to which a gentleman might be subject to in order to make himself presentable to society are listed with due solemnity by the author of *The Miseries of Human Life*. Only a few are given here but many are still just as pertinent today.

> After putting on your clean shirt, finding the two bottom buttons of the collar minus…)
>
> A coat tight and short in the sleeves
>
> Mis-buttoning your waistcoat, (which you do not discover till you have gone into company,)- so that the bottom button seems to be sent to Coventry by the rest, wringing the shoulder by the tug on that side
>
> The points of the knee-buckle curving outwards, instead of inwards; and so raking your leg, and tearing your stocking, every time you cross your legs
>
> In dressing to dine out- Your last shoe string breaking- one knee buckle lost- the wrong coat brushed- hole found in your stocking after you are dressed, & &- all this, and

WALKING DRESSES

FULL DRESS

R.Sands. del. et sc.

Published May 1 1806 by Vernor Hood & Sharp Poultry

Walking and full dress for May 1806.

much more, invariably coming upon you like hail, at the moment when you are most belated

Brushing your own coat, on an emergency, and perceiving, as you get on that every rub completely fixes in, instead of fetching out, the powder with which it is covered

Loudly bursting three or four buttons of your waist-coat, and the strings of your pantaloons behind in fetching a deep sigh!- dead silence in the company, at the moment of the melancholy explosion

The sudden necessity of going to a shoe-maker's shop, on the desperate enterprise of trying to suit yourself, extempore, with a pair of ready-made boots; then, after dragging on and off his whole stock in trade, without once approaching to the mark, being fated to shuffle, or hobble away, in a pair which you seem to have stolen.

Occupational and vernacular costume for 1807 is best studied in W H Pyne's *Costume of Great Britain* that was published the following year. This remarkable volume, with its hand-coloured aquatint plates, covers all sorts of professional costume and varied aspects of contemporary life from dustmen and knife grinders to the national lottery and Guy Fawkes celebrations. Most of the trade costumes, street sellers, pedlars and vehicles found in the book would have been seen in the streets of Bristol.

Hungry and bare-foot
Poverty and its alleviation

The Beggar Girl

Over the mountain and over the moor,
Hungry and bare-foot, I wander forlorn,
My father is dead and my mother is poor,
And she grieves for the days that will never return.
Pity, kind gentlemen! Friends of humanity!
Cold blows the wind, and the night's coming on,
Give me some food, for my mother in charity,
Give me some food, and then I will be gone.
The Old Bath Songster

WITH A HISTORY OF GREAT PRIVATE BENEVOLENCE TO THE POOR GOING back some 500 years, Bristol was well furnished with almshouses, hospitals and wealthy charities to alleviate distress. Many merchants and others had left large sums from their fortunes to charitable organisations set up to commemorate their names and to benefit the most helpless of their fellow citizens. The charities gradually came under the aegis of the Bristol Corporation as the council was then called, and by the early years of the nineteenth century were producing an annual income of £13,000 per annum. Inevitably there were charges of corruption levelled against the Corporation for presumed misuse of the funds which resulted in the Municipal Corporations Act of 1835. This set up the Bristol Charities to manage the vast network of properties and funds that had accumulated. In 1807 more than thirty almshouses existed as well as charity schools and the asylums for the blind and orphan girls. The two main hospitals for the poor were St Peter's in St Peter's Street and the Bristol Royal Infirmary. St

Peter's was the general hospital, or charitable institution, for the poor of the whole city. The 1804 *Bristol Guide* informs us that it also catered for superannuated persons, orphans and idiots:

> and has a ward for lunatics. Vagrants and beggars are taken up and sent hither. The building is ancient and very spacious, and was the mansion of Thomas Norton, Esq M.P. for Bristol, in 1399; afterwards it was the Mint for coinage of money, which is now its most general title.

It became the hospital in the eighth year of William III's reign. The *Bristol and Hotwell Guide* of 1805 tells us more:

> It is under the direction of a Governor, Deputy-Governor, Treasurer, and other Officers. Besides these there are an Apothecary, Chaplain, Master, Matron, Clerk, Officers, Baker, Brewer, &c. There are also many inferior officers and attendants. For the support of this hospital an annual assessment is made on the several parishes in Bristol.

The Bristol Royal Infirmary was opened in 1737 as a result of the charitable efforts of a group of well disposed persons who, reflecting upon the miseries and hardships to which the poor and labouring men of Bristol were exposed in the case of accident and disease, determined to establish an institution for their medical needs. The 1805 guide continues:

> BRISTOL INFIRMARY, situate in Marlborough-street, St James's, a handsome, spacious and lofty building, wanting a south wing. This charity is supported by subscription, and is conducted on the most liberal plan. Here all real

Child match-sellers by JT Smith.

objects from any part of the world, who have the misfortune to meet with accidental injuries, are immediately admitted without any recommendation whatever, and all proper objects recommended by a subscriber, are admitted on Monday and Thursday weekly, and every assistance and comfort administered to alleviate their distress. The ablest physicians and surgeons attend regularly, and there is an apothecary in the house, who is supplied with every kind of medicine of the best quality. The provisions and all other necessaries are the best that can be procured; and proper nurses are appointed to take care of the sick. A charity so universal and benevolent, cannot fail to claim support from every individual possessed of ability, who has any feeling for the sufferings of humanity.

The Bristol Dispensary on Castle Green was founded in 1775. Its main objective was to provide medical officers to give advice at the dispensary or visit the sick in their own homes and then to supply all needed medicines. The other main aim was to provide assistance during 'lying in' to poor married women. The dispensary was funded by subscribers who could then recommend deserving cases requiring assistance.

The problem of the poor in the city was however greater than all these well-meaning organisations could cope with. Although officially outlawed, beggars were rife. Many were unfortunate servicemen maimed in the current war or in earlier conflicts. Some black sailors took to wearing model ships on their hats to show that they had once fought for Britain. Much the same situation with ex-service men cut adrift from the forces after a conflict

'All in full bloom!' *The artificial flower seller* and *the Staffordshire chinaman.* JT Smith.

far right: Spencer's almshouses erected 1493. JS Prout.

still exists today, but then it was even more desperate. The numbers of beggars in 1807 prompted a visitor to write a letter of complaint to the editor of the *Bristol Mirror*.

Sir – Having been obliged to come to Bristol to transact some business, I could not avoid being struck by the number of beggars with which your city is infested. Curiosity induced me to make a minute of them, and here is the list.

Imprimis, A tall dirty-looking fellow, with a small hat, and a large sack at his back.

Item, Three mutilated sailors, one on each pavement, and the third in the middle of the street.

Item, A short fellow with one leg, and an old soldier's jacket and cap, shouldering a crutch.

Item, A fellow, paralytic, or pretending to be so, whose body and crutch form precisely the angle of the letter A.

Item, A sailor, a great part of whose thigh has been removed, exposing the remainder by sitting upon the pavement, especially at the door of the theatre.

Item, A sailor with 3 or 4 pidgeons upon his head.

Item, A negro with a ship fastened to his hat.

Item, A lad who having lost both his hands, attracts a crowd by picking up, with his stumps, such halfpence as are thrown to him.

Item, A man with a petition pinned to his breast, and

a lighted candle in his hand.

Item, A man with a red garter twisted round a shrivelled leg.

Item, A lad who asks you 'If you know of ever a place for a poor boy?'

Item, A lad who walks upon his knees with two short sticks, one in each hand.

Item, An Irishman, six feet and a half high, who desires the passengers to <u>look down</u> with an eye of pity upon the poor blind.

Item, But I will trouble you with no more items, otherwise the females would swell the account to a column! Now, Sir, I have heard the magistracy very freely abused, for suffering these nuisances, and I cannot myself think them altogether blameless; but the chief cause of beggary is not with the police, but with the public; for as long as the people are fools enough to give, there will always be knaves holding out their hands to receive.

A TRAVELLER

Vagabondiana, a rare illustrated survey of the types of beggars as seen and drawn in the London of 1815 by John Thomas Smith is in the Bristol Reference Library's Stuckey Lean collection (3657). It is pertinent to Bristol and contains an illustration of a black ex-sailor wearing a ship hat.

Not everyone of course was a professional beggar. Many were thrown on to the streets through the death of husbands and fathers. The newspapers are full of deaths caused by road accidents or work-related tragedies that often resulted in ruin to the whole family. The thick fogs experienced when weather combined with the city's pollution also killed many who either

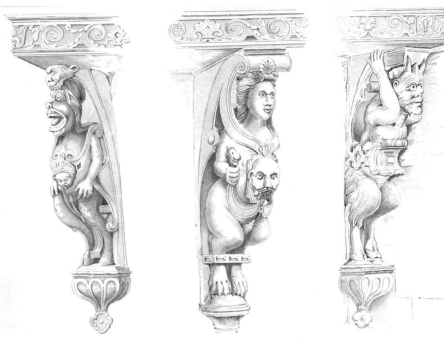

Carved brackets from the façade of St Peter's Hospital. Hugh O'Neill.

walked off the dock walls or fell under vehicles. A serious illness contracted by the bread-winner in the family could also result in disaster as could a woman's 'fall from grace'.

Goldsmith's poem, *The Deserted Village* tells of such a fall and sees the unfortunate condemned to sleeping on the streets,

Now lost to all, her friends, her virtue fled,
Near her betrayer's door she lays her head

The trade stagnation caused by the war resulted in bankruptcies in the city and previously prosperous individuals could find themselves destitute. The lines from another verse of the song *The Beggar Girl* that opened this section are particularly pertinent:

O think while you revel so careless and free,
   Secure from the wind and well cloathed and fed;
    Should fortune so change it, how hard would it be
To beg at a door for a morsel of bread

One particularly sad case was that of the Bristol sugar refiner and merchant William Gravenor. For him 1807 was a disaster. In September he was made bankrupt. By November his house, 14 Berkeley Square, was up for sale. All his household goods, including mahogany furniture and blue-and-white Staffordshire ware and Venetian carpets were also to be auctioned off. As if this were not enough his wife died in November as well. So those few months had seen him lose his business, his home, his wife and his liberty as he was incarcerated for debt. His wife Elizabeth came from the St Albyn family of Alfoxton in Somerset. William and Elizabeth's grandson, Langley, had inherited this estate in 1806. One wonders if William received any assistance from his relatives.

Occasionally those who had met with a reversal of fortune would advertise for situations, as did the anonymous farmer 'of respectable family' in *Felix Farley's Bristol Journal* of 14 February 1807, who wished for an engagement as a steward or manager of an estate.

Basic human emotions and relationships change very little over the centuries even if some ages and customs now seem either very brutal or cruel. Generally all stories of misfortune that one finds in the newspapers are written in a sympathetic style. There are various unselfish acts of kindness listed from ordinary Bristolians towards the less fortunate that illustrate that many had tender hearts and possessed as much humanity, if not more, than contemporary Britons. Malcolm in his account mentions the elderly Turk who was aided with an unsolicited gift of money from a lady in a carriage. Winter weather generally killed many on the streets and surrounding countryside, and two such occasions and the resulting actions of total strangers are chronicled in the local press:

On Tuesday a very deep snow fell in the vicinity of this city and the neighbouring counties. A poor old woman, on the Bath road, was found almost frozen to death, by the way side. She was conveyed to the first house, and by the well-meant, but imprudent humanity of some cottagers, placed close to a warm fire. She almost instantly died.
Felix Farley's Bristol Journal, 12 December 1807

Monday last a poor wretched woman was discovered sitting by the side of the turnpike-road, on Durdham Down, faint, apparently by disease, and shivering with the cold. Her forlorn and wretched appearance had attracted the attention and excited the sympathy of a gentleman walking that way; in the mean time a lady, who was driving along in her carriage, desired the coachman to stop, and alighting, wrapped up the poor shivering creature in a warm shawl, then assisting to raise her into the carriage, drove off with her towards town. The name of the fair philanthropist has not yet transpired.
Felix Farley's Bristol Journal, 19 December 1807

No ally in the world: Bristol at War

FROM 1796 THE PROSPECT THAT THE FRENCH MIGHT TRY TO INVADE and spread their republicanism throughout Albion galvanised Britain into a fever of self defence. The desire to arm the entire country arose and in Bristol on 18 February 1797, *Felix Farley's Bristol Journal* announced the formation of a body of 'provisional cavalry'. A number of merchants and tradesmen entered into association with the aim of guarding the 2,000 French prisoners-of-war held at Stapleton in the event that the existing militia should be sent away on active service. The corps was to be of Infantry and 1,000 strong. The name, the Bristol Volunteers, was chosen and at the founding meeting in the Guildhall, a fund was started to provide uniforms for the less wealthy volunteers. The mayor became the Hon Colonel and the two Lieutenant Colonels were Evan Baillie and William Gore. When, four days after the meeting, the French landed 1,400 troops in Pembrokeshire in what turned out to be a farcical invasion attempt, the urgency of the situation became apparent, as did the inefficiency of the navy in preventing an invasion. A second but ultimately spurious invasion was reported in March whilst the regiment was still unarmed and caused a great fuss in the city, with £100 collected amongst the crowds on College Green to aid the regiment. Soon the corps was joined by a cavalry regiment called the Bristol Light Horse Volunteers and two small corps based on Clifton and Westbury. The uniform of the Volunteers is captured in a water-colour in the Library's Braikenridge collection and also on Gore's magnificent tomb by Thomas Tyley of Bristol in the north transept of Bristol Cathedral, where two insouciantly elegant and life-sized soldiers relax. Gore was also painted in 1804 in his scarlet uniform by S F Downman of Bath, and a coloured aquatint produced.

In September of 1797 Admiral Nelson was awarded the freedom of the city for his successes against the French, but the vulnerability of the Bristol Channel to enemy shipping worried the citizens and a battery at the mouth of the Avon near Portishead was commenced, and provided with four large cannon for firing red-hot shot. It was finished in 1799.

In July 1806 Britain triumphed against Napoleon at the battle of Maida in Calabria, Italy. In Bath Mr John Ashley composed a stirring military song 'England's King and England's Glory' to commemorate this battle. The song was sung by the celebrated operatic tenor John Braham at Drury Lane 'with great applause', and no doubt in Bristol as well by others. It was published in April of the following year.

By 1807 the Napoleonic war had caused much interuption to the growth of trade in Bristol. The previous year Napoleon had passed a Decree of Blockade against Britain to cripple manufacturers and merchants. Shipping was constantly endangered by French privateers, both on the high seas and in the Bristol Channel. Trade with Europe had been seriously affected and the war entered a new phase following the Treaties of Tilsit in July. The treaties saw Napoleon make peace with Russia and Prussia and thus left Britain isolated in Europe. A putative petition to the King to also make peace with Napoleon was suggested by the merchants of Sheffield, but roundly condemned by the *Bristol Mercury* on 2 November 1807, saying 'nothing would so much disincline Bonaparte to make an honourable Peace with us as the concession on our parts that the situation of our Commerce has made Peace desirable and necessary to us.' The country prepared for a war of attrition and a renewal of the fear of invasion.

Bristol was full of military uniforms at this period with visiting regiments and those stationed around the city. It would have quite unsettled Lydia Bennett as it no doubt did others of both sexes in the city who were susceptible to uniforms. There are a number of marriage announcements in the local press between officers and ladies either living in or visiting the town. Regiments were reviewed on the Downs or in Queen Square, and military bands played music for the promenaders on College Green. The empty shells of the failed speculative houses in Royal York Crescent were partially converted into a barracks, whilst other encampments sprung up elsewhere in the surrounding countryside. Presumably there was a naval presence also in the area, although little is mentioned in the local press. Regimental anniversaries were celebrated in the city and Trafalgar Day saw the churches' steeples decorated with flags, like ships' masts, in the time-honoured Bristol custom. A rare survival in the library collection, and only discovered during the mounting of the 1807 exhibition, is the sealed document and covering letter from the

Members of the Royal Bristol Volunteers on Thomas Tyley's splendid, but sadly damaged, monument to William Gore in Bristol Cathedral. This is Bristol's finest artistic link with the Napoleonic wars.

Merchant Venturers granting the freedom of the City to Cuthbert, Lord Collingwood, who took charge of the English Fleet following the death of Nelson in 1805.

Like the rest of the country Bristol was saddened at the disastrous land campaign in South America but jubilant at the results of the naval Battle of Copenhagen against the Danish fleet in September.

The French prisoners at Stapleton Prison caused some annoyance to the local straw-plaiting industry, as they carried on the trade clandestinely, both to earn money for comforts and to pass the time in captivity. Two ornamental straw marquetry boxes are known that must have been produced at the prison and sold to visitors. One was in the Lloyd collection of prisoner-of-war work and the other is in the Bristol City Art Gallery collection. Both have views of the Dower House in Stoke Park, Stapleton, near the prison.

In 1805 the new prison at Stapleton had been completed providing accommodation for another 3,000 prisoners. This made the total there 5,000. The accommodation was said to be the equivalent of eight prison ships and the arrangements the most convenient of any prison in England.

The problem of prisoners escaping was a real one and sometimes, as in 1807, the guards could be bribed or persuaded to aid an escape. Sergeant Buckingham of the North Gloucester regiment had allowed a prisoner called Dare to escape early in the year. His ultimate fate is unknown but may be guessed at. Occasionally duels took place between the inmates using makeshift weapons. On 25 March 1808 a double duel resulted in the deaths of two prisoners. However, at the Gloucester Assizes the victors were acquitted of manslaughter.

A handbill warning of the horrors of a Napoleonic invasion. John Weeks' scrapbook.

A Year At War

PRIVATEERS

The Adventure, Jackson, from this port to Galway, is put back, having sprung a leak. On 29th ult. about 20 leagues westward of Lundy, was chased by a lugger privateer, when three vessels hove in sight, who bore down upon and boarded the Adventure, and proved to be the Serpent sloop of war and a frigate, with a French cutter privateer of 18 guns, captured the day before; after which they proceeded in pursuit of the lugger.

Bristol Mirror, 7 February 1807

TRADE WITH RUSSIA

We are happy to hear, that a Commercial Treaty is now upon the tapis between this country and Russia, by which the produce of our colonies, notwithstanding all the vengeful efforts of Bonaparte, is likely to have an extensive and ready market.

Felix Farley's Bristol Journal, 14 February 1807

SERGEANT BUCKINGHAM

Buckingham, a serjeant in the North Glocester militia, who was accessary to the escape of a French prisoner at Stapleton, some time since, was brought into this city on Monday last from Spithead, where he had entered on board a man of war.

Felix Farley's Bristol Journal, 14 February 1807

TRAINING ACT

We present our Readers with the following Abstract of the most material parts of the Training Act, for the execution of which directions have been issued by Government.

PERSONS LIABLE

All persons between the ages of 18 and 45, and liable to serve in

John Ashley of Bath's patriotic song that was published in 1807. It was sung to much acclaim by John Braham at Drury Lane.

the Militia, are liable to be trained and exercised under this Act. Also persons of the following descriptions, although exempt from serving in the Militia, viz. Articled Clerks or Apprentices, Persons employed in Docks, or Dock-yards, Tower of London, Woolwich Warren, gun-wharfs, at Portsmouth, Powder Mills and Store-houses, under the direction of the Board of Ordnance. Also persons being free of the Company of Waterman of the River Thames; poor persons having more than one child born in wedlock; persons serving by substitute in the Militia, or under any act or acts for raising any additional force for the defence of the Realm.

PERSONS EXEMPT

All licensed teachers of any separate congregation in holy orders, and not exercising any other trade except that of a schoolmaster; and all medical men actually practising as such, and being house-keepers, to be exempt from the operation of the Act, so long as they shall respectively continue within any of the descriptions aforesaid.

NUMBERS TO BE RAISED

His Majesty may raise any number, not exceeding 200,000 men, to be found by the Counties of England and Wales...
Bristol Mercury, 23 March 1807

THE STATE OF THE NAVY

ROYAL NAVY. — It appears from an authentic memoir that, in the year 1518, under Edward VI. The number of vessels was 53, and the tonnage 433,226. —In 1805, the vessels were 949, and in the present year about 1,200.

By the official report of the distribution of the British Naval Force, down to this day, it appears that there are now at sea, 83 sail of the line, seven ships from 50 to 44 guns, 121 frigates, 144 sloops, and 168 gun-brigs, &c. making a total of 523 ships of war, exclusive of those in ordinary, building, repairing, &c.
Bristol Gazette, 4 June 1807

ALONE IN EUROPE

We have now no friend, no support, no ally in the world, but our own courage and heroism.
Another year!-another deadly blow!
Another mighty Empire overthrown!
And we are left, or shall be left, alone.
The last that dares to struggle with the foe.
'Tis well! from this day forward we shall know
That in ourselves our safety must be sought;
That by our own right hand it must be wrought,
That we must stand unpropp'd or be laid low.

But if the difficulties of the times are unexampled, let the energies to meet them be equally vigorous; let us reflect that our existence as a free people is at stake; let there be no paltering for gain and office among our leaders; for, if the predominance of a party, instead of the preservation of the whole; if petty interests, and not the general weal; if the triumph of factions, rather than the honour of the country, is to be sought for, the game is already lost, and wretched indeed are the people who are under the guidance of such Statesmen...
Extract from a patriotic editorial *Felix Farley's Bristol Journal*, 18 July 1807

GOOD TIDINGS

Ship News. It is with pleasure we inform our readers of the safe arrival of the whole of the Jamaica fleet belonging to this port,

on Wednesday morning last; the remainder amounting to 165 have also reached their destinations in safety.
Felix Farley's Bristol Journal, 18 July 1807

CELEBRATIONS IN QUEEN SQUARE

Monday last the statue of King William, in Queen-square, was decorated by order of the Officers, &c. of the Lancashire Militia, quartered in this city, with orange and purple ribbons, being the anniversary of the battle of the Boyne, in which a corps of Lancastrians distinguished themselves under the command of Lord Stanley
Felix Farley's Bristol Journal, 18 July 1807

EMBARGO

Ship-News. The orders for laying an EMBARGO upon vessels of every description (except King's ships, and vessels employed in the service of the revenue) were yesterday received at this port. Similar orders have, we understand, been transmitted to all the sea ports throughout the kingdom.
Felix Farley's Bristol Journal, 25 July 1807

TOO MUCH SUGAR

Monday August 10. WEST-INDIA TRADE

Mr Magans rose to call the attention of the House to the present state of the West-India trade. The price of the commodities imported from the West India Colonies was not augmented in proportion to the great increase of the duties laid upon them. The price was, nevertheless, so high, as to check the home consumption, at a time when the exportation of foreign countries was almost absolutely prevented. The consequence was, that there was now a surplus of 100,000 hogsheads of sugar, which could not

A dragoon, WH Pyne

Stapleton prison where the French prisoners-of-war were kept. Malcolm tells us that the noise of their conversations in the yards could be heard some distance off. By JP Malcolm.

find a market. He concluded by moving a resolution, 'that the House would, early in the next session, take into consideration the report of the committee, for the purpose of considering the commercial state of the West-India colonies.'

The Chancellor of the Exchequer said, the subject was certainly of great importance, and required the most serious attention of the House. Resolution agreed to.

Felix Farley's Bristol Journal, 15 August 1807

BRISTOL MILITIA FUNDRAISING

The Bristol Militia Society, for Raising a Fund for supplying its Members with a proportional sum (which of course must depend on its resources) in case they should be ballotted to serve in the Glocestershire Militia, for the year 1807.

The inhabitants of Bristol, and every part of the County of Glocester, liable to serve in the Glocester-shire Militia, by the ensuing ballot, are respectfully informed, that Subscriptions are received and registered, and Certificates granted as under, viz.

FIRST CLASS Subscription of Two Guineas, will entitle each Member, ballotted to serve in the Glocestershire Militia, to an equal proportion of the funds of the Society, not exceeding £40.

SECOND CLASS Subscription of One Guinea, not exceeding £20.

THIRD CLASS Subscription of Half-a-Guinea, not exceeding £10.

When the ballot is completed and the men enrolled, which shall be ascertained by the Lord Lieutenant of the County, the surplus balance shall be divided, after deducting the necessary expences.

JOHN KNOTT ABBOTT, Secretary,
No.4 & 5, Denmark-street, StAugustine's Back, Bristol.
N.B. Messrs. STUCKEYS, LEAN and Co. being appointed Treasurers, the monies will, from time to time, be lodged in their Bank.
Felix Farley's Bristol Journal, 15 August 1807

ROYAL BRISTOL VOLUNTEERS INSPECTION

The Royal Bristol Volunteers were inspected in Queen-square, by Colonel Probyn, on Monday last. Gen. Champagny, his brother, and several officers of distinction, attended upon the occasion. The corps mustered 806 men rank and file, and upwards of 900,

including commissioned and non-commissioned officers were upon the ground. The report will, we understand, be highly honourable to the regiment. On Thursday it commenced garrison duty, when 206 men were under arms for that service; and yesterday, the same number marched from the College-green, to relieve their fellow-soldiers at the town guard and Stapleton prison. When the routine has passed through the regiment, it is probable that the Clifton and Westbury will take the duty, as we understand they have very handsomely volunteered their services.
Bristol Mirror, 22 August 1807

ARMED MERCHANTMAN
GRIFFIN WHARF, London, August 13, 1807.
For BRISTOL, The Fine BRIG BELINDA, (250 tons), ROBERT ROBERTS, MASTER;
Is now loading at the above Wharf, and will soon be ready for sea, a great part of her Cargo being engaged. The BELINDA is completely armed, and in consequence, can be insured at half per cent. less than otherwise.
Apply to Mr JOHN BEDWELL, 1, Castle-Court, Bridge Row OR PRICE AND CROSS. Bristol.
Bristol Mirror, 22 August 1807

FAST FOOD
The rapidity of the progress of the armies of Bonaparte has been greatly facilitated by the portable form of food by which they subsist. Biscuit, and a small case of brandy, is said to be the principle subsistance of the itinerant hosts of France. A more convenient sort of nourishment for such purposes is used by the natives of South-America. They burn the grain of Indian wheat in the same way that Europeans prepare coffee: they then macerate them; and every Indian, when he follows the chase, carries with him a little bag of this powder, of which a handful, thrown into a vessel of water, supplies a competent, palatable and salubrious meal.
Bristol Mirror, 5 September 1807

BRIBERY ATTEMPT AT STAPLETON PRISON
French Prison – In the course of last week, two officers in the French Prison, at Stapleton, attempted to bribe the centinels on duty, and offered them ten guineas to connive at their escape. The centinels, in a very honourable manner, acquainted their commanding-officer with the circumstance, who advised them to bring the business to maturity. When the prisoners, who had previously broken their parole, had passed all the centries but one, they were received by six file of men with fixed bayonets, previously posted in a convenient place for that purpose. They were consequently secured, and lodged again in the prison. The common men in the prison, we understand, also lately attempted to escape by undermining the walls, but their scheme was anticipated by the vigilance of the guard, and frustrated in due time.
Felix Farley's Bristol Journal, 5 September 1807

LUCRATIVE CONTRACT AT STAPLETON PRISON
To Bakers, Mealmen, &C
NOTICE is hereby given, that I shall be ready on WEDNESDAY, the 23rd instant, at Four o'Clock, in the Afternoon, at the BELL Inn, St Thomas-Street, Bristol. to receive sealed Tenders, and treat with such Persons as may be willing to Contract for the Supply of all such BREAD as may be wanted for the French Prisoners of War (in health) at Stapleton Prison, from the 1st October next, to the 31st December following. The Conditions of the Contract

may be known on applying at Messrs. HAYTER and Co's No.17, Old City Chambers, London or at the General Bank, Plymouth, or of Mr LEE, at the BELL INN, St Thomas-Street, Bristol.
SIMON LITTLE Contractor for Victualling the Prisoners at Stapleton London, 14th September, 1807
Bristol Mercury, 21 September 1807

VICTORY
Capture of Copenhagen and the Danish Fleet
The receipt of this intelligence (for the particulars of which see the Extraordinary and Supplemental Gazettes in another part of our paper) has spread a general satisfaction throughout the country, and dissipated, in a considerable degree, the gloom occasioned by our disaster in South America. Whatever may be the justice of the act, and however various the opinions upon this head, there can be but one sentiment as to the gallentry of the exploit, and the conduct of our army and navy upon the occasion. That our soldiers and sailors have acquitted themselves nobly, must give satisfaction to every English heart. They were sent to fight, and 'have fought and conquered'. We do not say they have retrieved the glory of the British army, for that has never been tarnished, but they certainly have established, on a firmer basis, our reputation, for discipline, moderation and honour. Whether the cause be just or not, the plan was certainly well conceived and well executed. Nothing intervened between the 'effect and the hit'. The destination of the expedition was kept a profound secret, and when its object was known, from the means provided, it contained in itself a moral certainty of success.
Bristol Gazette, 24 September 1807

ESCAPE
Yesterday se'nnight, about nine o'clock in the evening, fifteen French prisoners made an attempt to escape from Stapleton prison, of which number six got clear off, and have not since been heard of.
Bristol Mirror, 3 October 1807

A WELL-BEHAVED REGIMENT
On Monday the 5th October, the Royal North Glocester Militia, commenced its march from Plymouth garrison for Chicester and Arundel; the exemplary good behaviour of this regt. during their stay, is very handsomely noticed in the following general order:- Lieut. Gen. England in communicating the orders of the Commander in chief to the Royal North Glocester regt. Of Militia to march out of the Western district, desires to express his regret at losing so excellent a regiment, and begs them to accept of his best marks and good wishes for their orderly conduct and soldier-like behaviour, on every occasion, during the time they have been under his command.
Felix Farley's Bristol Journal, 10 October 1807

BEAUTEOUS DESERTERS
MALE BEAUTY. The following descriptions of two deserters from the 82d regiment, born at Southampton, appear in a late *Police Gazette*: 'William Thorn, labourer, aged 20 years, 5 feet 7.5 inches high, stout person, long head, oval face, hazle eyes, long eye-brows, long nose, wide mouth, long neck, light hair, square shoulders, long arms, large hands, stout legs, long feet, very handsome'. 'Geo. Stacey, labourer, 21 years old, 6 feet high, stout person, large head, broad face, blue eyes, light hair, broad shoulders, stout arms, large hands, stout legs, broad feet, very handsome.'

Will the ladies say, that this military description perfectly accords with their ideas of a very handsome man? 175 other deserters are advertised in the same *Gazette*, but none of these are stated to be handsome.

Bristol Gazette, 15 October 2007

TRAFALGAR DAY

The anniversary of the glorious victory of Trafalgar; was on Wednesday, commemorated in this city, in a manner becoming the country, and the solemnity of the occasion. The morning was ushered in by the ringing of bells; flags were suspended from the different churches and public buildings; and the remembrance of the loss of our immortal hero, appeared rather to consecrate than depress the emotions of national pride and patriotism. The Trafalgar Society met at Mr Reeves's hotel, and many other parties were assembled to pay their tributes of respect to the memory of the achievers of our naval glory.

Bristol Mirror, 24 October 1807

Nelson, The Victor of Trafalgar, CR Oak sprigs and Bay Laurel decorate a plinth to symbolise victory and fortitude. Nelson had been awarded the Freedom of the city in 1797 for his victories against the French. Trafalgar Day was celebrated in Bristol with much style.

NO RELIEF UNLESS YOU APPEAR

Merchants' Hall, Bristol

October 21, 1807

The Trustees for the relief of disabled SEA-MEN, intend meeting on TUESDAY the 3d of November next, at ten o'clock in the forenoon, in order to examine the several Pensioners, at which time they are all required to attend, or send sufficient reason for their non-attendance, and an account of their circumstances, otherwise they will be struck off the List.

By Order of the Trustees, OSBORNES.

Felix Farley's Bristol Journal, 31 October 1807

CHANGE OF REGIMENTS

The Royal Bristol Volunteers have again taken the garrison duty. The first detachment performed prison and town guards on Sunday. The second and third divisions of the W. York Militia, commanded by Earl Fitzwilliam, has arrived in this garrison, in the course of the week, to replace the Royal Lancashire, which has marched for Gosport.

Felix Farley's Bristol Journal, 7 November 1807

Robert Southey's Letters from England

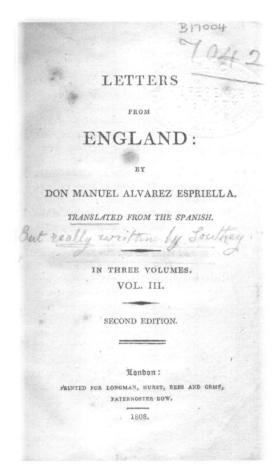

By Don Manuel Alvarez Espriella or (in pencil)
but really written by Southey.

LETTER LXXV.

Road from Bath to Bristol. – Cornu Ammonis. – Bristol. – Exchange. – Market. – Cathedral. – The Brazen Eagle. – Clifton. – Bristol-Wells. – Anecdote of Kosciusko.

From Bath to Bristol is three leagues; the road crosses the river Avon by an old bridge, and continues for some way along its banks, or at little distance from them. Half a league from Bath is the house wherein Fielding is said to have written Tom Jones; it stands by the way side, in a village called Twyverton, and I did not look at it without respect. We had a fine view of the river winding under a hill which is covered with old trees, and has a mansion on its brow, opposite to which, on our side the water, was the largest and finest meadow I have seen in England, in which an immense herd was feeding, as in a savannah. A little dirty town, called Keynsham, stands about half way. I noticed the Cornu-Ammonis built up in the walls of many of the houses, or, if it happened to be a fine specimen, placed over the door-way, as an ornament. This, I find, has given rise to a fabulous legend, which says that St Keyna, from whom the place takes its name, resided here in a solitary wood full of venomous serpents, and her prayers converted them into these stones, which still retain their shape. Beyond this there is a fantastic building, more like a castle than any thing else: I could neither guess for what it was intended, nor of what it was built. It proved to be the stables belonging to a great house on the opposite side of the road, from which there is a subterranean passage, and the materials were the scoria from some neighbouring iron-works, with which I soon perceived that the walls by the road side were capt: for this it is excellently adapted, as nothing will vegetate upon it, and it is undecomposable by the weather. Here we once more approached the river, which was now a dirty stream, flowing through wide banks of mud. Bristol was presently in sight, - a huge city in the bottom, and extending up all the adjoining hills, with many steeples, one of which inclines so much from the perpendicular, that I should be sorry to live within reach of its fall, - and the black towers of many glass-houses rolling up black smoke. We entered through a gate of modern and mean architecture into a street which displayed as much filth, and as much poverty, as I have seen in any English town. Here, for the first time, I saw something like a public fountain, with a painted statue of Neptune above it, which is as little creditable to the decency of the magistrates as to the state of arts in the city. The entrance into Bristol is, however, the worst part of it. We crossed the bridge, where there is a fine opening, and full in view a modern church and spire, so beautifully proportioned, and therefore so fine, that you do not at first perceive that the whole building is perfectly plain and unornamented.

D. was awaiting my arrival. He had secured our places for Exeter in to-morrow's coach, and I lost no time in seeing what he, as being acquainted with the place, thought most worthy to be seen. The exchange, a fine edifice, about half a century old, was opposite to the inn door at which the stage had stopped: its inclosed square is exceedingly beautiful, more so than any thing of the kind which I have seen elsewhere: yet, it seems, the citizens choose to assemble in the street, in front, where some friend in the city, in old times, erected four brazen tables, on which his town's-folk might count out their money in their public dealings. On one of these a man was selling newspapers, on another a cage

Robert Southey from a drawing by Hancock, 1796. As he himself often told people, the name is pronounced to rhyme with 'mouthey'.

of goldfinches was exposed to sale. Behind the exchange is the market, which is even finer than that of Bath. It contains three market-houses, to which cheese, butter, pork, poultry, &c. are brought by women from the country. The shambles stand in another part; and another is appropriated for vegetables, secured from the weather by a range of slated sheds. I never saw, even at a fair, a busier or more crowded scene, and every thing was going on with that order and dispatch which characterize this extraordinary nation.

We crossed a wooden draw-bridge over the bed of a river, where the ships were lying on a bed of mud, and the water was not wider than a common street gutter: it was full of small craft; the view on

'We entered through a gate of modern and mean architecture.'
Temple Gate by Edward Bird.

one side extended down the river into the country: there was the bustle of business along the quays and in the streets; one church tower of singular beauty was in sight, and the whole scene was fine and rememberable. The cathedral stands in a place with old trees in front; it is a poor building, excepting Chester, the least interesting in England. The entrance is disfigured by a door-way in the very worst style of modern architecture. A fine cross, which formerly stood in the square, has been sold by the corporation to a gentleman, who has re-erected it at his country-seat, and thus rescued it from destruction! This was about thirty years ago; the person who told me this, said he did not remember it, but had often in his childhood eaten it in gingerbread. Instead of ascending, you descend into this church, by several steps; the

pavement is therefore necessarily damp, and, what is truly abominable, stinks of the abominations which are, in contempt of all decency, committed against the doors, and find their way down.

It is, as I have elsewhere mentioned, a part of the service of the English Church to read a portion of the scriptures, one chapter from the Old Testament, and another from the New. In common parochial churches, the whole of the service is performed by the officiating priest, and he does this in his desk: but, in cathedrals, one of the minor priests takes this part of the duty, and performs it in the middle of the choir: here the bible is usually placed upon the outspread wings of a brazen eagle, the handsomest of all their church ornaments. Such an eagle they had in this cathedral, and a remarkably handsome one it was; but last year the dean and chapter thought proper to sell it, for the sake of applying the paltry sum which it would produce as old brass in ornaments for the altar. [See page 180]. So the eagle went as the cross had gone before it. There happened to be a man in the city whose humour it is to attend service whenever it is performed in this cathedral: on week days this is considered by the priests as a mere matter of form; and having few or none to attend them, they omit parts of the liturgy, and hurry over the rest, to get through their task as speedily as possible. During many years it had been the main business of this person to watch them, and endeavour to bring them to a sense of their duty; for which purpose he wrote to them whenever he found them offending, and also to the dean and to the bishop, calling upon them to interfere, and see that the service of the church was duly performed. He missed the eagle, inquired for it, traced it to the brazier's, and rescued it from the furnace. Here was a fine subject for his zeal! He wrote a circular letter to all the bishops, of which they took no notice; offered the eagle again to the cathedral at the price which he had paid for it, which they refused, being, as might have been expected, obstinate in their misconduct – and lastly put it up to sale, [see pages 180-181] in the hope that it might be purchased for some other church, and not utterly desecrated. What has been its fate I know not; but it seems that the respect which the English pay to their cathedrals is confined to the buildings, and does not extend to any thing in them. At one time all the monumental figures and inscriptions were cut in brass: a large collection of these, which were taken up from another cathedral while it was repaired, have gone the way of the eagle, and been cast into candlesticks and warming-pans.

The monuments in the church are numerous; that nearest the entrance is the finest and the most remarkable, as being Mrs Draper's, the Eliza of Sterne and of the Abbé Raynal. The rhapsody about her, in the latter's work, is as excellent a specimen of every thing that is absurd, as it would be easy to find even in his Histoire Philosophique. Some parts of the architecture are beautiful in their kind. At a little distance from the church is a Saxon gateway: the upper part is in admirable preservation – the bottom has been corroded by a practice as indecent as it is sacrilegious – the more to be regretted, as this is one of the finest specimens of the style.

The views in the neighbourhood of this city are singularly

A view of the High Cross and Cathedral, College Green from John Rocque's map of the city published in 1750. The cross was removed after agitation from certain influential Bristolians because it hampered their promenading on the Green.

pleasing. The adjoining village of Clifton was once the most beautiful village in England, and may now be said to be the finest suburb. Here too, as well as at Bath, is the dismal sight of streets and crescents which have never been finished, the most dolorous of all ruins. It stands upon a hill above the river, which runs between high rocks and a hanging wood; a scene truly magnificent, and wanting nothing but clearer water; the stream consists of liquid mud, and the banks are hideous unless the tide be full, for the tide rises here not less than forty English feet. The beauty of this scene is yearly diminishing; the rocks which formerly rose so immediately from the river side, as only to allow room for a

Canynges monuments in St Mary Redcliffe, by J Willis.

path, are used as quarries. The people of Bristol seem to sell every thing that can be sold. They sold their cross, by what species of weight or measurement I know not, they sold their eagle by the pound, and here they are selling the sublime and beautiful by the boat-load! One grand crag which has been left untouched shows what mischief has already been done. There is a cavern near the summit of this, of which the arch appeared remarkably fine as we looked up to it from the side of the river.

I tasted their famous medicinal water which rises at the foot of these rocks; it is tepid, and so completely without any medicinal flavour, as to be excellent water. In cases of diabetes it possesses some virtue; for consumption, which it is usually prescribed for, none whatsoever. Several unhappy patients, who had been sent here to die at a distance from home, were crawling out upon the parade as if to take their last gasp of sunshine. It was shocking to see them, and it is shocking to hear how thoroughly the people here regard death as a matter of trade. The same persons who keep the hotels furnish the funerals; entertain patients while they are living, and then, that they may accommodate them all through, bury them when they die. There came here a young man from the North, dying, with his sister to attend him. The disease sometimes, when it assumes its gentlest form, seems to terminate suddenly; and one morning, when the sister rose to breakfast and inquired for him, she found he was dead. He had expired during the night; the people of the house said they thought they might as well not disturb her, so they had laid out the body, dressed it in the shroud, measured it for the coffin, and given all the orders – to take all trouble off her hands. You will think it scarcely possible that this scene of disease and death should be a place of amusement, where idlers of fashion resort to spend the summer, mingle in the pump-room and in the walks with the dying, and have their card-parties and dances within hearing of every passing bell.

Half a century ago Bristol was in size the second city in England. Manchester now holds that rank, and several other towns have outstripped it in population. There is less mercantile enterprise here than in any other trading English city: like the old Italians, the Bristol merchants go on in the track of their fathers, and, succeeding to enormous fortunes, find the regular profits so great that they have no temptation to deviate from the beaten way. The port is therefore yielding its foreign trade to bolder competitors; but it will always remain the centre of a great commerce with the Welsh coast, with Ireland, and all those inland counties which communicate with the Severn, a river navigable into the very heart of the kingdom.

There is in the streets nothing like the bustle of London, nor like

The Red Lion Inn, Redcliffe Street.
Lithograph by S G Tovey, 1841.

the business of Liverpool on the quays. The Quay, however, is still a busy as well as a striking scene, and remains a noble monument of the old citizens, who made it in the thirteenth century. On one side, the shipping, the bridges, the church towers, and the neighbouring hill, which overlooks the town of which it now makes a part, form a fine picture. On the other, there is the cathedral with the old trees in its front, and the distant country. A third view has a wider foreground with cranes and trees, and piles of goods intermingled, shipping of larger size, a fine row of houses upon a high terrace on the opposite side, and apart from them the Church of St Mary Redclift, which is the finest parochial church in the kingdom, and is indeed far more beautiful than the cathedral. It is remarkable also, on this account, that it is the place wherein certain poems were said to have been found, attributed to a priest in the fifteenth century, which have occasioned as great a controversy as the Granada Relicks, and with as little reason. It is now admitted that they were the production of Chatterton, the son of the sexton of the church, who poisoned himself at the age of eighteen, and is considered by the English as the most extraordinary genius that has ever appeared among them.

A few years ago, when Kosciusko came to this city on his way to America, great marks of honour were shown him, and many presents made him, both by the municipality, and by individuals. – Among others, an honest gingerbread-baker thought, as he was going to sea, nothing could be more acceptable to him than a noble plum-cake for the voyage: he made him the very best which could be made, and a valiant one it was. It was as big as he could carry; and on the top, which was as usual covered with a crust of sugar, was written in coloured sugar-plums: To the gallant Kosciusko. With this burthen the good man proceeded to the house of the American consul, where Kosciusko was lodged, and inquired for the general. He was told that he was lying on the sofa (for his wounds were not at that time healed), and was too much fatigued and too unwell to see any one. 'Oh!' said the gingerbread-baker, 'he won't be angry at seeing me, I warrant, to show me the way up,' and pushing the servant forward, he followed him up stairs into the room. When however he saw the great man whom he was come to honour, lying on a couch, with his countenance pale, painful, and emaciated, yet full of benevolence, the sight overpowered him; he put down his cake, burst into tears like a child, and ran out of the room without speaking a single word. Having set out on my return, a natural impatience hurries me forward. I should else regret that I have not procured letters to Bristol, and allowed myself sufficient time to see thoroughly a city which contains many interesting objects of curiosity, and of which the vicinity is so exceedingly beautiful.

Robert Southey's Letters from England: the Brazen Eagle

As the notice for this sale is not less curious than the occasion, I have transcribed it from the city newspaper. One of the many conveniencies attending the English coffee-houses is, that the newspapers are regularly filed in them, so that they may always be referred to:

THE EAGLE FROM THE BRISTOL CATHEDRAL.

TO BE SOLD AT AUCTION,

At the Exchange Coffee-room, in this City,

On Thursday, the 2d of September, 1802, between the hours of one and two o'clock in the afternoon, (unless previously disposed of by private contract,)

A BEAUTIFUL BRAZEN SPREAD EAGLE,

With a Ledge at the Tail, Standing on a brass pedestal,

Supported by four lions, one at each corner.

This elegant piece of workmanship was sold, last June, by the dean and chapter of the cathedral church of the Holy and Undivided Trinity, of Bristol, or their agents or servants, as old brass, and weighed 6cwt. 20lb. or 692lb. and has since been purchased at an advanced price, by a native of this city, in order to prevent it being broken up, and to give the inhabitants a chance of buying it.

It was given to the cathedral, in the reign of Charles II, by one of the prebendaries, who had been there 40 years; and is supposed, by the following Latin inscription, (*which was engraved* on the pillar or pedestal,) to have stood in the choir 119 years:

"Ex Dono Georgij Williamson, S. T. B. Hujus Ecclesias Cathedralis Bristoll: Vice-Decani, 1683."

That is, 'The Gift of George Williamson, Bachelor of Divinity, Sub-Dean of this Cathedral Church of Bristol, 1683.

The whole of the inscription, except the figures 1683, has been taken off the pedestal, without the consent of the buyer; which he has since had re-engraved.

This piece of antiquity, which is of the most exquisite shape, is made of the best and purest brass, and worth the attention of *ministers and church-wardens*, or any gentleman or lady who would wish to make a present of it to their parish church: traders, also, to foreign parts, may find it worth their while to purchase, *as a like opportunity may never offer again.*

Such a handsome bird would be, as it has hitherto been, a very great ornament to the middle aisle of a church. It for many years stood in the choir of the Bristol cathedral, and *upheld with its wings the Sacred Truths of the Blessed Gospel.* The minor-canons formerly read the lessons on it, and in most cathedrals the custom is kept up to this day.

This superb image is *now* at King-street Hall, and may be inspected three days previous to the day of sale.

N. B. The purchaser offered, previous to any advertisement, to re-sell the eagle at the price he paid for it, provided it were replaced in the *choir*; which offer was rejected.

THOMAS KIFT, Broker.

A bill advertising the auction of the eagle.

The Scandal of the Brazen Eagle

IN 1807 THE SCANDAL OF BRISTOL'S EAGLE LECTERN WAS STILL MUCH IN PEOPLE'S minds. Several years earlier the Dean and Chapter of Bristol Cathedral decided to sell their superb eagle lectern for scrap. The lectern had been given to the Cathedral in 1683 during the reign of Charles II and was widely admired. It was sold to a brazier for £27 and was to be melted down, when a parishioner, William Ady, who had enquired as to its whereabouts, rescued it. Appalled by this example of clerical Philistinism, and believing that it must have been sold without the full knowledge of the Cathedral authorities he then offered to sell it back to the Cathedral at the same price. They obstinately refused to buy it. In the end he put it up for auction in the hope that someone would purchase it for another church and save it from being melted down. The affair caused uproar amongst those interested in Bristol's historical and religious traditions and only served to confirm the contempt with which the Cathedral authorities were held. Finding no buyers, Ady donated the eagle to St Mary-le-Port, in 1802.

Unfortunately it was severely damaged in the blitz when that church was bombed and the pieces were sent to the crypt of St John's church in the city. In 1979 sections of it were still there but could not be traced by the editor during the preparation for this book.

The lectern bore a great similarity to one in York Minster, dated 1686, that was by the hand of a London brazier, and it has been surmised that both may have come from the same workshop.

The Brazen Eagle. A sixpenny print engraved and issued by T Deeble, Bristol 1802.

Robert Southey's Letters from England: filling pitchers from a fountain

[ex Letter LXXVI]

We took our seats on the coach roof at five in the morning, and before we got out of the city received positive and painful proof that the streets of Bristol are worse paved than those of any other city in England. The road passes by the church of St Mary Redclift, which is indeed wonderfully fine; it is built upon broken ground, and there are steps ascending to it in several directions. I remember nothing equal to the effect which this produces. Women were filling their pitchers below it from a fountain, the water of which passes through the cemetery! The houses formed a continued street for nearly half a league; then the views became very striking, behind us was the city, on one side the rocks of Clifton, and as we advanced we came in sight of the Bristol Channel...

Temple Street, J S Prout.

Redcliffe Hill and the fountain in 1829. Southey remarked on the drinking water here having first flowed through the cemetery. A dray approaches up the hill and the shot tower appears at the far left.

Habitual Irritation of Mind James Malcolm, a Londoner in Bristol

THIRD EXCURSION.

The court-yard of the Swan with Two Necks, Ladd-lane, exhibits a scene every evening at seven o'clock highly illustrative of the rapid communication between distant places in Great Britain. A range of handsome mail-coaches faces the gate, surrounded by passengers and spectators. These radii of the great circle dart from London, the centre, at the same moment that many more depart from other inns. I seated myself in that destined for the antient city of Bristol, on the 13th of June 1805, and very soon arrived at the Gloucester coffee-house, Piccadilly. There three fellow-travellers entered the coach; and a fourth person, regardless of the intimation 'Licensed to carry not exceeding four inside,' would have prevailed on us, after obtaining the coachman's consent, to admit him; but the law of the land and the law of convenience forbad, and the application was unanimously rejected.

The disadvantages attending travelling in the mail are not numerous; yet those are of some importance: the fatigue is considerable, and the intervals of rest much too short; besides, the rapidity of their motion sometimes occasions an overturn. I observed our coach appeared to be perfectly new; but I felt the more secure on reflection, till the cause was explained by the self-congratulation of a gentleman, who said he should doze the night away in security, as he had never heard of the overturning of the *same person* a second time in the space of three days. This observation naturally produced enquiries; which were immediately answered, though not *satisfactorily* to us. He said the horses were trotting at the rate of near nine miles an hour, on their way to London, when the reins of the leaders broke; and, thus released, they deviated from the road, fell into a ditch, and threw the coach on its side. The narrator was asleep at the instant the vehicle fell; and, pitching forward with the violence of the concussion, his head met that of a fellow-traveller, and caused the latter a bleeding at the nose for some time. The coachman, guard, and the other passengers, received no injury; but the coach was so completely destroyed as to be unfit for further use.

HABITUAL IRRITATION OF MIND.

Why should we create imaginary vexations when many sources of satisfaction invite favourable comparisons between present and possible situations? Our new coach might have been overturned, yet we reached the inn where the director of our passage decreed we should sup, or breakfast, which the reader pleases, in perfect safety. The clock had told the third hour, and we entered what appeared to me a good apartment, where tables were spread with tea-cups, bread, butter, and various kinds of meat. I declare every article invited my approach; and, if any difficulty arose in my mind, it was whether I was to undergo the fate of Tantalus, through the impatience of the driver. My companions, however, proceeded to remove that apprehension from themselves by an immediate attack on the viands; an attack which they accompanied by a volley of words, directed at the unfortunate, interesting, and fatigued young woman who attended.

What, are these tea-cups fit to touch? – Oh! shameful, shameful! – What is this? minced sugar? – This tea-kettle did not boil. The dirtiest house, without exception, I ever entered!

But enough has been repeated to remind the reader how wrong it is to wound the feelings even of a servant at an inn, when facts do not warrant correction. Perhaps, indeed, the subject may be pronounced unworthy of serious reprehension; but I represent man as I find him, and repeat his words verbatim.
Curiosity, and a desire to proceed with due caution, on my first visit to Bristol, induced me to ask several questions of these gentlemen.

Sir, Bristol is one hundred years behind the rest of the world in improvements: men of immense, nay princely fortune, *dine at two o'clock*; money is obtained with avidity, with eagerness, but is buried and lost in the hands of the possessor, through want of spirit to enjoy it; in short, the city is a mere sink of filth and smoke, and the best inn within it is the nastiest in England.

You cannot cross the streets without danger from the sledges, used instead of wheeled vehicles. – I dined with my family at the ----: it is true, we had turtle; but it was served in dishes, and eaten from plates, which had not been cleaned after previous use.
So, Bristol is without one solitary recommendation. Neither its churches, streets, or domestic buildings, its trade or opulence, can save it from the reproach of the citizens dining at two o'clock.
O! ye brave warriors, our noble ancestors, I invoke your shades to witness this treason against manhood, this dereliction from your dining hours of eleven and twelve, to the modern six, seven, and eight.

A typical dinner invitation from 1808 that was sent to George Weare Braikenridge by the Church Warden of St Mary Redcliffe. Bristolians were sneered at for dining unfashionably early. Some surviving invitations state 4 o'clock but this requests three. Malcolm comments on fellow passengers saying Bristolians dined at two!

Mark the difference; the champions of early hours carried terror to the centre of France; now Frenchmen threaten a march to London.

BRISTOL.
The first view of Bristol, from the London road, is at the distance of one mile. Hence it appears an extensive range of roofs, almost level. When the air is nearly calm, the numerous chimneys of the various manufactories are confused, by the streams of smoke issuing from them, with the towers and steeples; nor are they readily distinguished from each other. This circumstance occasions a visual increase of distance, so much that Bristol might be readily supposed almost double its real size, and crowded with churches.
But, previous to the observations on, and description of this

respectable city, with which I purpose to present the reader, it will be necessary to mention the government, and some other particulars.

The High Steward of the corporation is the Duke of Portland. Next to whom, in civic importance, are the mayor, the recorder, and the court of aldermen, two sheriffs, and 24 common-councilmen; the town-clerk and clerk of the peace, the chamberlain, steward of the Sheriff's court, and two coroners; and the corporation has a sword-bearer.

Besides the above officers, there are, a clerk of arraigns, a clerk to the town-clerk, a deputy chamberlain, a registrar of the Court of Conscience, his deputy, a collector of the town dues, an under-sheriff, a clerk of the markets, and two inspectors of nuisances.

The city sends two delegates to parliament; who are, the Right Hon. Charles Bathurst, and Evan Baillie, Esq.

The cathedral, and its dependencies, are protected by a dean, a chancellor, an archdeacon, five prebendaries, a precentor, three other minor canons, and a chapter-clerk. And, exclusive of the above reverend gentlemen, there are 39 resident clergymen, of the established church, within the city and vicinity.

The ecclesiastical court consists of the chancellor, three surrogates, a registrar, two deputy registrars, four proctors, and an apparitor.

Sixteen Dissenting teachers in addition honour Bristol with their labours.

Neither is this flourishing mart destitute of legal protectors; five of whom are barristers, and the remainder *eighty-one attorneys*. There are eighteen physicians, and sixty-seven surgeons, apothecaries, and acoucheurs.

The Charitable Institutions are numerous and flourishing.

Temple Gate by J Skelton. Following complaints of the medieval gate restricting traffic it was rebuilt in a rustic classical style in 1734. However, the new gate was even narrower and so the corporation restricted the type of vehicles that could use it. The gate was finally demolished in 1808.

The Infirmary, for the reception of persons afflicted with acute or chronic disorders, has a treasurer, four physicians and five surgeons, an apothecary, a chaplain, a secretary, and a matron, who superintend others accidentally injured, and admitted without enquiry, in this noble, airy, and excellent building; consisting of a centre and one wing, to which another will very soon be added.

The Dispensary, a treasurer, three physicians, three man-midwives, three female practitioners, two apothecaries, and a secretary.

A Medical Institution on the Broad Quay, and at the Hot Wells, has two physicians and a surgeon.

But the most benevolent and excellent establishment is that of the Asylum for the Indigent Blind. Poverty and blindness, united in one pitiable object! Can human misery extend beyond these inflictions? A wretch destitute of sustenance, and forbid to work for it! The Asylum for the Indigent Blind will plead trumpet-tongued at the Throne of Merch in favour of the Bristolians; and Sterne's recording Angel will weep away all their sins, for this beautiful and sublime expiation. The necessary buildings for the reception of the unfortunate applicants is situated in Lower Magdalen or Maudlin-street. There every practicable effort is adopted to teach them manual occupations; for the double purpose of amusing the almost blank mind, and diverting the attention from contemplating to madness the horrors of eternal darkness, and providing a permanent support for themselves. Subscriptions towards which are earnestly solicited by the treasurer and twenty-nine members of the committee presiding over the institution. A collection of very curious articles, consisting of flowers, baskets, mats for the table, &c. are exhibited for sale at the Asylum.

St Peter's Hospital particularly attracted my attention, which is situated near the street, and behind the church dedicated to that Saint. From the number of gables on the front, decorated with strange grotesque carving, it has evidently been the mansion of a person of consequence; and is appropriated to Thomas Norton, who lived in the reign of Henry IV.
This hospital, the general receptacle for almost every description of poor persons, even including lunaticks and idiots, is attended by a physician, three surgeons, an apothecary, a chaplain, and governed by a treasurer, master, and matron.
The citizens of Bristol have established several other hospitals and institutions for the relief of their fellow-beings, equally honourable to them as members of the great community of England and as Christians. Nor have they by any means been deficient in providing for the wants of youth of both sexes, who are taught and provided for in various ways, by different religious persuasions, to the number of a thousand; exclusive of the schools founded by the Thornes, Henry VIII. and Queen Elizabeth, Sunday schools, &c.

When the benevolence of Bristol is under consideration, it would be unpardonable not to mention Edward Colston, born there in 1636 whose unequalled liberality is still the constant theme of his grateful townsmen. This gentleman acquired a vast fortune by the profession of a merchant; which he did not reserve to be disposed of by will, through the uninterested hands of executors; but distributed it himself, as the prudence of the moment dictated, in founding a school for ever in St Augustine's place, for 100 boys; whom he wholly provided for, and presented with a fee at apprenticeship of £.15. each; another in Temple-street, for 40 boys; and an almshouse, for 48 men and women, on St Michael's hill. Such were the acts which procure him an anniversary from the inhabitants of Bristol; those he performed in London, when member of parliament for his native place, are recorded in the archives of Heaven, and will appear in large items in the hours of future rewards and punishments. Colston, evidently influenced by the genuine spirit of philanthropy, carefully avoided injuring his relatives when providing for the wants of strangers. The distribution of the whole of a man's possessions in charity evinces ostentation rather than benevolence; and his family and the publick despise his memory accordingly. Colston, on the contrary, left his relations £1.100,000; and used that only for the desolate which they could not wish for without incurring the charge of selfishness and avarice.

SITUATION OF BRISTOL.

The old city stands on a comparative level, but the new extends up the East and South-east sides of very considerable hills. The Avon enters it from the South-east, and proceeds in that direction to St Peter's hospital; whence it flows near due South to Ratcliff, then West, and afterwards in a serpentine line to Rownham meads; whence it turns again, and passes St Vincent's rocks to the North-north-west.

The Froom enters Bristol at the North-east quarter, and approaches the Avon near St Peter's hospital; where Bridge, St Peter's, and Wine streets, intervene between them. It then proceeds North-west, South-west, and South, till it falls into the Avon, at the base of St Michael's hill; forming a long projection of land, covered by Queen-square and several streets.

Whatever may be the beauties of the shores of the Avon beyond Bristol, truth compels me to say, the river by no means improves them. The tide, which rises even thirty feet within the city, brings with it an astonishing quantity of soil from the Severn. This deposits, and forms vast sloping banks, extremely disgusting at low water, when the Avon becomes a mere canal, not more in breadth than four times the length of the ferry-boat you enter to cross it at the Gibb.

A bank of mud faces the pier-head at the junction of the two rivers, which is considered by mariners as a most convenient bed to receive the bottoms of vessels when rushing up the Avon at a rate that has frequently occasioned their total loss against the pier.

'Vast sloping banks extremely disgusting at low water.' View from Canon's Marsh towards St Augustines at mid-tide, by F Nicholson, 1799.

Can a river only 105 feet in breadth, discoloured with filth, be an agreeable object, even at high water? or can it, by the most extravagant strains of panegyrick, be converted into a safe navigation, when a sail cannot be used without hazard of depositing the vessel on a bank, where she may overturn at the ebb of the tide? or what can be more absurd than to assert it is one of the 'deepest, safest, and most convenient for navigation, in England,' when ships and small craft are seen up to their wales in mud, and full ten feet below the surface of the indented quays?

Persons who are infatuated by prejudices arising from long residence, and that have seen little of the world, speak of Bristol as one of the best ports in Europe; those who are ship-owners, and have visited London, Liverpool, and Hull, have at length been convinced of their error. In short, Bristol decidedly required an improved port: and that improvement is now in progress, on a very extended scale indeed, which will cost full £.300,000.

The rates levied to raise part of this immense sum are, six-pence in the pound on the same rents as are assessed for the poor; the remainder to be procured by subscriptions, at four, and not exceeding eight *per cent.* profit. The returns for which are to be charged on the tonnage of boats frequenting the bason; and duties upon every separate article imported, from *anchovies* to *yarn*, in alphabetical progression.

The corporation and society of merchants who formed the plan, estimate the general return thus:

> Tonnage £.8600.
> Rates on goods and merchandize £.3340.
> Annual rate on houses £.2400.
> Tonnage on the canal £.1830.
> And the licence for craft £.400.
> In all £.16,570. *per annum.*

After a certain term of years has expired, the whole concern is to revert to the corporation.

A thousand arguments were urged in favour of the undertaking by one class of the inhabitants; to which an equal number of replies and objections were made by another. Indeed, I much doubt whether there was a *neutral* in the city. Hand-bills replete with arguments, and sarcastic paragraphs in the news-papers, must have amused the stranger; though not one, I am confident, made a proselyte on either side in the parties concerned.

The intention is, to convert the *river*, from Rownham ferry nearly to St Anne's mill, into *wet docks*, and *to turn the river into a new channel* South of the present. Besides this vast undertaking, the projectors intend to excavate a large entrance-basin in Rownham meadows, a second auxiliary entrance-bason at Trim mills, a tide dam, and land-flood dam at the Northern extremity, and an overfall sluice at Rownham. The latter is to serve to carry off ice in winter, *which is to be broken by raising and falling the water suddenly.*

The canal, by the scale annexed to the plan, appears to be near four miles in length, and the depth will be greater than that of the bed of the river.

The principal objections to these improvements were, the excessive flow of the tide, and the consequent pressure on the gates, the amazing deposit of mud, and the accumulation of ice. The first is an inconvenience which can in no other way be remedied than by excessive strength in the construction of the walls and gates, as in the docks at Liverpool, where the weight of water in the Mersey must be tenfold beyond that of the Avon. The mud floating in with the vessels, in defiance of every precaution, will certainly accumulate, and must be removed at intervals. But, as the expence cannot yet be estimated, the objection is by no means serious.

The wet-docks of Bristol may not be frozen on an average more than one winter in five; and even then the concern will suffer only in proportion with every other in the kingdom founded on fresh water. As to the proposed method of breaking and discharging the ice, I believe that project will completely fail.

The Froom is a beautiful little pellucid stream, in Earl's mead, North of Bristol, and thence to its source deserves most honourable mention, from the rich variety of its shores: but I must trace it through Bristol, and describe it as it is there. Numerous willows overhang the banks near Froom bridge, and some few houses on the South-east side are tolerably neat. Yet, even there, the water stagnates, and becomes impregnated with the offal of manufactories.

In its progress through the heart of the city it is seldom seen, and is frequently almost arched by the avarice of antient builders, who suspended some of the vilest erections above it I think I have ever witnessed. At the Quay-head the river emerges from its concealment, and becomes a spacious dock; and hence, to the Avon, both above and below the draw-bridge, are numerous small vessels, generally coasters, or traders to Wales and Ireland; but those lay in a bed of mud, except during the short interval of flood-tide.

Large vessels may float to Bristol, and ships of the line have been built there; but most of the heavy merchantmen unload at the mouth of the Avon. The reader will perceive a ship-yard in the view of the church of St Mary Redcliff; besides which there are several others, and dry-docks for repairing, and two wet-docks; but the latter were sadly clogged with mud when I saw them.

The projection of land already mentioned, between the Avon and Froom, is bounded on the East, West, and South, by an excellent wall, indented for the reception of vessels; between which and the warehouses are large spaces for cranes, and arranging the various articles of import and export previous to their removal by the owners, or placing them in the shipping.

No vessels pass Bristol bridge, and small ones only approach it.

Some silly prejudice has operated with the traders of this city to the present moment, and induced them to prefer sledges for drawing the most ponderous articles; hogsheads of sugar and rum, numerous bars of iron, casks and bales, are invariably removed in this manner. And, although every stranger immedi-

A bastion and part of the city wall looking towards Union Street by JS Prout. The house in the right foreground stands on one of the bastions from the walls that bordered the Froom, which flows beneath Fairfax Street. The bridge carrying Union Street down the hill may be seen beyond.

ately perceives the long lines of metal streaked on the stones, demonstrating the resistance occasioned by their inequalities, yet the Bristolian walks over them without reflection, and dodges in zigzags to avoid the rapid turns of the machine, which frequently moves as if on a centre. Nor doth he imagine for a moment the difficulties he creates in the progress of his business.

The Custom-house, on the North side of Queen-square, is very conveniently situated, almost in the midst of the circuit of trade;

On the Froom opposite Bridewell, by JS Prout. Encrusted with privies and flowing with filth and effluent, the Froom was to contribute to the cholera outbreaks later in the century. A man draws water from it for household use.

divided into a centre and wings; whence an arch leads to the quadrangle intended for the reception of merchants. But the foreigner may seek them there in vain: let him search in the *adjacent street*, and he may be more successful. Wonderful! that the citizens of Bristol should expend £.50,000. on an Exchange erected by Wood of Bath, and yet prefer the rough stones of the street to the smooth ones of their piazzas, and the casual torrents of a British climate to the arches which would protect them from repeated wettings.

However, some method and contrivance is discoverable in arranging the above-mentioned necessary buildings; and it would be unfair, in censuring, not to praise the foresight which induced the community to add the Post-office to the West wing of the Exchange, from which a narrow passage only divides it.

Merchants-hall, at the North end of Prince's-street, deserves notice as a neat edifice, and as it contains a portrait of the celebrated Edward Colston.

St MICHAEL'S AND BRANDON HILLS.

The ground rises rapidly from Canons' marsh on the Avon, and the Quay on the West side of the Froom, and is termed St Michael's hill. The East side of this hill is entirely covered with buildings, which spread quite to the summit, but terminate there for the present.

South-west of St Michael's is Brandon hill, said to be 250 feet above the level of the city. The hill is a perfect cone, and bears strong marks of having been formed by a subterraneous cause, probably volcanic. The rock which composes it is a mass of matter resembling the dross of iron, mixed with red-ochre, and fragments of very hard stone, the whole evidently combined by fire. But, whatever the once-fluid substance may have consisted of

and the duties of the port of Bristol are near *£.300,000. per annum*, on an average. The same square contains the Excise-office. But neither of these buildings are very creditable to the city.

The Exchange, in Corn-street, stands at a very trifling distance from the Quay, and is a most respectable structure, composed of a rustic basement, supporting a range of Corinthian pillars, pilasters, an entablature, a pediment, and balustrade, with vases, originally, the strongest spirit of nitre has now no kind of effect on it. The manner in which the matter alluded to is disposed seems to favour the supposition that some violent cause urged burning masses upward from the earth, through a small aperture in the centre of the hill, which still impelled, and cooling on the surface, split in every direction, and rent the stones carried with it. St Michael's hill, though separated from it only by a small valley, has nothing indicative of ebullition; but St Vincent's rocks, though essentially different in their component parts, may be adduced in support of my conjectures. These consist of long strata, which answer each other on the sides of the river Avon so exactly, that they may be readily supposed to have been rent asunder. Indeed, the bed of the river forms the extreme point of an angle, to be completed by an horizontal line from Durdham Downs to the opposite summits of the rocks.

In addition to this evidence I shall adduce the warm-springs of Clifton, situated between Brandon hill and St Vincent's rocks. How are those springs heated, which are of the temperature of 70 degrees by Farenheit's scale, as all springs of *pure* water which gush from rocks are extremely cold? A subterraneous fire must therefore still exist in this neighbourhood, though probably at a very great depth beneath them, yet sufficiently near to produce a very sensible heat after puffing a long distance through *cold substances*. The last, and as it appears to me conclusive evidence, terrified the inhabitants of Bristol, on the 1st of November, 1755, when the water of the hot-well became red, perhaps with the ochre before mentioned, and utterly unfit for use, and continued so for some time. This effect was produced by the dreadful earthquake at Lisbon, and demonstrates a remote connection with the cause of that horrible convulsion of Nature.

It would be futile to say the concussion of the earth roused a deposit of soil from the sides and bottom of the spring, and spread it through the water, because but one other spring was so affected, which was at Kingswood. Had the impurity originated only from motion, every well in the circuit of Europe must have been more or less impure after the earthquake.

To conclude, I cannot but suppose an earthquake, proceeding from subterraneous fire yet unextinguished, split St Vincent's rocks, filled some previous channel of the Avon, admitted the waters of that river through them, raised the isolated Brandon, and still heats the mineral waters of Clifton.

It is said that the name is derived from a chapel, dedicated to St Bredanus, which once occupied the narrow point of the cone; but it seems by no means probable that was the first use made of it. The Romans, skilful beyond competition, cannot have passed Brandon hill as a point suited for a military post; and I think the reader will agree with me, after consulting the panorama I shall lay before him from it, that they must have used it as a place for observation at least.

Charles I. sensible of its advantages, caused the hill to be fortified; and some traces of lines are still visible.

The base exhibits a circle of red congealed matter, mixed with rocks, and the sides are nearly covered with soil, enlivened by short grass and scattered bushes. The path to it from St Michael's passes through a magnificent street, of white stone, unfinished, uninhabited, desolate, and almost in ruins; the houses of which consist of rustic basements, handsome cornices, and Doric doors. The ascent is an angle of very many degrees, and the lines of the houses and their copings form complete steps.

To commence this grand view, from the left; a mansion of the purest white, and of the Doric order, buried in dark foliage, on the summit of a beautiful slope, has the effect of a most retired country villa, although separated from the suburbs of Bristol merely by a grove of elms, judiciously disposed. The lawn, descending from the front, planted at intervals, grouped with an imitation of one of the ruined towers of a castle, the grove, and the house, strongly evince the taste of Mr Tindal the proprietor. The horizon beyond Mr Tindal's house retires full twenty miles; and from the base of St Michael's hill the city extends in a semicircle; but sadly immersed in smoke, even in the month of June, which, rising from numerous manufactories, clouds the atmosphere and obscures the nearest outlines, burying the more distant in impenetrable confusion. Yet Devonshire-buildings, Bath, may be observed in the evening, after the hours of labour are past; and then the fourteen spires and towers of Bristol become visible, and the lines of the streets may be traced, with thirteen huge cones interspersed, the chimneys of kilns.

The cathedral appears from this elevation as if immersed in foliage, and has a very fine effect. This venerable fane demands attentive examination, though deprived of the nave, and in other respects mutilated. The tower is large, but not of considerable altitude. Three of the angles are supported by buttresses, and the fourth has a turret. Beneath the battlements are ranges of pointed arcades; and, lower, two of rich windows, partially filled with modern masonry. The great arch of the nave has been converted into a vast window.
A row of handsome houses, intersected by the masts of vessels, and a second grove, separate the cathedral from the church of St Mary Redcliff; which might be mistaken for a grand monastic structure, of the most splendid description, but the spire unfinished injures the grace of the general outline.

Beyond that majestic pile the hills retire in gentle ascent, marked by numerous green boundaries, each containing the various gifts of nature to the laborious farmer; and at their bases are terraces of neat mansions. Hence westward the Avon emerges from the city in a semicircle, and flows through meadows almost to the edge of Brandon hill; where a dense black smoke issues from a glass-house. The South side of the stream is diversified by trees, and the vast excavations for the improvement of the port. Those are of a bright red, and wonderfully enliven the verdure of the beautiful rising landscape, closed by the hills of Dundry, and the richly-ornamented tower of the church there.

The abrupt middle distance of Belle-vue and Clifton, formed of hanging woods, white mansions and terraces, with the remote meadows covered by white cloth for bleaching, strongly resembling sheets of water, is extremely fascinating, and conducts the eye to glimpses of mountains in Wales, beyond Durdham downs, and the intervening suburbs of Bristol.

The ground immediately before Brandon hill, on this side, deserves particular notice, and is broken into those picturesque inequalities which were so well represented by the late artist Morland, who would have correctly and finely delineated the rich groups of trees, the verdant slopes of grass, and the houses elevated above each other to the summit of Clifton.
Such is the view from Brandon hill: those less extensive obtained from St Michael's, through the avenues of streets, have their attractions on an evening when the sun is nearly set, and the tints become purple and gold. At that serene and pleasing hour the

Laundresses drying linen on Brandon Hill by George Fennel Robson. Although local tradition states that Queen Elizabeth I granted the Hotwells side of the hill to washerwomen to dry linen on, the privilege was old in her father's reign. Malcolm mentions distant fields beyond white with bleaching linen.

houses spread before the spectator, and appear to approach his feet: the spires seem as if they might be touched by an extended arm, and the superb St Mary's glows with all the attractions of sculpture gilt by Nature.

The morning sun silvers the objects on Brandon and St Michael's. Then every street, every house, every tree, the cathedral, the laundress spreading her dazzling white linens on the cone, the nursery maid and the infant, may be observed far above the house-tops of the city.

There are few cities which exhibit a greater contrast in the disposition of their streets, and in the form of their houses, than Bristol. The antient and unaltered parts are inconceivably unpleasant, dark, and dirty; and the suburbs consist of numberless lanes, lined by houses inhabited by a wild race, whose countenances indicate wretchedness and affright. These are the wives and offspring of the labourers at copper and iron-works, glass-houses, and many other manufactories; where they are buried from the world, amidst fire, smoke, and dust; and when released, sufficient leisure is denied them to humanize themselves and families.

Let the reader imagine a cellar, of considerable dimensions, lighted and ventilated by inconsiderable apertures, on one side has the vast grate for the tremendous fire necessary to melt the materials without the cone, yet connected with it: boys have been known to crawl on the burning ashes, falling from the ignited coals on the grate, *beyond the fire,* and there seat themselves till they chose to return, or were dislodged by the workmen.

Such is the state of society at present, that a majority of the community would starve were not people of this description to be found. I may lament that men should be compelled to undergo hardships almost too dreadful for contemplation; but I do not by any means wish to be understood as blaming the citizens of Bristol for employing the inhabitants in the production of those articles which support the labourer, the artisan, the retailer, and the merchant, and contribute to the honour and independence of the island.

As the opulence caused by the industry of the Bristolian increases, we are agreeably reminded that his conceptions expand in proportion. Hundreds of sound yet inconvenient houses have been rebuilt in consequence, where the tradesman resides in the midst of his family, surrounded by comforts his neighbours determine henceforward to realize; and I cannot but anticipate the time when those strange, grotesque, encroaching, yet interesting, antient buildings, now very numerous, which darken the narrow streets, shall become as rare at Bristol as they are at present in London through the casualty of 1666.

Several streets have been widened within a few years past, to the great improvement of the city; and others will in all probability be rebuilt.

It is much to be lamented that part of the *furor* for building, which lately prevailed at Bristol, had not been directed into a

The Neptune statue as it once stood at the public conduit in Temple Street by J S Prout. At this period the statue was still naturalistically painted in the manner of a ship's figurehead.

only, containing a huge furnace flaming with intense heat, maintained by men; and then let him conjecture what the feelings of those men must be, when they are assured they are for ever condemned to those and similar regions of despair and misery.

The following fact will serve to evince how the youth of this class of persons are, voluntarily, trained to hardships we shrink from with horror. One of the glass-houses in the environs of Bristol more useful channel than extending the city Westward, when half of the sums expended on absurd speculations, applied to improve the streets, and rebuild the old houses, would have repaid the builder great interest, without risking his principal. A rich merchant or tradesman, who determines to continue his money-increasing pursuits, cannot be tempted from his favourite house or shop by splendid mansions on St Michael's hill, where it is out of his power to converse with others of Bristol, soon felt that all their squares, crescents, and magnificence, would be destitute of residents, though certainly highly desirable. Those mistaken men appear to have followed the pernicious example of London builders, who often ruin themselves, but sometimes make great fortunes, by erecting rows of four houses *in the fields*, forgetting that London possesses a magnetic power of attraction of which Bristol is entirely destitute. The former, being the seat of government, and the seat of a thousand other inducements to residence, has a constant supply of fresh inhabitants, who speedily occupy new houses; but the reverse has been found to be the case in a very great measure in Bristol.

I do not recollect a more melancholy spectacle, independent of human sufferings, than a walk on a dull day through the silent and falling houses in the Western environs of this city; almost all of which are so nearly finished as to represent the deserted streets occasioned by a siege, or the ravages of a plague. Nor can one fail of reflecting on the ruin many families must have suffered, to occasion such a picture of desolation.

Even the beautiful park already mentioned as belonging to Mr Tindal was let on building leases; and grand avenues of architecture were projected, and actually commenced, when misfortune interfered, and restored the domain to the owner; who has since effaced every mark, and returned his soil to the bountiful hand of Nature, now happily employed in renewing her embellishments. If the infatuation, which too long prevailed, had ceased when inhabitants no longer offered for the new houses, the beauty of the Western suburb would have demanded that admiration which I shall not attempt to deny to Park-street, almost perpendicular, and of the Doric order, Berkely-square, and Charlotte-street, all of freestone, commanding from their great elevation most fascinating views.

Two objections prevail against this portion of the city, which are beyond redress, the fatigue of ascent, and the danger attending the foot-way in frosty weather. The former is a shocking inconvenience to the inhabitants of the extensive, broad, and generally well-built, road, or rather street, strangely called St Michael's hill, when criminals are conveyed for execution to the summit; who are detained an incredible length of time, during the repeated yet necessary rests of the horses.

Numbers of extremely pleasant residences, shaded by foliage, are scattered on the hill; and many streets, but a greater number of lanes, intersect it, most of which command the finest prospects. The longest streets on the level, or in antient Bristol, are Redcliff, Temple, the Old Market, Corn, Wine, Broad Mead, and Marlborough; to which may be added many others of considerable, but inferior, length and breadth.

The inhabitants say there are nine squares; but the reader who has never visited Bristol must by no means think of Portman or Grosvenor squares in London, when estimating their size and buildings. Queen-square certainly ranks in the first class; but is not quite so well built as we could wish, nor as the area demands;

After the partial demolition of the Abbey church at the Dissolution, and until the new Cathedral nave was built in 1868 to 1877, its site was covered by houses and gardens as is shown in this rare view by James Storer.

the remainder is covered with grass, oddly enough protected from the deviating steps of pedestrians by rough stakes driven along the borders; which practice is common in other squares of this city, and has a strange and disagreeable effect. The mansion-house, or permanent residence for the mayor, is situated in the North-east corner of Queen-square, and may be pronounced a comfortable and spacious, if not a superb building.

Prince's-street, parallel with the West side of the Square, deserves notice, as it contains several fine houses; and the Assembly-room, of white stone, fronted by a rustic basement, and four Corinthian pillars, supporting a frieze, inscribed 'Curas cithara tollit,' a cornice, and very handsome pediment.

A modern square, dedicated to the Duke of Portland, at the Northern extremity of Bristol, is a second memento of speculation in freestone, which remains unfinished, and nods in concert with one or two streets near it. The fronts of the houses have pilasters and atticks; but I am by no means determined which of the five Grecian orders claims the capitals of the former.

The increase of inhabitants in this neighbourhood occasioned the division of the parish of St James, and the erection of a new church on the East side of the square, dedicated to St Paul, in 1794.

The architect asserts the neat structure thus situated to be in the Gothic, or, if you please, in the antient English Pointed style. I certainly agree with him, and admit that the arches of every description are Pointed; yet, with this concession, he must permit me to add, that the tower resembles a Grecian building at a distance, and, when examined, an attempt to imitate the Pointed style is observable, which it as little resembles as the tower of St Mary Redcliff does the dome of St Paul's London.

which is railed, and has an avenue of fine elms on each side, that shade a broad gravelled walk. The centre contains an equestrian statue of William III. in bronze, by Rysbrack, of considerable merit, and the head of the horse deserves praise. Eight walks diverge from the pedestal to the sides and angles of the area; and

THE CATHEDRAL

occupies the South side of a triangular space called the College-green, which is intersected by walks, and very pleasantly ornamented by large trees, where the soldiers in garrison parade morning and evening, while the bands perform martial airs, and the citizens walk and converse, or listen in groupes to the musick. It will be sufficient for me to describe this venerable building as it now remains.

A gateway of Saxon architecture, in the South-west corner of the College-green, consists of the most curious ornaments in that style, and cannot fail of exciting the warmest praises from the admirer of antiquity. The mouldings are covered with a great variety of interlaced reliefs; which are as correctly and accurately arranged as it would be practicable to entwine ribands; and the stone is fortunately so durable that the sculpture is now sharp, and nearly as well defined as if just completed. But the super-structure is in the Pointed style, with niches, pinnacles, and battlements. After passing through it to the lower green, a passage introduces the visitor to the antient cloisters, with a modern house in the centre of the quadrangle; where he may observe many peculiarities of Saxon origin in the pillars, capitals, and arches, which are interesting through their age and comparative rarity.

Though this cathedral is smaller than those of many other dioceses, it has a most prepossessing effect from the intersection of the transepts, and must have been extremely magnificent before the destruction of the nave. The side ailes of the choir, contrary to generally-established rules in the arrangement of conventual churches, are elevated to the height of the middle aile; and hence arises an air of spacious grandeur sometimes denied to larger structures.

The East window remains, I should imagine, nearly if not quite

Boys play and elegant ladies are enticed to the Chapter House in James Storer's delightful engraving of the Cathedral cloister in the days when it served as an all-weather promenade. The Chapter House then served as the library for the Dean and Chapter.

in its original state; and is very richly and brilliantly filled with representations of saints, monarchs, devices, and arms, in painted glass. The outline may be said to include three large windows. Those on the sides are composed of trefoil divisions, with clusters of ovals in the arches; each of the former containing three small trefoils; and the centre has six divisions; with quatre and trefoils above them. The remainder of the great outline spreads into six leaves, filled with a repetition of the trefoil.

Niches containing coroneted busts, perhaps of the then reigning monarch and his queen, are introduced on each side, and in the depth of the window.

The altar-piece, elevated on five steps of marble, is almost as the architect of the choir left it. One alteration indeed has occurred; but I am inclined to forgive the innovators, as they have by no means committed all the injury in their power.

Three magnificent arcades, separated by buttresses of three gradations, enriched with crockets and finials, filled the space from the pavement to the base of the East window. Two of those are perfect; but the centre is covered by a modern altar-piece, composed of four Corinthian columns, inclosing an arch, painted with a nimbus, by Van Somers, supporting an entablature, and circular divided pediment. The arcades have neat mouldings, which are studded with rosettes, and ornamented with crockets, and terminate in foliage. The angles on the sides of the arches contain shields of arms; and the frieze has four vast heads, projecting in high relief. The cornice, set with roses, forms the base of a range of arches of various breadths, and lozenges, each filled with shields of arms, quatrefoils, and the rebus of a tree issuing from a ton, with the initials W. B. annexed. The arms and regal crown of England adorn the centre.

The termination is extremely beautiful, and serves to prove the skill and ingenuity of our antient sculptors, who spared neither time nor labour in piercing exquisite ornaments. Forty-seven niches, with trefoils in the arches, compose the parapet; the mouldings of which are contrived to form lozenges, crowned with foliage. In each are quatrefoils; and between the foliage are heads of bishops or abbots, and roses.

Let the votary of Grecian architecture visit this antient altar-piece and window; and, if he returns with all his prejudices, I resign him as hopeless, and beyond the reach of the remedy of British art.

There are two windows on the sides of this part of the choir.

Those next the altar are divided by one horizontal mullion, and the width by three perpendicular, which form a double range of cinquefoil arches, with two quatrefoils in each; and the great arches of the windows have four. The others contain two horizontal, and the same number of perpendicular mullions; but the former are branched in the midst, so as to form ovals over and under the ranges of cinquefoil arches.

A variety of subjects, in painted glass, give a rich effect in those windows; and, though greatly subordinate to the Eastern, they make a fine groupe with it. The piers have pierced passages, and busts of bishops and monks over them. Under each are strings of roses; and three clustered pillars, on the fronts of the piers, ascend to the roof; where nine ribs diverge from the capitals, and, intersecting in the vault, composes a series of lozenges in the apex, and others in the ramifications above the windows.

Under them, and near the pavement, are large recesses, composed by four sides of a pierced octagon, with escalops on the interior outline; and on the exterior are four semicircles, and two halves reversed, with foliage on the points and mouldings. Three contain effigies of bishops, or mitred abbots; but the fourth has been destroyed, to admit a monument, dated in the reign of Queen Elizabeth.

The remainder of the church has four pillars on each side, besides others which support the tower, and are placed on vast mouldings, turning into Pointed arches, that form part of the roof. The capitals are enriched with foliage, and the same description of ribs diverge from them as those already mentioned. The pillars that face the side ailes have a singularity attached, which I have no where else observed; the strong arches supported by them ascend from stones placed horizontally across the ailes, that resemble

Engraved view of the 'Saxon Gateway', College Green by J Heath, 1808. This engraving shows part of the Deanery that stretched across what is now Deanery Road and the proximity of the Georgian houses to the Abbey Gateway.

beams; busts on them are the bases of small mouldings; and a double row of arches is thus inserted, East and West, *within the vaults* of the ailes. We should condemn a modern architect for such an exploit.

The windows are the whole height of the walls. The Eastern, where the church increases in breadth, has three ranges of arches and quatrefoils in the great arch. The rest are similar to those in the chancel.

Three niches in the South wall resemble the recesses already described. One contains the effigies of a Crusader, the second a knight, and the third is empty.

A beautiful door, ornamented with buttresses, niches, finials, and foliage, opens into a small anti-chapel, highly enriched on the sides and roof, which leads to St Mary's, or the oratory of the Berkeleys, paved with glazed tiles, and decorated with a cieling covered by tracery, and three very fine windows.

There are two antient sepulchred niches in the North wall empty; but a third is pierced through to the elder Lady chapel, and contains an altar-tomb, with the effigies of a man in armour and his lady, alluded to in the following inscription, placed near it:

The monument of Robert Fitzharding, lord of Berkeley, descended from the kings of Denmark; and Eva his wife; by whom he had five sons and two daughters. Maurice, his eldest son, was the first of the family that took the name of Berkeley. This Robert Fitzharding laid the foundation of this church and monastery of St Augustine, in the year 1140, the fifth of King Stephen, dedicated and endowed it in 1148.

He died in the year 1170, in the 17 of King Henry II.

This monument was repaired A.D. 1742.
From the said Robert Fitzharding, lord of Berkeley, Augustus, the present earl, is the two-and-twentieth in descent.

The architecture of this chapel evinces a remoter date than the rest of the cathedral, and has a range of arcades on the side, separated by clustered pillars, and the arches are ornamented with foliage and busts. Three single columns on the walls support the vault, intersected by plain groins. The four windows in the North are each three pyramidal lancets, faced within by isolated pillars. The Eastern has five, with quatrefoils above them.
There are several handsome modern monuments, and two for well-known characters:

Sacred to the memory of Mrs Elizabeth Draper, in whom genius and benevolence were united.

Sterne's celebrated *Eliza*, commemorated by figures emblematic of the genii mentioned in the above short inscription.
George Colman, senior, the dramatic author, inscribed the second monument, erected by his widow, to William Powell, patentee of Covent Garden theatre, who died in 1769:

Bristol! to worth and genius ever just,
To thee our Powell's dear remains we trust:
Soft as the streams thy sacred springs impart,
The milk of human kindness warm'd his heart;
That heart, which every tender feeling knew,
The foil where pity, love, and friendship grew.
Oh! let a faithful friend, with grief sincere,

Inscribe his tomb, and drop the heartfelt tear;
Here rest his praise, here found his noblest fame,
All else a bubble, or an empty name.

Mr Powell was one of the managers of the theatre erected in King-street about 1766, which is said to be handsome and convenient; but I had not an opportunity of seeing it.

CUSTOMS OF THE BRISTOLIANS
An antient house situated at the North end of Frogmore-street has an empty niche on the angle, where the statue of some saint has evidently stood, in the manner they are placed in the streets of cities on the continent; and I am the more convinced of the correctness of this supposition, as the building, which is of timber and plaster, has no resemblance to the appendages of a religious structure.
Hence to the drawbridge every circumstance reminds the stranger of a populous trading city: numerous hackney-coaches interrupt his steps, and great numbers of persons glide rapidly on each side of the streets. The male inhabitants of Bristol are generally well formed; but the females are short, and few have handsome features. Neither have they that elegance of exterior which distinguishes even the nursery-maids and shop-women of London. Let me, however, be understood to speak of the aggregate in this particular, as thousands of exceptions occur, and present us with exquisite beauty, embellished with all the attributes of the Graces.
Were we to confine our observations to the youth and adults of the male sex only, it would be difficult to discover any material difference in their manners and appearance from those of the metropolis.

Neither sex has yet adopted that convenient method of passing through the streets which renders our movements nearly uninterrupted even in Cheapside. The citizens of Bristol politely endeavour to give each other the wall, and thus constantly impede their progress in a direct line, forgetting that no rudeness can possibly be imputed to individuals where every person invariably inclines to the right when meeting others.

Should a small portion of the 100,000 people who inhabit this city meet with my work, let them profit by the gentle reprehension I now convey for their excess of good-breeding.

On passing through Clare, Corn, and Wine, named as if three, though one street, numbers of large and excellent shops attract the attention very forcibly to the best articles of dress, gold, silver, and jewellery, and books and prints by the most eminent authors and artists, which are continued down High-street to Bristol-bridge.

Those, the Exchange, the Post-office, the Stage-coach-office, and the Exchange market, constantly assemble numbers of persons; and this focus is the point where character may be observed, and inferences drawn. Mine are, that regularity, industry, and civility, distinguish the citizens of Bristol and its rural environs.

The display of meat and vegetables, cheese, &c. &c. in the different markets, is plentiful; but those articles almost reach the London prices. Coals and house-rent, however, compensate the inhabitant, and are very reasonable. Indeed, the former abounds even under the city, and the vicinity of Kingswood reduces them to 14s. per ton.

The whole body of the people emerge from their houses in the evenings of fine Sundays, and walk to the various heights in the neighbourhood; where they breathe a salubrious air, or pass through luxuriant meadows to the tea-gardens near Stapleton. But I observed, during my residence, that very few indeed of the richest inhabitants were pedestrians beyond the limits of the city.

An anniversary of the charity-children, held in the parish of St James, enabled me to observe the spirit with which celebrations of that nature are entered into. The steeple of the church was literally dressed, in the nautical phrase, with large ensigns and pendants, and made a most gaudy appearance, compared with the solitary and ragged flags exhibited upon a few of our London steeples on rejoicing days.

A very considerable degree of interest and expectation fruitlessly agitated the Bristolians when I was there, in consequence of an intimation that the Royal Family would honour the city with a visit. The first upon record from a crowned head was involuntary, and occurred in the person of King Stephen, as a prisoner to the Empress Maud, whom he had previously entertained there, when duped by her pacific professions.

Since the Revolution of 1688 the citizens have had the honour of receiving Queen Anne and the Prince of Denmark in 1703; and the former again in 1710. But, though every attention was paid the royal guests, much disloyalty appears to have been shewn to the Queen's successor, George I. which afterwards subsided, as will be evinced by the following account of the splendid honours rendered to Frederick prince of Wales, and his lady, in 1738, extracted from the *General Evening Post* of November 11:

Bristol, Nov. 11. The neighbouring parishes have been busy all the week in mending and cleaning the roads (which were grown almost impassable) through which their Royal Highnesses were to pass, in their way to the city; and the better to accommodate them in their journey, Colonel Bridges, of Keynsham, gave their Royal Highnesses an invitation to come through his park, which extends almost to Bussleton common; and, at the same time, made a present to their Royal Highnesses of a brace of deer, hares, partridges, &c.

Yesterday, about noon, their Royal Highnesses the Prince and Princess of Wales paid their promised visit to this city, accompanied by my Lord Baltimore, Sir Thomas Saunderson, and other persons of quality.

At their departure from Bath Mr Thompkins, the boatman, saluted them with a discharge of several small cannon. A great many of the citizens of Bath accompanied their Highnesses hither. The roads were lined with a vast concourse of country people, belonging to the several parishes on the road, who testified their joy by firing small guns, &c.

At length they arrived at Temple Gate; within-side of which, under the town wall, scaffolding was erected for the Mayor and Corporation. As soon as their Royal Highnesses had entered the city, they were congratulated by our Recorder in a very eloquent manner. Then the gentlemen of the corporation went into their coaches, which were near at hand, and so the grand cavalcade began.

The companies of the city made a magnificent appearance in their formalities, marching two by two, preceding the Corporation and the royal guests.

The Company of Glassmen went first, dressed in white Holland shirts, on horseback, some with swords, others with crowns and sceptres in their hands, made of glass. Then followed the Wool-Combers, on foot, dressed also in white, with woollen caps, dyed in different colours, and wands in their hands. Next came the Weavers, likewise in white, and on foot; in the midst of whom was a new loom, erected on a pageant, with a boy in it weaving a piece of shag along the streets, to whom his Highness was pleased to make a present of five guineas. Then proceeded the several other companies, consisting of 21 in number, all in their formalities; among whom was the Sadlers', who made a splendid appearance, on horseback, with rich cockades in their hats, who complimented the Prince in a very particular manner, and who was pleased to return them his thanks.

Mr Nash, the Sir Clement of Bath, attended their Royal Highnesses hither, and proceeded in the cavalcade.

Along our spacious key were planted 121 pieces of cannon, which were regularly discharged during the procession. A great number of guns were also discharged from the opposite sides; but the first salute was given by the cannon planted on Brandon hill.

The cavalcade passed round the key, that the royal visitors might have a full view of the shipping, and the beauty of the harbour.

The companies ranged themselves in two columns in the square, under cover of the horse; so that their Highnesses had a compleat view of the whole cavalcade, as they proceeded to their lodgings, where the clergy, and body of merchants, congratulated them on their happy arrival; the Rev Dr Harcourt, in the name of the clergy, and Mr John Coysgarne, master of the hall, in the name of the merchants; being introduced, at the request of his Royal Highness, by the Right Worshipful William Jefferies, Esq. mayor; who had all the honour of kissing their Royal Highnesses hands. As soon as the Prince had got up stairs, the sashes were thrown up, and his Highness was pleased to stand some time at the window, perusing the Freedom of the City, which was presented by the Mayor and Corporation in a beautiful gold box of excellent workmanship.

The visit of the Prince of Wales in 1807 occasioned a special performance at the Theatre Royal in King Street. This bill is just one example from Bristol Reference Library's huge collection of theatrical memorabilia.

After their Highnesses had refreshed themselves, they were preceded to the Merchants'-hall by a grand band of musick, and the Corporation on foot, bare-headed, in all their formalities. Their Highnesses stood some time at the entrance of the hall, and seemed mightily delighted with the thronging concourse of spectators.

The entertainment at the hall was very grand; upwards of 500 ladies and gentlemen were present; and £.5. apiece was offered for tickets.

After the ball there was a very handsome firework in the square, which was played off on a scaffold erected round King William's statue; and it was carried on in the following manner: Upon giving the signal, 21 guns were fired from three of the sides inclosing the statue. Then from all the four parts of the scaffold rose a great number of rockets, which broke into stars, grenadoes, and gold and silver rain. Then three girandolas, or fire-wheels, were played off. The runners upon lines concluded this first part of the fire-work.

After a small pause, another signal being given, the 21 guns were fired as before; then a large parcel of rockets from all parts of the scaffold, went up as before, with stars, &c. Then three more girandolas, or fire-wheels, as before; concluding with four runners on lines.

Then, after a second pause, a third signal was given, when the last part of the fire-work began; first with the 21 guns, then very large rockets from all parts, in a great number, succeeded by three more wheels, and four runners on lines. All this while the figure of the sun appeared upon the top of a pyramid, 20 feet high. Now the whole pyramid began to blaze out in fountains of fire; and the sun threw out his rays in streams of fire also. The conclusion was a great number of fountains of fire, throwing out stars continually; and ending in several mines, which were sprung, and filled the air with a great number of different fire-works, &c.

This fire-work was, at the desire of the Mayor and Corporation, undertaken by Dr Defaguliers, who having but very small notice, and but four days time to prepare it in, was very unwilling to undertake it; but, as the citizens were desirous of such a thing to entertain their Royal Highnesses with, the Doctor was prevailed upon the give them what the time would afford.

The signal that was given at each part of the firework was from the Doctor, at a window adjacent to the Prince.

The houses in the several streets through which their Highnesses passed were adorned with scarlet, &c.

Upon the whole, never were grander doings in this city. And his

Royal Highness was so condescending as to bow to the populace as he passed; who in return ushered them along with the loudest acclamation. The shops were shut throughout the city; and the whole ceremony was conducted with the utmost magnificence, decency, and good order.

This morning the Prince visited the Hot Wells; and about noon their Royal Highnesses set out on their return to Bath, the Corporation attending them to the city gates in their coaches and formalities.

Copy of the Address presented by the Company of Sadlers of the City of Bristol, to his Royal Highness the Prince of Wales, at Bath, which was very graciously received:

Sir,
From a grateful sense of the great favours which your Royal Highness has been pleased to confer upon the Sadlers in the City of London, those of the same occupation in the City of Bristol humbly beg leave to congratulate you upon your safe arrival in these parts. They ardently wish, that the waters of the Bath may answer all the intentions that can be desired by your Royal Highness and the Princess your Royal Consort; and that the same kind Providence that has hitherto attended you, may ever continue to be so propitious, that there may never be wanting a royal branch, lineally descended from the illustrious house of Hanover, to adorn the British throne.

The Duke of York made a public entry over the new bridge in 1761, and remained at Bristol several days; but since that period no part of the royal family have visited the city, to the great disappointment of the majority of the inhabitants.

Fairs are still held, which are probably very beneficial to the town and neighbourhood; and if confined to the sale of great varieties of manufactures brought from Birmingham, Sheffield, Tewksbury, Wolverhampton, London, &c. &c. must undoubtedly be so; but I am afraid there are drawbacks that almost counterbalance the advantages.

That which commences on the first of September, and is termed St James's, requires great preparations. Those, when completed, exhibit streets of shops filled with cloth, blankets, stockings of wool and cotton, carpets, rugs, linen, every description of hardware, haberdashery, millinery, and trinkets; and even cattle, and vast quantities of leather are sold during this period, and in March at the Temple fair.

I have often had occasion to observe that improprieties are suffered to exist in full force by bodies politick, of which they appear to be insensible, though a stranger feels shocked at the first glance on them. Such an impropriety occurs annually at Bristol, before the church of St James, when the church-yard is converted into the site of the fair named from the patron Saint. The area, of very considerable extent, is situated on the side of a hill; but the lower portion has no appearance of interments; occasioned, as I have been informed, by the possible danger which might ensue from disturbing the remains of persons deposited there who died of the plague. Through this circumstance the bodies of numbers of parishioners are crowded in the upper part, where an incredible assemblage of grave-stones and graves cover the surface.

When we reflect on the necessary consequences proceeding from the movements of the multitude who frequent the fair, sufficient cause appears why a cemetery is an improper receptacle of articles for buying and selling. This, however, may be pronounced a slight objection; but there are others, of great importance, which I shall take the liberty of noticing. Posts or stakes used in erecting the shops cannot be inserted within the church-yard without disturbing the ashes of the dead. It surely must be admitted that those ashes ought not to be disturbed, unless through necessity. Are there, besides, no arts of trade practised in the disposal of property? and are such to be permitted where a solemn act of consecration has once occurred? To conclude, is the depositary of mortality of so little importance with us, as to make the exhibition of the most contemptible shews, contortions, grimaces, and even obscenity, by the most abandoned wretches of both sexes, a matter of indifference, where the priest performs the last offices of religion daily?

An inhabitant of the square inclosing this area observed to me, that his whole family viewed the approach of September with dismay. 'How,' said his lady,

'shall I express the effects of the scene as it appeared from our windows? Tombs covered with cloths, toys, and ginger-bread, children and servants admiring the follies of a great city, and at the same moment treading upon fragments of the dead, but too often exposed after recent interments, stages supporting puppets, ridiculous yet innocent, inter-mingled with painted hideous males and females, their drummers, fidlers, and trumpeters; when the constant roar of sounds was at intervals interrupted by the tolling of the church-bell for a funeral.'

After having thus freely expressed my disapprobation of the site of the fair of St James, I feel it incumbent to declare that I mean no censure towards the members of the present Corporation, whose remote predecessors were alone to blame. The populace would by no means have compelled them to appoint the church-yard for such a purpose; but I am extremely doubtful whether the fair could now be removed without their interference, and possibly in a manner that might shake the very vitals of the city. Popular insurrections should be guarded against with the utmost caution, and those reforms avoided which are calculated to excite them. Several instances have occurred in the history of Bristol that fully justify fears on this point; particularly when we remember the vicinity of Kingswood, the affair of incendiary letters, and that of the toll on Bristol bridge.

The church of St James, originally a priory, and situated on the summit of the hill, has nothing remarkably attractive on the exterior; but the houses and trees on St Michael's hill, far beyond, have a very good effect grouped with it.

The Temple fair is held in and near Temple-street, on the South side of the Avon; where it must unquestionably greatly impede the communication with the London road. Temple-street, generally filthy, and badly built, derived its name from the Temple church, on the North-east side; erected, according to Barrett, by the Knights Templars, on ground presented to them by Robert of Gloucester, in the reign of King Stephen, and dedicated to the Holy Cross.

No part of the original building is now visible; and I should incline to think the architecture belongs to the time of Henry V. or VI. The length is considerable, and the nave contains three ailes, without clerestory windows. The pillars are generally more ornamented with mullions than those of parish churches.

The North and South walls lean outwards, and the arches of the middle aile are full two feet farther asunder than the bases of the pillars which support them.

A curious antient lustre of brass is suspended from the cieling, consisting of a double row of leaves for sockets, which spring from pierced buttresses, inclosing St Michael slaying the dragon; and on the apex is a figure of the Holy Virgin, with the infant Jesus held beyond her breast.

The inducement to visit Temple church proceeds from the very singular inclination of the tower to the West, evidently occasioned by the insecurity of the marshy earth which supports the foundation on that side. Many arguments might be brought to prove the solidity and general excellence of our venerable ecclesiastical structures, deduced from probable inferences; but the tower now under notice is an indisputable evidence of the skill of antient artisans, and the durability of their materials, which are so well cemented in this instance as to actually overhang the base, without deranging the continuity of the rich sculpture near the battlements.

The tower of the church of Holy Cross is 25 feet square, about 114 feet high, and deviates three feet nine inches from a perpendicular line. There are buttresses at each angle, and a semi-octagon turret, inclosed by those at the South-east. The former reach to the summit, in four gradations, and terminate in finials, and others proceed from grotesque heads on the third cornice, beneath which are pointed windows, in two ranges, with cinquefoil arches, and a quatrefoil above them.

From the cornice just mentioned upwards, the decorations are minute and beautiful, commencing with a range of zigzags, each containing a trefoil, bounded by a string of rosettes. The sills of two windows (similar on the four fronts) have small quatrefoils under them, and the angles of their arches are ornamented with others. Over those are cinquefoil arcades and a cornice. The reader, upon referring to the plate of this interesting subject, will find other appendages, too minute for description, and will perceive the exact appearance of this leaning wonder of Bristol. Barrett says that Brunius, in his *Theatrum Urbium*, Cologn. 1576, mentions the church of Holy Cross as then having a deranged Tower, through the vibration of the bells; who adds, that Abraham Ortelius informed him, he had put a stone as large as the egg of a goose in the fissure between the church and tower which was broke by the motion thus occasioned.

Several strange traditions and assertions have their origin from the present state of the tower, erected originally in 1390, and rebuilt in 1460, which are worth recording as instances of credulity and ignorance. One of primitive date asserts that the ringing of the bells caused so violent a concussion in the walls of the church, before the crack appeared, that the oil undulated over the sides of the lamps, and extinguished the flames; but after that event happened they remained unshaken.

A more modern supposition accounts for the motion, by placing the foundation on certain *woolpacks, the elasticity of which* causes the tower to vibrate on ringing of peals.

Others say that the foundation sunk on the West side, when the tower was half completed, with a sudden shock, which threw the scaffolds and men on them to the ground; and that it remained thus twenty years, and was then completed.

To conclude, it is generally believed, that a basin filled with water will be completely emptied by the mere concussion, if placed on the roof during a peal; but that assertion is untrue, as the sexton informed me he had deposited a bason full of water there, and found that the vibration caused but very little to run over the declining side.

The fact, as explained by this inoffensive man, may be depended on. Had he attempted observations beyond the sight and touch, his authority could have had but little weight with me, subsequent to his directing my attention to several tombs which he said belonged to persons 'be-knighted by Queen Anne and Queen James.'

A plumber of respectability was employed a few years past in mending the lead on the roof of the tower, when a peal commenced unknown to him. He afterwards declared the tremulation was so dreadful that he should never forget it, though he instantly hurried down.

St MARY REDCLIFF

is situated on the East side of Redcliff-street; principally occupied for large warehouses, and very considerable retail shops, yet dirty and badly paved. That parsimonious spirit which I have often had occasion to condemn and deplore, operated in full force facing and on the North side of St Mary's. The street ascends immediately before the West front, where it is extremely narrow, and wretchedly built; and houses project at the North-west angle, which entirely impede a view of the superb porch on that quarter of the church. Had this glorious specimen of antient British art been granted as much ground on the front and North sides as the South faces, the effect of the flight of steps near the tower, on which it appears to be elevated, would have been grand beyond parallel.

Under these disadvantages, there is but one point of view where the general outline of the building can be observed; and even

there all the front of the South aile, and the Western doors, are obscured by intervening foliage. The reader will perceive by the annexed view, that Camden was right in pronouncing St Mary's 'like a cathedral': the vast window of the nave, the turret at the angle, the flying buttresses from the South aile, and the rich tower and mutilated spire, broken by lightning, fully justify his comparison.

A tall square building intercepts the South transept, which is Watts's patent-shot manufactory. This person is said to have been indebted to his wife for the discovery of his manner of casting shot; who often thinking intensely of her husband's conversations on the subject, dreamed that she had made those diminutive globes very perfect, by dropping melted lead from a great height into water. Such at least is the story circulated at Bristol: whether it is founded on facts I cannot pretend to decide; but of this I am certain, I have, when a boy, often made pear-shaped shot by the same means, though I never held the lead at a distance from the receptacle; which, if increased, must doubtlessly render the globular outline more perfect.

The rock and earth ascending from the river, represented in the plate, is the Red-cliff whence the South suburb of Bristol derives its name; but I have, for obvious reasons, drawn the view at high-water; which in a great measure conceals the elevation.

Near the boat, on the right, is the landing-place of the ferry from the Gibb; whence a romantic flight of steps, cut in the rock, and shaded by foliage, leads to the railed terrace before Redcliff parade, the houses on the summit.

The most delicate and elaborate ornaments on the exterior of St Mary's church are placed where they are least observed. I would therefore recommend the visitor to enter the North yard; when he will discover several angles, discoloured by smoke from the

The length, including the Lady-chapel, is said to be 239 feet, that of the transept 117; the breadth of the nave and ailes 59, the transepts 44; and the height of the middle and side ailes 54, and 25 feet.

I had the curiosity to ascend the stair-case in the Western turret, in order, if possible, to discover the manner in which the stones of the vault of the nave were placed; but was completely disappointed on finding the whole surface next the roof covered with a deep circular bed of cement, evidently intended to carry off any water that might penetrate through the lead above, and thus injure the ribs and intervening arches. Let the modern imitator of the Pointed style imitate

adjacent glass-houses, adorned with the very acme of ecclesiastical sculpture, particularly on two doors faintly sketched on the illustrative plate. The decorations on those are actually isolated, in vines of stone, and fret-work of incredible slightness. Nor will he be less entertained with the grotesque brackets, two of which are represented.

As I have never professed to enter into the history of places and buildings in this work, but merely to detail the effects of first impressions from them on my mental tablet, I shall only mention, from Barrett, that Simon de Burton is supposed to have begun the church in 1292, the remnant of which is the North porch; and that Canynges, an opulent merchant, erected the nave, choir, transepts, and Lady chapel (now a school), circa 1376; repaired by his grandson, after a storm had destroyed the steeple, and injured the church, in 1445.

such, and other precautions, that have preserved our antient buildings for centuries.

The proportions of this beautiful structure are so correct, that it may be justly pronounced one of the finest parish-churches in England; yet it must be acknowledged, that the workmanship of some of the parts has been exceeded in other instances. There certainly is not that delicacy and minuteness in the pillars and mouldings of the arches which is generally observable in the florid style. The architect formed an admirable plan; but the masons and sculptors were not uniformly proficient in their respective arts; and recent white-washings have contributed to enlarge the swells, and close the cavities, in a most provoking manner.

There is a capricious deviation from symmetry at the commencement of the nave, by the introduction of a vast arch, opposed to

two smaller; within which is the belfry, lighted by plain pointed windows. But there is a rich cieling, of filleted tracery, surrounding a circle; and the intersections are covered with fanciful, yet whimsical sculptures, very neatly executed.

A bracket, inserted on the angle of the arch of the North aile, formed of a head with foliage in the mouth, supports the celebrated rib of the enormous dun cow said to have been killed by Guy earl of Warwick, which is unquestionably a bone, but of what animal I am not naturalist enough to determine; nor shall I bewilder myself and the reader by entering into conjectures when and why it was placed in the church.

The first arch of the aile just mentioned has an angular door, communicating with the North porch, part of the original church. On the sides are arcades and pinnacles; and above an enriched string, and foliaged battlements; still higher four cinque-foil arcades; and behind them three ovals; each containing quatrefoils, and trefoil divisions of the aile windows. Those, however, have a poor effect, caused by the excessive breadth, and their angular mouldings.

The cielings of the ailes, and that of the nave, nearly resemble each other; except that the latter is extremely rich and elaborate. The filletings, with the ribs, forming a great variety of pleasing figures, have their intersections finely decorated.

The nave contains seven arches on the South side, and but six on the North. Those are plain, and the mouldings between them are without capitals; and two small pillars on each side of them contribute to expose this defect. Besides, they are exceedingly clumsy. However, the depths have clusters of pillars.

Between the arches and the bases of the clerestory windows are ranges of arcades; and five mullions are inserted in the former, the arches of which are filled by thirty-two small divisions, trefoiled, and quatrefoils.

The antient porch is a sexagon, with seats, arcades, a strong of busts, and foliage, intermixed with figures; and the principal door has an arch, of numerous escaloped mouldings. The piers are pierced between the windows, for passages; and higher are niches, which have contained statues or pedestals, of high relief; but the windows are two-thirds filled by the external ornaments of the porch. The arches have escaloped quatrefoils and trefoils.

The cieling is intersected with great taste, and nothing can exceed the beauty of the sculpture of the intersections. On the West side a door communicates with an apartment described by the attendant as an original confessional; but the circular aperture, supposed to be intended for the penitent, appears modern. Besides, there are two closed arches. I do not, however, pretend to assert the place was not used for the purpose mentioned.

Several steps lead to an arch supported by isolated clusters of pillars; and two large niches adorn the sides. The pedestals to those are monks' heads attached to the bodies of animals, and the pinnacles rest on others extremely grotesque.

The square passage before the entrance to the nave has a range of arcades, separated by isolated pillars, and a plain cieling of two groins. A door on the left-hand opens to the stairs which conduct to the room where Chatterton asserted he found Rowley's manuscripts, forged by himself, and in a manner so decidedly unlike those soiled by age, that an antiquary could not possibly be deceived for an instant.

Many of the scraps alluded to have found their way to the British Museum; where they will long remain as mementos of Chatterton's perversion of his supereminent abilities, and of the extreme facility with which extraordinary tales are imposed on the credulity of the publick. 'Look,' said a gentleman who shewed them to me at the Museum, 'and wonder how the most superficial could be deceived by these streaks of bistre, mixed with Indian ink, so decidedly transparent, and washed on old parchment and paper.' I gazed, and was astonished.

I detest the cheat, as an otherwise valuable history of Bristol has been polluted by long quotations from Rowley.

The South porch has several rich niches, with canopies and pillars in the angles; which support a cieling of elegant tracery.

There are four great arches at the intersection of the Cross, the pillars and mouldings of which are delicate; and the vault has a cross of tracery, and angles filled by enrichments. Those of the transepts are very beautiful.

There are side ailes, and six arches in each transept. Between the angles above them and the string are trefoils, and arcades still higher. The clerestory windows of the South are uncommonly pleasing, with each a border of fifteen quatrefoils, inclosing an arch, within which are two escaloped arches, two quatrefoils, and four arched divisions in ovals, all glazed. Tall windows, at the extremities of the transepts, have both three mullions, with quatrefoils and trios of trefoils in the midst. The arch is divided into two parts by the centre mullion, and the intervals contain quatre and trefoils. The lower portions of these windows have paintings of the Virgin and Saints, in dull glass.

The chancel, or choir, consists of five arches. Those and the cieling resemble the nave.

The side ailes are separated from the choir by skreens of arcades; and there are three steps at the chancel gate, and four lead to the altar. The vast pile of wood, or altar-piece, is a most disagreeable foil to the slender proportions of the church, and as ponderous as the rest of the building is taper and graceful. This, like all our modern appendages to the East wall, is of Grecian architecture, with the usual pillars, pediments, &c. But the greatest misfortune attending the sacred spot is the eclipse of the fine East window, by Hogarth's painting of the Ascension; in which, to use the attendant's words, 'the white men are angels, and the red man one of the Saints;' accompanied by two others on the side walls, representing the High Priest sealing the stone, and the women informed of the Ascension. Below them is a smaller picture of the raising of the widow's child, by Tresham; presented to the church by Sir Clifton Wintringham, bart. the artists uncle.

I shall mention but two of the numerous monuments, in order to avoid prolixity. That of William Canynges is an altar-tomb, under a canopy, and situated at the base of the wall of the South end of the South transept. The sketch of his life and property given in the inscription cannot fail of interesting the reader:

Mr William Canings, the richest merchant of the town of Bristow; afterwards chosen five times mayor of the said town, for the good of the commonwealth of the same. He was in order of priesthood seven years, and afterwards Dean of Westbury, and died the 7th of November, 1474. Which said William did build, within the said town of Westbury, a college (with his canons); and the said William did maintain, by space of eight years, 800 handycrafts men, besides carpenters and masons every day 100 men.

Besides, King Edward the Fourth had of the said William 3000 marks for his peace, to be had in 2470 tons of shipping. These are the names of his shipping, with their burthens:

The Mary Canings,	400
The Mary Redcliff,	500
The Mary and John,	900 tons
The Galiot,	150
The Catharine,	140
The Mary Batt,	220
The Little Nicholas,	140
The Margaret,	200
The Catharine Boston,	22
A ship in Ireland,	100

No age nor time can wear out well-won fame;
The stones themselves a stately work doth shew;
From senseless grave we ground may men's good name;
And noble minds by ventrous deeds we know.
A lantern clear sets forth a candle light.
A worthy act declares a worthy wight.
The buildings rare, that here you may behold

To shrine his bones, deserves a tomb of gold;
The famous fabrick, that he here hath done,
Shines in its sphere as glorious as the Sun.
What needs more words? the future world he fought,
And set the pomp and pride of this at nought;
Heaven was his aim, let Heaven be still his station,
That leaves such work for other's imitation.

The second in importance is thus inscribed:

Sir William Penn, knight, born at Bristol, 1621, of the Penns of Penn's-lodge, in the county of Wilts. He was made a captain at 21; rear-admiral of Ireland at 23; vice-admiral of England at 31; and general, in the first Dutch war, at 32. Whence returning, in 1655, he was chosen a parliament-man for Weymouth; 1660 was made commissioner of the admiralty and navy, governor of the forts and town of Kingsale, vice-admiral of Munster, and a member of that provincial council; and in 1664 was chosen great captain-commander, under his Royal Highness, in that signal and most evidently successful fight against the Dutch fleet.

Thus he took leave of the sea, his old element; but continued his other employs till 1669; when, through bodily infirmities, contracted through the care and fatigue of publick affairs, he withdrew, prepared and made for his end; and, with a gentle and even gale, in much peace, arrived and anchored in his last and best port, at Wanstead, in the county of Essex, 16 September, 1670, being then but 49 years of age and four months. To whose name and merit his surviving lady erected this remembrance.

The brave exploits of Admiral Penn procured him a grant from Charles II. of a tract of country in North America, now Pennsylvania.

Bristol contains several excellent churches besides those already mentioned; but it cannot be expected that I should notice each, or the numerous neat chapels and meetings of the Dissenters. The disciples of Wesley seem to have a prescriptive right to Bristol and the vicinity. Indeed, the memory of that teacher of Methodism deserves real gratitude from the present citizens, and the inhabitants of Kingswood. To him they are indebted for the peaceable possession of their property, and the amelioration of the savage manners of the colliers who work the coal-mines Eastward of the City.

As those mines have been thus introduced, I cannot resist transcribing the ensuing narrative from the *Whitehall Evening Post* of November 22, 1735, which, if true, is most extraordinary:

Bristol, Nov. 22. Among the many and various accounts that have been given us of accidents happening to mankind, nothing has occurred more particular for many years than the following surprizing relation of three men and a boy, who were ten days and nineteen hours in a dark cavern of the earth, 39 fathom deep, besides the danger that otherwise attended them, of drowning, or falling from the heights of the mine, the very coal-work itself being 16 fathom deep.

The persons whom we relate this of are, viz. Joseph Smith, aged upwards of 60; Edward Peacock, Abraham Peacock, his son; all of the parish of Beeton; and Thomas Hemins, of Mangotsfield: all coal-miners.

On Friday the 7th instant, as they were wedging out the coal, in an old mine, near Two-Mile Hill, in King's wood (rented by lease of Thomas Chester, esq. by Joseph Jefferies, Edward Wilmot, and Thomas Nash), on a sudden, a prodigious torrent of water bursted out of the vein, that all of them were nigh immediate death, not knowing whither to escape for want of their lights, which were all extinguished by the water, each shifting for himself. Such was their consternation, that go which way they would, danger was near them of drowning or breaking their necks, the work being very large. In this distress they crawled, sometimes on their hands and knees, from place to place, to avoid the water, and getting on a rising ground, they continued there some time; when proceeding further, they at length came to what they call in the mines a hatchin, a high slant from whence coal had been dug, and in which the boy had secured himself, who made lamentable moan, and gave himself up for death. The three men came together by calling to each other. In their way to this hatchin, Joseph Peacock found a bit of beef, and a crust of bread, weighing, as they supposed, in all, about four ounces, which they equally divided. The boy's situation being the most secure, they continued there to the time of their relief, and made the boy fetch them water in his hat, as best knowing the way, which was but a little by the time he returned with it, the water shrinking considerably; and it became so dangerous to have a supply, that the boy could not be prevailed upon to fetch any more, which forced them to the necessity of drinking their own urine, and to chew some chips, which Joseph Smith had cut from a coal basket he accidentally found, which being all gone, and the old man losing his knife, they could get no more from the basket. Being all ready to perish for want, Joseph Smith chewed a piece of his shoe, which not answering his end, he took a resolution of endeavouring to come at the water, in which he tumbled twice, and would have been drowned each time, had not Edward Peacock

saved him. What with the heat of the place they were in, the nauseous fumes of their own bodies, their want of water, meat, &c. during so long a time, it cannot be looked upon otherwise than a miracle their being alive. One would think it impossible four persons should sustain life after so long a hardship, and with only the small portion of four ounces of meat and bread.

Towards the close of their deplorable misery, which was till Monday the 17th instant, when they were taken out of their dismal cell, the old man, Joseph Smith, began to yield to nature, and grew delirious; and indeed all the rest gave over all hopes of relief, and began to decline too by weakness.

At the first bursting of the vein, there were four other boys in the mine, but being at what they call the tip of the work, and hearing the noise of the water, made the best of their way to the rope, crying to the people on the surface to pull them up; which was not so speedy but the water was at the last boy's heels; who, as the others were hauling up, catched hold of one of his companion's feet, and all got safe to the top.

This being noised in the neighbouring hamlets, great numbers of people resorted daily to the pit, and divers colliers ventured down at different times, in order to relieve their unfortunate brethren; but perceiving a black damp in the work, which they reckon the more dangerous, as admitting of no lighted candles, were as often obliged to return, till Providence had ordered others to a more successful attempt, viz. Sampson Phips, Thomas Somers, Moses Reynolds, and Thomas Smith, son to old Joseph Smith, who prudently carrying down a parcel of coals on fire, so draughted the damp, that they got to their miserable brethren, except one Thomas Bolison, who was all the time missing, and supposed to be drowned.

When they were hawled up to the open air, their sight entirely failed them for some time, and were all very weak and feeble; but after having some comfortable refreshment, they all walked to their homes, to the great surprize of the people present. Being told the long time of their calamity, they were under a consternation, not thinking it had been but about five or six days. The morning of their never-to-be-forgotten preservation Thomas Smith, son to old Joseph Smith, intended to bespeak a coffin for his father, and his mother had made preparations for his funeral.

P.S. We formerly mentioned the above persons to be drowned in a coal-work at Timsbury; but the account now given was taken from Joseph Smith's son, who was one of the last persons that went down to their relief, and from their own mouths.

The reader has now received a general description of Bristol, which will enable him in a great measure to appreciate its advantages and defects; I shall therefore conclude my notices of it with an extract from a manuscript, numbered 4206 in Ayscough's catalogue of additional articles, preserved in the British Museum:

There is no mention made of this town in the Saxon Chronicles. Aylward, earl of Gloucester, in the time of King Athelstan, was the principal founder thereof. From which time the earls of Gloucester continued lords of Bristowe, until it was incorporated.
William earl of Gloucester founded and annexed Redcliff to Bristowe.
Robert Fitz Parnel, earl of Gloucester, built at Bristowe the priory of St James, which was made a member or college of the Abbey of Tewkesbury.

The castle of Bristowe also was built by the Earl of Gloucester, and hath been of reputation ever since the time of King Stephen, against whom Robert earl of Gloucester held it, when other nobles offended with the prince held others.
Also King Henry II. and Robert Fitzharding were the first founders of St Augustine's church, of Bristowe; which, by King Henry VIII. was made to be a cathedral church; and the borough of Bristowe was then made to be a city.

EXCURSION TO DUNDRY.
I crossed the Avon at the Gibb, at low water, and observed that the boat was pulled with a pole applied to the bottom of the river. The stream did not then appear to be more than four times the boat's length in breadth; and a large ship, the Mermaid of New York, lay at a wharf, with her stern towards Redcliff, full seven feet deep in the soft mud, by which the vessel was supported erect, as if water-borne, ten feet above the water.
An unpleasant lane leads from the ferry to the verge of the new canal. As I passed this, a labourer advanced, and requested that I would return, as a person had at that instant fired the train of a ball of gunpowder, by means of which the workmen loosen the otherwise immoveable rocks of the fire. In an instant the explosion occurred, and I saw a thousand splinters of various sizes hurled into the air, that as instantaneously fell, in a dangerous shower, in a circle probably 400 feet in diameter.
The shock had not only rifted the rock immediately surrounding the powder, but immense fragments were removed from their beds, where wedges were driven into them, and they are thus reduced small enough to be raised with cranes by four men, into the carts which are conveyed up the sides of the banks on stages,

by the operation of steam-engines erected on the verge of the canal, that turn several wheels, and those two others, with chains of vast length and strength round them, which by their revolutions lower, empty, and raise the filled carts attached to the chains.

The variety of strata in the canal between the Bath road and Rownham meads are highly interesting. Part consists of fine sand, almost as bright as vermilion, others of a chocolate-coloured rock, connected in some instances with a buff-coloured. It is the latter which cannot be broken without the use of gunpowder, or infinite labour, by wedges. And there is, besides, a lead-coloured clay, and some gravel. The excavation made through the rocks, though attended with great difficulty, has saved the proprietors a very considerable sum, as the stone was immediately used for the walls of the canal; and indeed this rock, cut perpendicular, serves as a wall for at least one quarter of a mile. The sand is admirably calculated for mixing mortar; and the company had merely to burn their lime, which they were preparing to do on the spot when I saw the works.

A temporary bridge, erected with the stone and intended mortar, crossed the canal at that time; but the fierce red of the sand in the latter ruined the appearance of the work. Iron bridges are, however, to be exclusively preferred.

'An indifferent suburb termed Bedminster, closely but meanly built'
A cottage dated 1653 in Bedminster. Sepia watercolour, by William Muller, 1830. This previously unknown watercolour was painted when Muller was 18 but shows little of his later ability. It is, however, a rare record of architecture in the hamlet.

An indifferent suburb, termed Bedminster, closely but meanly built, extends a considerable distance on each side of the Bridge-water road. Numbers of one-horse-carts, and lasses seated on horseback, between large baskets, were returning from market; and a recruiting party proceeded nearly at my pace, with fifteen lads whom they escorted, with the honours of war, to the branching of the road, two miles and a half from Bristol; where they were committed to the care of three soldiers; and the martial musick, with the fine gentlemen bedecked with ribands, returned to the city to ensnare others.

The drums and fifes roused the inhabitants of Bedminster, and brought them to their doors.

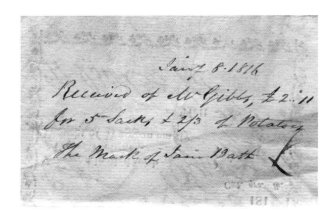

The back of a turnpike ticket issued at the Stoke's Croft Turnpike in 1817. It has been used as a receipt for £2 11s for the delivery of five sacks of potatoes at 2s 3d a sack. The ticket tells us that the cart weighed 6 cwt 2qrs empty and 18cwt 3qrs loaded.

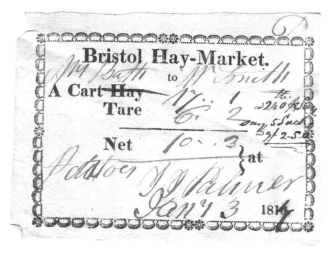

A turnpike ticket from 1817. This rare survival was issued at Hay Market Turnpike for a cart travelling with a load of potatoes. The weight of a load on the privately maintained toll roads affected the tariff.

Three labourers balanced themselves on a stile. 'Ay.' said one, 'go to slaughter, like the brutes in Smithfield. God keep I, and all my family, from that!'

I readily perceived that the senses of the recruits were disordered by excessive drinking. Their countenances indicated wildness, and their actions were frantic. They threw heavy stones at each other, accompanied by curses and peals of laughter; and one of them possessing a little dog, they set him barking at a flock of sheep that grazed on the Downs. When the animals fled, and sprung from eminence to eminence, a shout occurred that equalled the yell of a chace. The embryo soldiers joined in the pursuit, to the terror of their guards, who eagerly followed them, justly fearful of an escape.

One touch from the pencil of Nature illustrated this brutal picture. A serjeant stationed himself on the road side, and the recruits passed him. At the moment of separation they offered him their hands to a man; and each with silence and earnestness shook his, while their features individually exclaimed – farewell. The motions of the serjeant reminded me of the ridiculous custom of taking hands, and violently disengaging them, when two exasperated men are about to fight – but, a recruiting officer ought not to possess humane feelings.

This elevated spot commands a most extensive compass of country, the mid-distance of which is the vale of Bristol and St Vincent's rocks. The city, enriched by various spires, and the tower of the cathedral, spreads at the base of the Western hills, and is seen in long white lines of handsome houses on their sides, almost over-hanging the immense cliffs above the Hot Wells. The eye, descending those stupendous walls, meets glances of the Avon, bounded on the South by a beautiful hanging wood, which renders that bank of the river most picturesque. Hence, to the left, the sameness of the verdure is agreeably broken by clumps of trees, and several white mansions are half obscured by their shades.

The natives of Bristol observe, that when Dundry tower is enveloped in mist, there will probably be much bad weather. I have seen clouds involve it, and glide along below the base of the church. When I visited the village, a violent South wind howled amongst the branches of the trees, and the fleeces of vapour rushed, like white smoke, not an hundred feet above the pinnacles. This circumstance prevented the pleasure I had promised myself in ascending to the battlements of the tower, and thence viewing Bristol, four miles and an half distant, Bristol Channel, the Severn, Wales, Gloucester, the Malvern hills, Bath, the White Horse in Wiltshire, at the distance of 35 miles, &c. &c.

Heavy clouds cast their dusky shadows over the mountains of Wales; the Severn sparkled in a bright line; and to the South-east and North-east streams of rain fell in torrents; the wind whistled through the pierced-work of the tower; and I descended, vexed, and chilled with the rarified air.

Dundry is situated on a range of hills, or indeed one vast hill, which may be said to commence at Bedminster; and, though an inconsiderable village, has been honoured with a most magnificent tower, appended to a most insignificant church. The former, erected in the reign of Edward IV. is a land-mark for an amazing extent, and seems to have almost been intended as such by the founder or founders, rather than as necessary to so contemptible a structure as that which shrinks beneath it.

A turret covers the North-east angle, and buttresses of eight gradations support the three others. Four horizontal strings separate the height into four stories, each of which contain pointed windows, with neat mullions. The upper string, or cornice, has projecting grotesque heads of animals on every angle but the North-east, and one over each window to the cardinal points. The former support beautiful pierced flying buttresses to the four lanterns, or pierced turrets, and the latter octagon columns embattled; but the print will illustrate this rich masonry better than any description possibly can.

KINGSWESTON.

The road to the above place, and beyond it, is very pleasant; but, previous to the commencement of Durdham Downs, opulence has exerted her utmost means in securing her domains from depredation, and the operations of human vision. Those means are doubtless fully adequate; and yet they demonstrate, that opulence prefers security to taste, and even convenience; for her stone walls inclose the road, and confine the sun-beams and dust to a most pernicious degree.

Several houses have been erected on the Eastern extremity of the Downs; and a handsome terrace, the lamps before which are secured from injury by a netting, or cage of wire, a common practice in and near Bristol.

The Downs are covered with short grass, and very near level. Many sheep graze there; and I observed two waggons crossing it, drawn by six oxen each. An avenue of elms shade the road, and open on the brow of a hill at the Western termination; where a neat mansion, buried in firs and laurel, faces an extensive park. The opening of the road admits the eye to a beautiful level of verdure, broken by groups of distant trees; beyond them flows the Severn; and the mountains of Wales close the view.

When on this part of my way I met a novel exhibition *trotting on the path*. This, gentle reader, was two *John Bottoms*, bearing burthens far more important than usually fall to the share of those enduring and patient animals. The foremost had a neat saddle, on which sat (not a sweep, with legs dragging on the earth, or rude and ragged brute, kicking and beating as we see them with indignation in London), but an elegant young lady, clad in black silk, with a white beaver bonnet, and laced veil, bearing a parasol of green silk, which shaded her fair features from the rays of Sol in his meridian glory. Her brother *followed*, as the path admitted but one ass abreast.

I have mentioned *the novelty of the sight*; but let me be understood merely to mean I never before *saw a lady* on an ass. I should be shocked were I for a moment supposed *ignorant* of this important trait in the manners of the day, through the medium of our diurnal details of the progress of folly and dissipation.

As an admirer of antiquity, permit me to examine how Queen Elizabeth would have treated a cavalcade of her female subjects had she met them thus mounted – Elizabeth, who appeared in the front of her army, and swore she would punish the coward, conquer the enemy, or perish sword in hand. The 'first impressions' must have been insufferably acute on her imperial mind. The dignity of her sex, the honour of her crown, demanded that she should immediately – *box their ears*; and, my life on it, such would have been the first impulses of her resentment.

Our improvements in the mode of governing have rendered absolute monarchs unnecessary. The virtuous and the sedate now follow the example of the Sovereign and their families; and the reigning house of Brunswick must be allowed, in three successions, to have afforded the most amiable for public and private life.

The Monarch, and his illustrious relatives, need not now – box or imprison their erring subjects; the smile of derision, from those who commit no follies, cuts deeper than the lash on slumbering reflection; and they who are not to be recovered by that smile are not worth serious correction.

Caricaturists and the Stage flagellate those who cannot be noticed from the Pulpit. Even Astley's exhibition of the dowager on assback, attended by her gigantic footman, must have had some effect; and severe falls may perhaps cure the mania of ass-racing. The populace have prevented this new mode of taking the air near London. John Bull's family has that general sense of decorum, that they would hunt the riders, and restore poor Donkey to brick-dust bags, foot, carrots, turnips, potatoes, and apples; and to riders who always consider the vertebrae and ribs of those animals too weak for the support of an adult, and therefore ever mount him without a saddle, and sit on the hams.

On the right side of the road, two miles from Bristol, there is an antient and singular mansion, worth describing, which consists of a centre turret, with a balustrade, like those on Hatfield house; and a door of the Corinthian order, most extravagantly ornamented. The wings are surmounted by the same number of domes, and each has three arched gables, with intervening battlements, and three ranges of windows. This I believe to be Stoke-Bishop, once the residence of Sir Henry Lippincot, bart.

The descent near it glances on a valley at the base of Kingsweston hill; which, with the foliage of the foreground, is extremely beautiful.

At some distance from the hill just mentioned I was overtaken by a venerable Turk, whose scattered grey hairs were partly concealed on the neck by his turban. He wore a blue cloth vest, with a red collar and cuffs, and round his waist an embroidered apron of the order of Freemasons.

A chaise, containing two young ladies, had previously passed us;

but soon after stopped. When the Turk arrived within hearing, the driver said, 'Master, the lady wants you.' The old man proceeded to the door, with his turban in his right hand. The fair female within the chaise dropped money into it: the lad spurred his horses, and the donor and receiver were instantly, and perhaps for ever, separated.

Why should the novelist seek for strained scenes of philanthropy in the exhausted receptacles of his own brain? Have we not touches of exquisite delicacy and benevolence daily before us? We generally need only observe, and record. The blooming Briton beheld an oppressed, aged, and weary stranger, labouring through the dust, burnt by the midsummer and mid-day Sun. An appeal from the Divinity, directed to the heart, whispered, 'Should I not sink under these circumstances, without relief, were I in Turkey?' The truth was indisputable, and the hand executed the dictates of compassion. Who can doubt but that every prospect brightened around the inmates of this chaise from that instant?

An example so forcible was instantly imitated by me, a poor copyist. When I enquired of the Turk whether he understood the language, he replied in the affirmative, in tolerable English; and I thought his accent very like that of a Frenchman.

'Are you a Mussulman?'
'Yes.'

'Have you visited Mecca?' 'No. I am de Freemason, and come from Constantinople; a merchant. I have met with very great loss. I am cast away upon de coast of Norway, and loose every ting: much above 1200 guinea. I come, I travel, I go to my country!'

'Have you been in London?'
'Yes.'

'..on the Eastern extremity of the Downs.. a handsome terrace, the lamps before which are secured from injury by a netting.' King's Parade, Whiteladies Road, c.1865. This was the grandest terrace erected in what was then the hamlet of Durdham Down, now called Blackboy Hill. Edward Bird died at number 8 in 1819.

'Well, how do you like that city?'
'Ah! London very good town, but no good like Constantinople. There de poor man live cheap: here my breakfast cost one shilling sixpence, my din – two tre. At Constantinople fowl six-pence, meat two pence, butter two pence. It is war ruin England.'

I could not but observe, after I had separated from the Turk, who was proceeding to Wales, that his mind was most disagreeably tinctured with national prejudice; and I confess that circumstance led me to doubt, whether he was not a mere itinerant pedlar, rather than a merchant of Turkey; and yet his manners and appearance were dignified beyond those of persons of inferior station. Kingsweston hill is the segment of a large circle, extending nearly North and south, parallel with the Severn. The surface, from East to West, is almost angular, and covered by short grass, nibbled with avidity by numerous sheep. Kingsweston inn, to which parties continually resort to enjoy the prospect, and where the citizens of Bristol relax on Sunday evenings over a dish of tea, is pleasantly situated, at the Southern extremity of the hill; and the ruins of a windmill, in the centre, serve to point out the greatest elevation. At the North verge a cloud of white smoke announces a lime-kiln; erected under the almost perpendicular, verdant, and smooth, descent, which forms the South side of a valley exceedingly wild and romantic, beneath Blaize castle. This valley, proceeding North and West, forms an angle, on which the structure just mentioned is situated.

The characteristics of the Northern vale consist of a hanging wood, interspersed with crags. Those of the Western are a precipice of grass, opposed to another of rocks, shaded by small trees. Those rocks are the foundation of the triangular building erected by Thomas Farr, esq. mayor of Bristol in 1775, on or near the site of a chapel dedicated to St Blasius, which is a tolerable imitation of a citadel, with towers on the angles.

The Eastern half of the circular view from Kingsweston hill is very extensive and beautiful; and yet the objects are such as are to be met with in an hundred instances; but the Western has a foreground of superior attractions, though level. The park of Lord De Clifford, and the upper part of his mansion, built by Sir John Vanbrugh, lay at the base, to the left, with the mouth of the Avon, the Eastern banks of the Severn, Portbury, and, to the right, the whole extent of Wales. The mountains of Wales are the most sublime termination of the view imaginable, on the Western horizon; a soft blue tint, approaching to purple, cloaths the summits, and their outlines vanish almost imperceptibly into the thin air; the sides are faintly marked by ravines, and lesser hills intervene. As the eye approaches the Severn, objects become more defined, yet not sufficiently so to ascertain what they are. The river, about three miles in width at the Aust passage, flows North and South, separating the kingdom and principality. Two fine hills intercept part of the English shore; but the various vessels at anchor and under sail animate the scene for a very considerable distance.

COOK'S FOLLY.

It has long been the stupid practice of the vulgar to stigmatize every attempt to depart from the mere ploddings of life. When an opulent landholder observes that he possesses an elevated situation, commanding an extensive view, he dare not erect a tower, or other edifice, to improve those advantages, without risking obloquy, and the certainty of having his name attached to a word which sounds extremely disagreeable. Thus, a Mr Cook, desirous of tracing the beauties of Nature from an erection on the North bank of the Avon, has had his disgraced by the multitude, who term his imitation of an antient tower 'Cook's folly'. Nay, they even dishonour the memory of that gentleman by the following ridiculous story.

Esquire Cook fancied that he should die by the sting of an adder: to avoid which cruel death, he determined to elevate himself as far as possible from his native earth. But mark the facility of tradition. Cook burnt wood instead of coal; and the sagacious reptile, finding this fact in its favour, concealed itself in a bundle of faggots; and at a proper opportunity effected the destruction of the victim.

A singular chasm, or gully, occurs on the Downs near the tower alluded to, which commences in a gentle declination of the soil where covered with grass; whence it becomes rugged, and scattered with crags; and, finally, millions of fragments of stone lay heaped together, resembling those broken for mending roads;

but the rocks above are in large masses, and form striking contrasts to the shivered piles on both sides of the ravine; which ends in an acute angle, clogged by thorn-bushes washed down by rains, and walled by stupendous rocks.

From the levels intended as towing-paths, on each side the Avon, the precipices are very abrupt; but from those down to the water the banks are disagreeable shelves of mud.

The mountain almost opposite to the Hot Well is transcendently beautiful. The crags of rock resemble ruins, and every fissure affords an asylum for vegetation, which springs vigorously from them, and shades the surfaces, covered with mosses of the richest tints. In many places the soil is so thin that the sapling inclines with its own weight. In those instances their leaves are of a light green; and the wind bows them over the darker shades of more healthful foliage, with infinite effect. The hanging wood on the side consists of many species of trees. The firs are very fine; and the blossom of the thorn relieves, with wonderful beauty, from the velvet-like appearance of the grass and moss beneath them.

St Vincent's rocks, with one exception, are no longer the sublime and frowning fronts formed by the convulsion that originally split them asunder. Restless man has even dared the terrors of these precipices, and we see him perched an hundred and fifty feet from the base on terraces of horrible danger, where he stands and sports with desperation, amidst the ruin he is daily increasing. Consequently, the face of one portion of these rocks represents a true picture of supernatural convulsion, in masses of stone projected from the parent stock, which hang in frightful positions, supported by mere angles, that are loosened with incredible hazard, when they plunge through the air to the bottom.

The old man who rents the rocks, and converts them to fragments for burning into lime, has worked and superintended forty-five years. His principal inducement and emolument, however, appears to arise from the spar and Bristol stones discovered after every explosion in the fissures of the rock; whence he always cautiously conveys them himself, in order to sell each for decorating grottos, and furnishing naturalists with curiosities.

I ascended the side, about 80 feet, by a rope, to the terrace, where the operation of preparing a chamber for a blast was performing. A level of about four feet in breadth enabled the men to proceed with their labours. One is seated on the rock, and holds a huge chisel, three or four inches in diameter, and about three feet six inches in length, wrapped with hay, in order to prevent the disagreeable jarring of the hand, through an unsteady blow, perpendicular on the rock. Another man strikes it with a large sledge-hammer, fitted to a very short handle. By this means, and turning the chisel at every stroke, a cylindrical excavation, three feet in depth, is accomplished, in about three days. A certain quantity of gunpowder is then introduced; which they ram very tight; and the surface is closed with clay, as compact as possible, except where the communication with the train is preserved. When that is fired, the whole mass of rock trembles, and hollow echoes rebound from surface to surface; the solid bed of stone is convulsed, and opens; large fragments rush to the bottom; and the neighbourhood rings with thunder.

The shrill sound produced by the hammer and chisel at the vast elevation where chambers are sometimes made, has an effect almost musical, when reflected by echo; and when the labourers are seen reduced by perspective to mere infants, the whole seems almost the effect of enchantment.

After I had reached the little level where the men sat at work, I

Clifton and Hotwells from Bedminster in 1805, by James Malcolm. From a sketch made on his excursion to Dundry. The broken, unfinished, lines of Royal York Crescent appear on the right side of the engraving.

observed to them,

    'This is a dangerous employment of yours?'

    'Ees, Sir, but we do na mind it.'

    'I should suppose you sometimes receive dangerous hurts, if none of you are killed.'

    'About four years sin a man were killed.'

    'How did the accident happen?'

    'Why, sir, a stood, with three others, upon a loose stone, not minding, when it fell, and all four went down together. Three were only a little bruised, but one cut his scull all open. A never spoke, but a was not dead. He died a matter of twelve hour after we had un to the Firmary. But you see that are wall: a father and son were killed under that wall by one stone, by a blast.'

Such are the horrors attending the rifting of St Vincent's rocks. During the conversation just related, I riveted my eyes on the chissel held by one of the men, justly dreading a glance downwards, when the person unfortunately enquired the time of day. I involuntarily turned to examine my watch. At that instant my brain whirled, and I recovered my recollection just in time to seize the rope, by which I half slipped, half fell along the projections to terra firma, sufficiently alarmed to have made a vow to build a monastery, and dedicate it to my patron Saint -, had I been a prince of ancient days, or a feudal baron.

The rocks that remain in their original state are of stupendous height, and strongly resemble vast walls crumbling with decay, and tinged with moss. Viewed by twilight, turrets, watch-towers, and loop-holes, may be imagined throughout the surface; and, descending, the Avon might be supposed the most of an immense castle, calculated for the reception of the Titans.

At that silent and serene hour a friend and myself amused ourselves by seeking amongst the piles of fragments for spar and Bristol stones, when we observed a party of five ladies and a gentleman on the opposite shore, who seated themselves beneath a tree, and immediately sung several hymns in parts, and concluded with that of 'God save the King'. I was astonished at the delightful effect of this vocal musick, reverberated from the rocks above me, and the trees opposite, and sincerely applauded the piety of the performers.

The precipices decline rapidly near the Hot Wells, and the room there closes the passage between it and the Avon. A colonade extends from the river, and an avenue of young trees have been planted along the banks; but the lodging-rooms above the former are too near the water; and the exhalations from the shoals of mud, heated by the concentrated beams of the Sun, cannot fail of being prejudicial to the valetudinarian. Besides, the streets and houses between Bristol and the Wells are dirty and badly paved, and the latter meanly inhabited. The hills above are however far otherwise: there invention appears to have been exhausted in contriving fascinating residences; and some adventurous projector has commenced a row of houses of the Corinthian order; and his unfinished memento is not only exalted on a mountain, but rises proudly from a terrace at least thirty feet in height.

What more can I possibly add of the different Hot Wells and Clifton? The subject is exhausted; nor should I have ventured to notice those celebrated scenes of disease, death, sublimity, pleasantness, and dissipation, had I not remarked there were chasms in the best descriptions of Nature, which might always be filled by the last observer.

STAPLETON.

The prison at this village is situated on high ground, and has the advantage of an excellent air, and uncommonly beautiful prospects from the upper rows of windows. The road to it from Bristol is very pleasant; but a path along the Froom has superior attractions, and introduces the pedestrian to the most romantic groupes of trees, rocks, and meadows.

The gentleman and lady who were my guides to Stapleton, and myself, had ocular proof of the truth of the adage, that 'when wine is in, wit is out;' as we ascended a steep eminence, covered with short grass, near the prison, where two young gentlemen, a little inebriated, chased each other rapidly; and one falling, the other tripped over him. In this situation they drew their swords, and actually entertained themselves with a contest of more skill than discretion, which sometimes threatened consequences not altogether unlike the effects of anger.

'This,' said I, 'is indeed jesting with edged tools.' 'Yes,' answered my friend; 'and to make the folly worse, their hands are almost as ungovernable as we have observed their feet to be; and I shall think them fortunate if we escape the honour of going back to Bristol for a surgeon.' More than half a century past such a rencontre would have excited far different emotions in the breasts of the generality of observers than those we experienced. Then it was the barbarous amusement of the day to witness Figg, and other men of skill in the use of the sword, cut each other severely, but not dangerously, as they acted upon the principle of Butler's coward, and lived 'to fight another day.'

The strange conduct of these young men led me afterwards to reflect on the disagreeable effects of intoxication; to which, I am sorry to say, very little censure is attached: particularly when it occurs in company. Many shocking consequences might be enumerated; but the late burning of the miserable man in Chandos-street, Covent Garden, seems to eclipse every modern example of casualty during inebriation. It is in every man's power to guard against the inordinate use of wine; and it becomes doubly necessary for officers, who are obliged to wear weapons.

THE PRISON
is about two miles North-east of Bristol, and commands an exceeding fine view of Stoke-house, rebuilt in the last century by Lord Botetourt, and since one of the seats of the dukes of Beaufort; which stands on the summit of a hill, shaded by noble trees. Such of the prisoners of war confined at Stapleton as possess a taste for the attractions of Nature, have at least the gratification of contemplating them at leisure, and thus obtaining some small recompence for the horrors of confinement. The

majority, however, of the 2,600 inclosed by the walls of this prison seem not at all calculated for the enjoyment of the pleasures of imagination, as they proved, by an uproar surpassing every noise I had before heard produced by the voices of men, and which is distinctly audible at a quarter of a mile from the place. As I advanced, a constant murmur interrupted the general repose of the fields and woods, and I at last exclaimed, 'What strange sound can this possibly be?' My friend smiled, and said, 'The prisoners in conversation.' When under the walls, the strongest lungs may be distinguished from the mass in loud songs and vehement utterance, very much resembling dissention; which, without doubt, prevails, though we had not an opportunity of ascertaining, as the publick have very judiciously been recently denied admittance. One hundred and seven men and officers were on duty at the guard-house in June 1805; who have pairs of boxes, elevated on platforms, provided with flights of steps, near the top of the wall which incloses the yard of the prison; whence they command the whole range of the area, in case it should be necessary to fire, on an attempt of the prisoners to escape.

REDLAND,

within a mile of St Michael's hill, deserves honourable notice for its situation, and the beauty of the chapel; which is, I think, without exception, one of the best specimens of Grecian architecture in the kingdom. The ichnography is a parallelogram, with an Ionick front, of four pilasters, an entablature, pediment, rustick angles, and a door and niche in the centre intercolumniation. Immediately over the pediment is a cupola of uncommon elegance, composed of a basement, on the angles of which are pedestals and enriched vases, inclosing circular windows. From the pedestals upward the outline becomes an octagon, with brackets to an entablature; whence a fluted dome terminates in a ball and cross.

BATH.

The leap from Clifton to Bath is perfectly natural. Indeed, the former is but a cabinet picture copied from the latter; and the miniature movements of the Master of the Lilliputian ceremonies swelled to those of the Brobdignags. With the amusements of the vigorous and healthful I do not mean to intermeddle, and it would be cruel to examine whether they interfere with the recovery of the disordered and miserable. When fever and the plague carry desolation and death in their train through a populous city, the survivors fly with dismay from the victims, and the offices of humanity are neglected. How decidedly contrary are the effects produced by other diseases! The commiserative and benevolent fashionable world sympathize with the sufferers through palsies, convulsions, contractions, rheumatisms, the gout, scurvy, bilious complaints, obstructions of the liver and spleen, the jaundice, the leprosy, all cutaneous disorders, weakness of the stomach, and hysteric and hypochondriac affections; and fly to console them at Bath from every quarter of the kingdom. There the afflicted patient gulps the health-restoring fluid, and bathes, surrounded by eyes sparkling with hope, in which he may read the pleasant anticipation of his future convalescence and strength, and progress towards Heaven.

The natives of Bath exult in the certainty that all the Deities whose smiles have contributed to bless the lives of man since the days of good old Homer preside there at this instant. Every luxury that inventive art exhibits to the votaries of pleasure may be found in this favoured city, and amusements of endless variety blend night with day, during the season. One of them exclaims, with conscious pride, that the gay visitor witnesses the astonishing improvements made there in the mode of diverting the mind, and compares with complacency cards, balls, and the theatre, to the exploded pastimes of bull-baiting, cock-fighting, pig-racing, and grinning through a horse-collar.

When we reflect on the generally-received opinion that the springs which issue from the earth at Bath are highly sanative, it is impossible we should experience the least surprise that numbers resort there, in every stage of disease, to try their efficacy. Relatives and attendants increase the crowd, and affection doubtlessly often induces the friend to visit the sufferer. Persons in health, and possessed of affluence, cannot be supposed to remain inactive; the mind must relax; nor did the Divinity ever intend innocent amusement and gaiety should be expelled from the breast. Instead of condemning I applaud the diversions of dancing, riding, and the theatre; but gaming I class with the vices. Let me therefore not be mistaken for a fanatick when I smile at the excess of amusement to be met with at Bath; and wonder at the odd mixture of groans, musick, and flippancy.

Were a stranger to walk directly through this city, he would observe that the High-street consists of a narrow avenue of churches, palaces, inns, ale-houses, shops, and the worst-description of habitations strangely interwoven, with a pavement calculated to break the heads of those who jolt over it, in coaches and other vehicles, amidst a constant noise and rattle of wheels. Every church in Bath appears to have been purposely placed in disgraceful situations. To commence from the North entrance: Walcot church, at an angle of two streets, each narrow enough to occasion the sprinkling of soil on the walls from the feet of horses. St Michael's, with a portico, at a second angle. This church is constantly surrounded by stage-coaches, gigs, chaises, coachmen, and postillions.

The Abbey is invisible from High, Cheap, and Hall streets; indeed from every street and place, except an inconsiderable court.

And the church of St James stands at some distance from Horse-street, eclipsed by intervening houses. Each of those structures, exclusive of the Abbey, though not remarkably superb, would do honour to the modern squares and crescents. In their present situations they obstruct the progress of carriages, and their congregations cannot be free from the noise of wheels constantly passing.

The principal errors observable in the recent improvements of Bath lies in the naked grandeur of the structures, and their uniformity. Crescents, and lines, of magnificent buildings, extend in every direction; but not a tree shades them. The Sun glares on the white stone, and nothing is picturesque. The public buildings in Oxford are surrounded by the richest foliage, and what city can vie with that in beauty? Had Bath the same advantages, the site would improve them.

Queen's-square may be pronounced the commencement of Wood's architecture, and the houses deserve great praise; but the obelisk, erected by Nash, in honour of Frederick Prince of Wales, is one of the most disagreeable fancies I have ever seen. It is not an easy matter to decide what it resembles, as it proceeds from the earth, to the height of 70 feet, without the smallest break in the surface, and terminates as sharp as a needle. This silly Master of the Ceremonies might have discovered in the works of the antients, forms far more beautiful than an Egyptian conceived from the rays of the Sun. Besides, what possible reference could this obelisk have to that raised by Ramises, king of Egypt, at

Heliopolis, when Troy was taken, from which it was imitated, at least according to Pliny's description?

Gay-street, though very steep, is finely built, and an appropriate avenue to the King's Circus; a most noble circle of palaces, rather than the residences of private families. The regular gradation of the orders is admirably preserved; and one only objection applies, which is the omission of cornices, pediments, and enrichments, to the Doric, Ionic, and Corinthian ranges of windows. The streets diverging from the Circus are such as should proceed from such an area; and I should be guilty of injustice did I not add, that this quarter of Bath surpasses every other city I have seen. As every building from the Abbey to the Chapel, and every other public structure, has been repeatedly described, it is by no means necessary that I should dwell on them; I shall, therefore, merely request the reader to ascend with me to the Eastern and Western hills, to survey the town and vicinity, and then bid him farewell for the present.

There is a magnificent but incomplete crescent, on a stupendous and rugged mountain, almost immediately above Walcot church; the Eastern extremity of which superb pile appears to have been finished, and a chasm left between it and the remainder of the completed semicircle. The detached fragment, of beautiful white stone, consists of a triple basement, the upper rustic, on which are four three-quarter columns, of the Corinthian order, with an enriched entablature, including a principal story and an attick. This house may have been accidentally burnt. However, that, or some other cause, has made it a grand ruin, perhaps fifty feet in height from the base, and situated on an elevation of several hundreds more above the level of the meadows, through which the Avon glides. The general effect of the Grecian architecture, and the swells of the pillars, forcibly reminded me of the remains of an antient Roman villa, particularly when grouped with the romantic scenery on every side. Gardens divided by shrubs, and bright broken ground, tufted with grass, enliven the descent before the ruin to the backs of the streets of the city; which extend Southward, and are terminated by the mountains in that direction, partially shaded by hanging woods. But the most pleasing view is along the valley, inclining to the North-east. There Nature spreads all her treasures; and the cultivator has contributed his best efforts to improve her gifts.

The Avon, a clear and serpentine stream above Bath, flows through this vale; and its banks are crowded with willows, and other trees, which dip their branches into the transparent fluid, at the same time that their roots cling to the rich soil of the meadows, of the most brilliant green, sprinkled with millions of yellow flowers. Those meadows, divided and subdivided by hedges, interspersed with tall trees, appear one vast pleasure-ground, inclosed by steep ascents, covered with groupes of trees, elegant villas, and cultivation almost to their barren summits. Back of the ruin the surface of the hill is broken into numerous ravines, that give an excellent background from the city.

The view from the Southern hills is deprived of the valley just mentioned. Thence Bath appears the arena of a vast amphitheatre of mountains; not fertilized and broken by projecting crags and foliage, like the Clifton and St Vincent's hills; but covered with short grass, lines of hedges, intersected by roads, and scattered with small houses. Thus each hill has

- its brother,
And one half the *amphitheatre* reflects the other.

The builders seem to have adopted this uniformity in the repetition of crescents and places; and they may not unaptly be compared to the *feelers* attached to some animals, extended at full-length, as if reaching to a remote height. The white stone of the buildings and roofs, and the smoke of the city, do not accord with my taste. They produce a dazzling appearance, which my eyes left with pleasure for the verdure Westward of Bath, improved as it approaches the Avon.

The Abbey, with ten large windows on the South side and transept, and the tower appear to much advantage; but the other steeples are not remarkable.

All change: in the 1830s the railway came to Bristol.

Bibliography

Bristol Public Library was founded in 1613 and is the third oldest library in the country, being beaten only by Norwich in 1608 and Ipswich in 1612. In the nineteenth century it was the first library in Britain to establish a 'Local Collection' or a special collection of books and other material solely devoted to the history of its city and surrounding area. As a result of its early interest in the subject and with the acquisition of private collections of Bristoliana, it now holds unparalleled textual and visual resources for the researcher. All of the items listed below are held in stock by either the Reference or Art Reference Collections in the Central Library at College Green, Bristol. Some of the rarer items may only be available by application made prior to a visit. In some cases below, items have been given their accession number in brackets after the entry to facilitate location.

NEWSPAPERS FOR 1807
LOCAL:
Bristol Gazette
Felix Farley's Bristol Journal
The Mirror
NATIONAL:
The Courier
Morning Chronicle (electronic resources)
The Times (microfilm and electronic resource)

BOOK, MANUSCRIPT AND ILLUSTRATIVE MATERIAL
ANON *A Birthday Book and Other Dates.* (A scrapbook ornamented with fernwork and local and international photographs, containing birthdays of the Prichard and Pocock families). Bristol c 1860-1870. (B19200)
ANON *The Milliner. A Poem: dedicated, Without Permission, to the Beautiful Miss George.* Bristol, 1807 (B929)
ANON *One Hour after Marriage, A Tale. Town and Country Magazine,* Supplement to the Year 1770. Pages 701-703. (27192733. Dup.Loc Pb.)

ANSTEY, Christopher *The New Bath Guide or, Memoirs of the B-n-r-d Family in a series of Poetical Epistles*. London, 1807

ANSTEY, Christopher *The New Bath Guide*…. Bath, 1807 (Illustrated by F. Eginton).

ASHLEY, John *England's King and England's Glory. A Military Song*. London, 1807.

ATKINSON, William *Views of Picturesque Cottages with Plans*. London, 1805.

BARRISTER (pseudonym) *A Tour in Quest of Genealogy through Several Parts of Wales, Somersetshire and Wiltshire*. London, 1811. Includes a description of a journey by sea in 1807 (pages 86-87) and a society dinner and entertainment in the same year (pages 102-104).

BARTELL, Edmund *Hints for Picturesque Improvements in Ornamental Cottages, and their Scenery*. London, 1804.

BARTH, Henry *Travels and Discoveries in North and Central Africa*. In 3 volumes. London, 1857.

BEESON, Anthony *Bristol Central Library and Charles Holden*. Bristol, 2006.

BERESFORD, James *The Miseries of Human Life*: London, 1806 (and 1810 edition).

BISS, John *Instructions for Measuring a Gentleman* mss Bristol c 1805, in Advertisements and Prospectuses. (B22763)

BLACK PRINCE (Bristol slaving ship of 150 tons) *A Journal Of an Intended Voyage in the Ship Black Prince From Bristol To The Gold Coast of Africa, Being her 7th To the Coast Commencing Aprill the 24th 1762*. Mss (B4764).

BRIGGS, Richard *The English Art of Cookery* London, 1794 (1788).

BRISTOL LIBRARY SOCIETY Bristol Library Society Registers of Book Loans and Borrowers. Mss. 1807 (B7478 and 7479).

BRISTOL MISCELLANEOUS. A collection of Trade Cards, Handbills and Property Details. Bristol (B6523) (BL4H).

BRISTOL PICTORIAL SURVEY. A vast collection of images of buildings and places in Bristol kept at the Reference Library, College Green.

BRISTOL PRESENTMENTS Exports 1807-8 (weekly list of ships and cargoes exported).

BRISTOL PRESENTMENTS Imports 1807-8 (weekly list of ships and cargoes imported).

BRISTOLIENSIS *The Bristol Guide*. Bristol, 1815.

BRITTON, John *The Architectural Antiquities of Great Britain*, 5 volumes. London, 1806-1826 (volume 3 contains the Abbey Gateway, College Green).

BUMPUS, John *A Complete Natural History; Containing Complete Delineations of Upwards of Three Hundred Animals*. London, 1813.

BUNBURY, Henry William *Annals of Horsemanship*. London, 1796 (34H3).

CARTER, George and others *Humphry Repton, Landscape Gardener. 1752-1818*. London, 1982

CIRKER, Blanche (Editor) *1800 Woodcuts by Thomas Bewick and his School*. New York, 1962.

CORRY, John and EVANS, John *The History of Bristol, Civil and Ecclesiastical; including Biographical Notices of Eminent and Distinguished Natives* . 2 volumes. Bristol, 1816

CRUTTWELL, Rev Clement *A Tour Through the Whole Island of Great Britain*. vol. 3. London, 1801.

DAGLEY, R *Death's Doings*. London, 1826.

DANIEL, William Barker *Rural sports*. Three volumes. 1807. Appendix, 1813 (W67).

DAVEY, George *Views in the Vicinity of Bristol and Chepstow*. Bristol. nd.

DAVIES, Edward *BLAISE CASTLE. A Prospective Poem*. Bristol, 1783.

DEARN, Thomas D.W. *Sketches in Architecture; consisting of Original Designs for Cottages and Rural Dwellings suitable to Persons of Moderate Fortune, and for Convenient Retirement*. London, 1807.

DICKSON, R. W. *Practical Agriculture: or, a Complete System of Modern Husbandry: with the Methods of Planting and the Management of Live Stock*. Two volumes, London, 1805.

E.J. *Photographic Album of Local and International Views*. Bristol. c1860-1895

EVANS, John *The Picture of Bristol*. Bristol, 1814.

EVANS, John *The New Guide, or Picture of Bristol*. 3rd Edition. Bristol. Nd.

FALCONER, William T*he Shipwreck* London, 1807 (RL30B).

FALCONER, William *The Shipwreck, A Poem. Embellished with Descriptive Engravings by Robert Dodd*, Marine Painter. London, 1808.

GLASSE, Hannah *The Art of Cookery Made Easy*. London, 1796.

GOLDSMITH, Oliver *The Poetical Works of Dr Goldsmith*. London, 1805 (RL30B).

GRAY, Thomas *The Poetical Works of Thomas Gray*. London, 1805 (RL30B).

GREENACRE, Francis *From Bristol to the Sea*. Bristol, 2005

GROSE, Francis *Advice to the Officers of the British Army, with the addition of some hints to the Drummer and Private Soldier*. London, 1946 (1782) (34c3).

GUY, J *A Pocket Encyclopaedia, or Miscellaneous Selections: being Useful Knowledge…Designed for Senior scholars in Schools, and for Young Persons in General*. Bristol, 1804.

GYE, H *The Goldfinch for 1803: being a Choice Selection of Songs as sung at The Theatres, Vauxhall etc*. Bath, 1803.

GYE, H *The Old Bath Songster* Bath, c 1805.

GYFFORD, Edward *Designs for Elegant Cottages and Small Villas, calculated for the Comfort and Convenience of Persons of Moderate and Ample Fortune*. London, 1806.

GYFFORD, Edward *Designs for Small Picturesque Cottages and Hunting Boxes adapted for Ornamental Retreats…* London, 1807.

HARRIS, J. *The Geographical Guide; A Poetical Nautical Trip round the Island of Great-Britain*. London, 1805.

HEATH, Charles *Historical and Descriptive Accounts of the Ancient and Present State of Chepstow Castle…the roads to Bristol...Monmouth* 1801.

HOBHOUSE Isaac *The African slave Trade of Bristol.. Letters to Isaac Hobhouse and Partners. Slave Estates*. Mss., Jefferies Collection. Volume 13 (SR48).

HOBHOUSE, Thomas *Kingsweston Hill. A Poem*. London, 1785 (B9843).

HORTON, Charles H *Horton's Photographs of Bristol Antiquities*. (photograph album) Bristol, 1908 (BL10 F).

IBBETSON, *Julius Caesar and others. A Picturesque Guide to Bath, Bristol Hot-Wells, the River Avon and the Adjacent Country….*London, 1793.

KEMP, James *Love And Law or The Orange Girl. A Satirical Poem*. Bristol, c 1800 (B9837).

KNIGHT, Charles *The Pictorial Gallery of Arts: Useful Arts*. London, 1845.

LATIMER, John *The Annals of Bristol in the Eighteenth Century*. Bristol, (privately printed) 1893. Unique Grangerised copy edited by its author (B5323).

LATIMER, John *The Annals of Bristol in the Nineteenth Century*. Bristol, 1887. Unique Grangerised edition edited by its author (B5324).

LEWES, Charles Lee *A Lecture on Heads*, by Geo. Alex. Steven, with additions by Mr Pilon as delivered by Mr Charles Lee Lewis, to which is added An Essay on Satire. London, 1799. Illustrated by Nesbit.

LOVELL, Robert *Bristol: A satire*. London, 1794.

LOVELL, Robert Lovell's last letter to his wife. Mss., 1796.

LOXTON, Samuel Loxton collection of pen-and-ink drawings of Bristol and surrounding counties. A large collection of images drawn by Loxton for inclusion in the local Bristol newspapers from the 1890s to around 1920.

LYSONS, Samuel *A collection of Gloucestershire Antiquities*. London, 1804.

LYSONS, Samuel *Remains of Two Temples and Other Roman Antiquities discovered at Bath*. London, 1802.

MALCOLM, James P. *First Impressions or Sketches from art and Nature. Animate and Inanimate*. London, 1807 (W13).

MALTON, James *An Essay on British Cottage Architecture*. London, 1798.

MANBY, G. W. *The History and Beauties of Clifton Hot-Wells, and Vicinity, near Bristol*. London, 1806.

MARKS, Hayward *Proofs of Some Early Nineteenth-Century Woodblocks for Tea and Tobacco Papers*. London, 1948 (Private Press).

MARSHALL, Mr *The Rural Economy of Glocestershire; including its Dairy*. 2 Volumes, Glo(u)cester, 1789.

MATTHEWS *Matthews's Complete Bristol Directory* continued to January 1807. Bristol, 1806.

MAVOR, William *The British Tourists*. 2nd edition. London, 1800 (Volume 3 page 48+ includes a Bristol tour. Vol 4, page 253 + includes a visit to Bristol).

MILLER AND SWEET A Catalogue of Forest Trees, Flowering Shrubs, and Evergreens; Fruit Trees: Herbaceous, Green-house and Hot House Plants, sold by Miller and Sweet. Bristol, 1808.

MILLER, William see *BLACK PRINCE*

MORE, Hannah *The Troubles of Life, or the Guinea and the Shilling*. London, 1799.

MORGAN, Edwin Thomas *A brief history of the Bristol Volunteers from their earliest recorded formation to the establishment of the territorial Army in 1908*. Bristol, 1909.

MORGAN, William *Long Ashton, a Poem, in two parts…*Bristol, 1814 (B9419).

MYERS, Harris *William Henry Pyne and his Microcosm*. Stroud, 1996.

NARRAWAY, John Original letters to Thomas Coutts, Mss., 1798 (B35253) (SRC4)

NEILD, James *An Account of the Rise, Progress and Present State of the Society for the discharge and Relief of Persons Imprisoned for Small Debts throughout England & Wales*. London, 1808. This includes a description of the conditions within Bristol City and County Gaol on pages 109-111.

NEWMAN, Jeremiah Whitaker Hot-Wells Anecdote in *The Lounger's Commonplace Book*, Vol 4 p180-181. London, 1799 (34E3).

NIGHTINGALE, J. *The Beauties of England and Wales or, Original Delineations, Topographical. Historical, and Descriptive, of Each County*. Somerset. London, 1813.

OBSERVER *The Observer, Part 1st; being a transient glance at about forty Youths of Bristol*. Bristol, c1794.

OLIVER, Richard W. *The Lloyd Collection at Unreserved Auction*. Maine, 1988.

PAIN, William *The Practical House Carpenter or, Youth's Instructor: containing a Great Variety of Useful Designs in Carpentry and Architecture*. London, 1792.

PATRIOTIC SOCIETY *Articles Containing the Rules, Orders and Regulations of the Patriotic Society instituted in the City of Bristol, the Twenty-Ninth Day of January, 1807, for the Benefit of Members during Sickness, Defraying the expences of their Burial; and Providing annuities for their Widows for their Widows and Orphan Children*. Bristol, 1808.

PLAW, John *Rural Architecture; or Designs, from The Simple Cottage to the Decorated Villa…* London, 1794 (another edition 1802).

PLAW, John *Ferme Ornée; or Rural improvements*. London, 1795.

PROUT, John Skinner *Picturesque Antiquities of Bristol*. Bristol, 1835 (B10134).

PROVERBS in verse, Or moral Instruction conveyed in Pictures for the Use of Schools.

London, c 1790 (SL 2446).

PYNE, WH *The Costume of Great Britain*. London, 1808 (SR44).

REPORT OF THE LORDS of the Committee of Council appointed for the Consideration of all matters relating to Trade and Foreign Plantations. 1789.

REPTON, Humphry *The Fort Near Bristol, A Seat of Thomas Tyndall Esq*. Romford. 1801 (Facsimile of the Red Book from the original at Yale Library. New Haven, Connecticut, SR 33).

REPTON, Humphry Red Book for Blaise Castle. Bristol, 1985.

REPTON, Humphry *Sketches and hints on Landscape Gardening*. London, 1794.

ROWLANDSON, Thomas *The Comforts of Bath*. London, 1798 (GC 4848) (BL 15G).

SHEPPARD, W. *The New Bristol Guide*. Bristol, 1804.

SHIERCLIFF, E. *The Bristol and Hotwell Guide, Containing an Account of the ancient and present State of THAT OPULENT CITY*. Bristol, 1805.

SKELTON, Joseph Skelton's *Etchings of the Antiquities of Bristol from original sketches by the late Hugh O'Neill*. Bristol, c 1825.

SMITH AND WOODALL Handbill alerting the public to fraudulent bottles of Hotwells' water. Bristol. Nd. (B28525).

SMITH, George *Collection of Designs for Household Furniture and Interior Decoration*. London, 1807.

SMITH, James Edward *An Introduction to Physiological and Systematical Botany*. London, 1814.

SMITH, John Thomas *The Cries of London*, 1839 (SL3656).

SMITH, John Thomas *Vagabondiana; or anecdotes of Mendicant wanderers through the Streets of London*. London, 1817 (SL 3657).

SOCIETY OF LADIES *Lady's Monthly Museum or Polite Repository Of Amusement and Instruction*. London, 1803. A women's magazine.

SOCIETY OF THE MERCHANT ADVENTURERS AT BRISTOL. Letter to Admiral Cuthbert Lord Collingwood from Thomas Daniel (Master) together with the sealed grant of the Freedom of the Society of Merchant Adventurers in recognition of his part in the defeat of the French at Trafalgar..Mss. Bristol, 1805/1806 (B35252) (SRC4).

SOUTHEY, Robert *Letters from England by Don Manuel Alvarez Espriella*. In three volumes. 2nd Edition. London, 1808.

STROUD, Dorothy *Humphry Repton.* London, 1962.

THOMSON, James *The Seasons.* London, 1807 (RL 30B).

THORN, Romaine Joseph *Bristolia, A Poem.* Bristol, 1794.

THORNTON, Robert *The Temple of Flora, Or the Garden of the Botanist, Poet, Painter and Philosopher.* London, 1799-1807.

TRUSLER, J. *Proverbs Exemplified and Illustrated by Pictures from Real Life.* London, 1790 (SL 2445).

WARBURTON, Elizabeth *The Experienced English Housekeeper, for the Use and Ease of Ladies, housekeepers, Cooks, etc.,* London, 1782.

WEEKS, John John Weeks' Scrap-Book Mss (B28209) (SR45).

WHITEHEAD, W. *An Hymn to the Nymph of Bristol Spring.* London, 1751 (B9838).

WILLS T. Thornton *A collection of Illustrations relating chiefly to Bristol.* Bristol, c1880-1910 (B17833).

Illustrations

The originals of all illustrations and objects used in this volume are in the collections of Bristol Reference Library with the exception of the following for which we gratefully acknowledge permission to reproduce.

MONOCHROME
Dyer Collection 1, 153, 157
Sotheby's 30, 31
Tozer Collection 40
Beeson Collection 22, 29, 68 right.

COLOUR
Bristol City Museum and Art Gallery 27, 30, 35, 36
Dyer Collection 16
Sotheby's 28
Stevens Collection 31, 32
Beeson Collection 4, 8, 13, 15, 37.

Index

The numbers in **bold type** refer to illustrations in the colour plate section of the volume.